PARENTING THE HURT CHILD

PARENTING THE HURT CHILD

HELPING ADOPTIVE FAMILIES HEAL AND GROW

BY GREGORY C. KECK, PH.D., AND REGINA M. KUPECKY, LSW

EDITED BY LYNDA GIANFORTE MANSFIELD

P.O. Box 35007, Colorado Springs, Colorado 80935

OUR GUARANTEE TO YOU

We believe so strongly in the message of our books that we are making this quality guarantee to you. If for any reason you are disappointed with the content of this book, return the title page to us with your name and address and we will refund to you the list price of the book. To help us serve you better, please briefly describe why you were disappointed. Mail your refund request to: Piñon Press, P.O. Box 35007, Colorado Springs, CO 80935.

ISBN 1-57683-314-3

Cover photo by ibid
Cover design by Steve Eames
Creative Team: Steve Eames, Lynda Mansfield, Amy Spencer, Glynese Northam

Some of the anecdotal illustrations in this book are true to life and are included with the permission of the persons involved. All other illustrations are composites of real situations, and any resemblance to people living or dead is coincidental.

This publication is designed to provide accurate and authoritative information in regard to the subject matter covered. It is sold with the understanding that the author and the publisher are not engaged in rendering legal, accounting, or other professional service. If legal advice or other expert assistance is required, the services of a competent professional person should be sought. *From a Declaration of Principles jointly adopted by a Committee of the American Bar Association and a Committee of Publishers.*

Keck, Gregory C.
  Parenting the hurt child : helping adoptive families heal and grow /
by Gregory C. Keck and Regina M. Kupecky ; edited by Lynda Gianforte Mansfield.
    p. cm.
  Includes bibliographical references and index.
  ISBN 1-57683-314-3
    1. Special needs adoption--United States. 2. Intercountry adoption--United States. 3. Adoptive parents--United States. 4. Parenting--United States. 5. Attachment disorder in children. I. Kupecky, Regina M. II. Mansfield, Lynda Gianforte. III. Title.
HV875.55 .K436 2002
649'.145--dc21   2002002114

Printed in the United States of America

1 2 3 4 5 6 7 8 9 10/ 06 05 04 03 02

To James,
Your enthusiasm and quick insights are amazing.

■

Solace

It isn't too late
To learn how to trust
To heal the invisible wounds
I know that I must
Let gnawing insecurities
Frustration and loss
Slip from my grasp
As water spills from fingers spread
To relinquish the stigma
So at home in my head
And the unresolved hurts
That make me push you away
When your greatest desire
Is to keep me from harm
Please help me find rest
In the solace of your arms
For it is only there I will feel safe enough
To build new dreams.

CONTENTS

FOREWORD

America is filled with hurt children. Dr. Keck and Mrs. Kupecky quote the figures that forty-two thousand children were adopted from foster care alone in 1999. There were sixteen thousand children adopted from countries overseas. Almost all of these children have suffered from trauma, be it movement from home to home, by parent or orphanage care, or abuse. Some of these children have fragile genetics. Many others were bathed in alcohol or drugs before birth. Some were left on porches, and more than a few were recovered from trash containers or rescued from homes in which most rooms appeared to be a trash container. Some have neurological problems from head trauma. In addition to these children arriving in families from social services, foster care, or orphanages, there are many more thousands who have had poor early parenting and are living with grandparents and other kin.

These are America's hurt children.

In today's world, few children, no matter how disturbed, are in residential treatment or group homes. Someone, somewhere, is living with these children and attempting to cope with their parenting needs. And it is almost always a rocky road. Many, if not most, of them are difficult to parent and resist all discipline.

Every person who makes the choice to parent a hurt child has a dream. These dreams vary, but many include the anticipated fulfillment of helping someone else out of a tough situation; the feelings of satisfaction when a grateful child returns our love; the joy of seeing a person flower from a child into an adult who reaches his or her full potential. These are the things that all parents hope for, based on their own backgrounds and their own childhoods. And therein lies a problem, for most who choose to parent hurt children are functional people without early abuse and neglect of their own. They often have a record of success in parenting birth children. But the discipline they successfully used with prior birth children may not be effective with their hurt children. And tragedy can result.

Nothing, but nothing, can turn a normal household into a nonfunctional—even dangerous and threatening—environment as fast as bringing into the home a rebellious hurt child who doesn't understand love. The child's attitude and behavior turns everything topsy-turvy. The other children often feel neglected, picked on, angry, or resentful. The children become inwardly sullen or outwardly rebellious or show an unhappy combination of the two. Loving couples who previously agreed on parenting approaches find themselves disagreeing and doubtful not only about the other's behavior but about the other's motive itself! Family, neighbors, and friends who considered a couple saintly for taking in the troubled children, upon seeing the children's continuing misbehavior, begin to question the couple's parenting competence and even their character. The best hope is *knowledge on parenting the hurt child.*

The world expects reciprocal responses. If one is nice to someone, one expects the other to be nice back. If one is mean, it is understandable that others are mean in return. If one smiles, he or she expects a smile in return. If one is giving, it is expected that others will probably be giving in return. All this makes perfect sense in our usual world. In the topsy-turvy world of hurt and disturbed children, all these normal responses may not occur; they have to be taught. Hurt children early in their lives learned that smiles are not to be trusted. They know that adult actions may end in pain. They are "hard-wired" by early experiences to know that the only safety is in total and complete control of their emotional and physical environment. The chaotic past living inside their heads becomes the chaos they project onto others in their home.

Because of the turmoil such children can produce, *Parenting the Hurt Child* is not simply a parenting book; it is tragedy prevention. Here parents will find the attitude, tools, techniques, and responses that make parenting special children especially rewarding.

The ideas you are about to read will help ensure that your time with your hurt child is interesting not frightening, rewarding not unhappy, effective not destructive.

FOSTER W. CLINE, M.D., coauthor of
Parenting with Love and Logic

THE CHANGING FACE OF ADOPTION

PLEASE NOTE: In order to prevent confusion, we have chosen to use the masculine gender when referring to generic situations throughout this book.

The face of adoption continues to change. Gone are the days when the policies of social-service agencies forbade foster parents to get close to their foster children, and when nurturing was to be reserved for the yet unidentified adoptive family. Gone are the days when the accepted belief was that withholding love and attention from an infant or child would serve him well.

As the winds change course through the adoption and child welfare world, children no longer have to be subjected to impermanence or frequent moves from foster home to foster home while awaiting the phantom magic of reunification. They can finally reap the sensible rewards of a fact that we have known for years: children need to be in one place with loving, protective, and nurturing people—whether birth parents, foster parents, adoptive parents, or kinship parents.

Today foster parents are encouraged to "keep" the children they have. So widespread is this updated belief that youngsters in foster care are now more likely to be adopted by their foster parents (64 percent) than by relatives (14 percent) or new adoptive families (21 percent).[1]

The Adoption and Safe Families Act of 1997 goes a long way toward addressing the many shortcomings of the earlier system. This law finally recognizes the critical need for permanency in a child's life and mandates that states move more expeditiously to obtain permanent homes for foster children. As a result, the number of finalized adoptions from foster care has soared—from 28,000 in 1996 to 42,375 in 1999.[2]

And the numbers will continue to grow. Irresponsible parents can no longer spend year after year ignoring the reunification expectations of their case plans, while their children move around the foster care system like endless chain letters.

No longer do agencies have to wait until the birth family does something injurious to an infant or child before removing him. If there has been a clear pattern of parental irresponsibility with other children, the state may now proactively protect a newborn. Social workers are freed from old laws that protected the rights of the birth parents while simultaneously endangering the lives of their innocent children.

The trend toward change is far-reaching. It is estimated that 16,396 children were adopted internationally by American families in 1999—an increase from 7,093 in 1990.[3] Many people pursue this path in an attempt to adopt a child who has not been hurt or damaged, but the child may be as hurt as a child from foster care. Most adoptable children from other countries share the same traumas as those experienced by children in our own system. The abandoned children found wandering the streets of Moscow most assuredly have not had good lives. In all probability, they were subjected to abuse, neglect, and sexualization, as opposed to nurturing, stimulation, and security.

Abandoned infants everywhere in the world have had iden-

---

1. Department of Health and Human Services, as quoted on Evan B. Donaldson Adoption Institute Web site, www.adoptioninstitute.org
2. Voluntary Cooperative Information System, as quoted on Evan B. Donaldson Adoption Institute Web site, www.adoptioninstitute.org
3. U.S. Immigration & Naturalization Services, as quoted on Evan B. Donaldson Adoption Institute Web site, www.adoptioninstitute.org

tical experiences, and the motivation for the abandonment is irrelevant. Whether the child's mother left him in China due to sociopolitical reasons—or if he was dumped in a U.S. high school bathroom because his mother was terrified to tell anyone about her pregnancy—the end result is the same: the infant was abandoned by the woman who gave him life.

While we are not suggesting that people avoid inter-country adoptions, we simply want to make it clear that most adoptable children—regardless of their country of origin—have experienced trauma. We also want to point out that the fear of a U.S. family reclaiming a birth child is not a sound sole motivator for seeking an international adoption. For the most part, there are very few situations in which a birth family regains custody of, or contact with, the child. This is particularly true of children adopted from the foster care system.

As changes in the adoption world continue, we are pleased to see the formal recognition of kinship placement. While this practice has always existed informally, families related to a child are now able to adopt him and receive the same kind of support—subsidies, medical care, and so on—that nonrelative adoptive families have always enjoyed. This movement opens up significant options for many children and negates years of undefined, nebulous existence in the foster care system.

Certainly, kinship families should be considered when they offer the child a chance for a secure, protective, and nurturing childhood. However, one should not assume that a new trend equals a solution for every case. Kinship placements may be superb, but they can also be abysmal, because there is not always a positive relationship between a biological tie and quality care. Kinship placements must be evaluated, utilizing the same factors as those employed in nonrelative placements. An aunt who is unknown to the child is more of a stranger than the foster family with whom the child has been living for two years. We think it is unwise to move a child simply because a blood relative has surfaced and indicates an interest in adopting him. This kind of thinking does not take into account some common-sense factors, even though it may flow with the current trend.

As we celebrate the numerous, positive changes that have occurred for hurt children, we must remain focused on a commitment to keep this process moving. Perhaps one day, a child who is removed from an abusive home will be able to have his first out-of-home placement as his final placement. While this may be a lofty goal, it may help the system refine its practices to enable children to "get where they're going" as quickly as possible. What's more, it will ensure that the child has the potential to experience continuity in his development. And that alone will reduce the lifelong difficulties for parents and their hurt children.

ACKNOWLEDGMENTS

When thinking of all of the people who have been involved in helping us help families with hurt children, it becomes difficult—actually impossible—to identify them individually. In fact, it is the integration of a host of factors, experiences, children, adolescents, parents, and professionals that has made this book possible.

There were times when we wondered out loud if we were addressing important issues. Were we providing the tools parents need to undertake the huge task of helping children heal from the traumas thrust upon them early in life? While we were sometimes able to answer our own queries, most of the time the answers came from others. To all of the people who shared their observations, a heartfelt thank-you.

Lynda Mansfield, our friend and editor, has helped make this book talk to the reader in the same voice as *Adopting the Hurt Child*. Thanks, Lynda.

We are grateful to Carol Blatnicky for her chapter "The School Dance." Families struggle so much with the situations she addresses. We are certain you will find her information helpful. Thanks, Carol.

Special thanks to all of the parents and children who shared their thoughts in chapter 11. We learn so much from the families with whom we work.

It is a privilege to include Launa's beautiful poem in our book, and we thank her.

Ohio is a special state for adoptive families. For years, there have been monies made available through the Post-Adoptive Special Services Subsidy (PASSS) program. These generous funds, supplemented by State Special Services Subsidies, allow adoptive families to access specialized services that their hurt children so desperately need. We know of no other place in the world that has such a post-adoptive program. Thank you, Ohio, and your eighty-eight counties.

We thank Piñon Press for receptivity to our thoughts and ideas, valuable ongoing input, and a simple and productive publishing process. A special thanks to Steve Eames, who first reviewed our proposal.

Additional thanks to all of the people at the Attachment and Bonding Center of Ohio, who keep the day-to-day operations running smoothly as they encounter extremely difficult work.

To Ann Winchester, who has been Regina's friend since they were toddlers—thank you for getting us out of all our computer glitches. You're right; it was easier than the way we did the first book—on legal pads!

Thank you to ATTACh, Jewel Among Jewels, and *Adoptive Families* magazine for publishing our articles and allowing them to be reprinted in "Authors' Smorgasbord." We would also like to give special thanks to Patty Hamblin, LSW, post-adoption social worker, and the Wayne County Children Services Board for allowing us to reprint questions and answers from their publication *The Connection* in our chapter "Ask An Expert."

And, just as we did in *Adopting The Hurt Child,* we thank our parents and grandparents for providing the kind of foundation that has allowed us to deeply understand the critical nature of family.

GREG: I often ask my son James for his thoughts and opinions. He, as most adolescents, usually has an answer that shows great insight and simplicity. Once, as I was getting ready to participate in a meeting to decide whether or not a sibling group should stay together, I asked James what he thought. His answer was direct and to the point, "If they can get along with each other, they should stay together." Made sense to me! I think of his answer each time I am asked to address this issue. Thank you, James. And to both of my sons, Brian and James, who keep providing me with new ideas and opportunities for me to be creative—thanks, guys!

REGINA: To my husband, Don, who has been patient and supportive during busy times. Thank you, Don.

■

We hope this sequel to *Adopting the Hurt Child* will give you, the reader, information and perspective that will strengthen your commitment to your hurt child. Most important, we hope it will provide you with renewed hope for that child's healing and growth.

HELPING YOUR HURT CHILD HEAL, GROW, AND DEVELOP

In the six years since *Adopting the Hurt Child* was published, we have been asked repeatedly about writing another book. Of course, we were flattered, but the mere thought of the undertaking was daunting.

Now we feel the time has come. We want to add to the information we have already imparted and give parents more tools to help them raise their hurt children. The past six years of ongoing work with families have given us new insights, ideas, and strategies that we want to share with parents to help their children heal, grow, and develop.

We want to make it clear that foster and adoptive parents are *not* responsible for the development of their children's problems. But they *are* responsible for creating the proper environment for change, the motivation for growth, the direction for improvement, and the security needed for comfortable attachment. Their roles are extensive, and if they are not fulfilled, their children cannot get well.

Parenting a hurt child may not be the kind of parenthood that some people envisioned when they responded to an advertisement about adding to their family. But anyone who wishes to take on the responsibility of fostering or adopting a child who has had early trauma needs to understand precisely what is to be expected. Once the choice is made to proceed, parents must know what they can do to help their new child heal.

It is our intent to give them information that will prepare them for troublesome—even dark—moments and to arm them for a loving battle. Many parents feel as if they are in combat, and most of them had no idea this is what the social worker meant when she said, "Jamie can be challenging and energetic."

Parenting hurt children can be difficult. But it can be less difficult . . . more fun . . . more effective . . . and more productive when you know who you are parenting and how to do it best. While your child may not always feel your help—or may not let on that he does—this is a normal part of the process. After all, how many of us recognized and appreciated what our own parents were doing for us as we were growing up?

As more and more adoptions of hurt children take place, there is a critical need to prepare the new parents for the challenges they will face. They require support from both the professional and the lay communities, because they are often misjudged and misinterpreted.

Early on, people speak of them as "saints." As time goes by, the child's disturbance begins to emerge. The parents' struggles and frustrations are revealed, and people pull away. They become judgmental, nonsupportive, and unsympathetic. These once "saintly" families withdraw, afraid to tell people what they are really going through. They think, "Who will understand?" "How could such a sweet child possibly be so much trouble?" "How could such a young child cause enormous turmoil among family members?"

These difficult situations are the ones that led us to write this book. We want to explore every option that will help families help their children. We want to enable parents to understand the very things that cause them distress . . . that cause them to reflect upon their capacity to parent. We want to give them as much hope as possible and to share some very specific strategies that may help make their journey smoother, more productive, and more enjoyable.

No single technique will solve all problems. There are no "tricks" that will abolish the hurt the child has experienced.

There are no strategies that will completely alleviate parental stress. Parenting a hurt child is a journey filled with surprise, pain, uncertainty, episodic joy, unparalleled excitement, and an ongoing sense of wonder—wondering what is just around the corner . . . wondering just how long the peace and love will last . . . wondering when the next crisis will hit.

When the carousel of placements finally stops, the roller coaster ride begins. We hope that what we have to share will give you the hope, strength, courage, and commitment to endure the ride with all of its unexpected turns and bumps. If you are able to complete the journey, you will have helped your child heal and grow. In the process, it is inevitable that you, as a parent, will also grow. We hope that what we have to share will inspire you to tap into your own resources and creativity and will allow you to become the parent you always wanted to be.

As you read this book, keep in mind the following facts. They will serve you well as you begin to understand parenting the hurt child.

- Parenting hurt children requires loving patience and clear expectations for improvement.
- Parenting hurt children is frequently painful.
- Hurt children bring their pain into their new families and share it with much vigor and regularity.
- Parents who did not cause the child's trauma often suffer the consequences of it.
- Even though the child may seek to anger the parent, children will not be able to securely attach to an angry parent.
- Anger prevents healing.
- Nurturing will promote growth, development, and trust.
- Parents do not need to have a consequence for a child's every misdeed.
- Family fun should not be contingent upon the child's behavior.
- Parents should expect difficult times, as well as a reduction of them.
- Parents must spend time—lots of it—with their children.
- Parenting involves sacrifices.
- While parents must take care of themselves, that care cannot be at the child's expense.

- Parents and children pay a price when parental short-cuts are taken.
- Expectations are more effective and powerful than dozens of rules.
- A child's history isn't only in the past. It affects the present and the future.
- Parents need to determine what information is private and what can or should be shared with people outside the family.
- Strong parenting does not need to be mean-spirited parenting.
- Angry parenting will help keep the mean child mean, the wild child wild, the scared child scared, and the hurt child hurt.
- If your child is from another country, his hurts and losses are the same as those of a child from the United States.
- Hurt children get better when their pain is soothed, their anger reduced, their fears quelled, and their environment contained.
- Reparenting is what hurt children need, regardless of their chronological age. Going back to pick up some pieces will be necessary before moving forward.

CHAPTER 1

WHO IS THE HURT CHILD?
Understanding the Attachment Cycle

For those who have read Adopting the Hurt Child *or have a good understanding of attachment issues, this chapter—condensed, with permission, from our first book—will serve as a review. For those new to the topic, this will provide an introduction to the hurt child.*

There is a common children's verse that says, "Sticks and stones may break my bones, but words will never hurt me." For the abused child, nothing could be further from the truth. While the effects of physical abuse usually heal over time, the psychological insults experienced by the child bring deep, long-lasting pain. These wounds fester within, creating ongoing difficulties for both the child and the adoptive family.

Many adoptive children did not experience early childhood trauma, neglect, or abuse. In these cases, the issues they face are common to all children and are supplemented by issues related directly to adoption. But for adoptive youngsters who lived through a difficult start, there is a range of developmental complications tied to the abuse, trauma, or neglect.

The problems that adoptive parents often see in their children are most likely the result of breaks in attachment that occur within the first three years of life. This condition is often diagnosed as Reactive Attachment Disorder, which impairs—and even cripples—a child's ability to trust and attach to other human beings.

Often mothers understand attachment issues before fathers do. This is because healthy children first attach to their mothers—beginning in the womb. Most adopted children blame the birth mothers for their abandonment, abuse, and/or neglect, and target adoptive mothers with their most negative behaviors.

AT THE BEGINNING OF LARA'S ASSESSMENT, HER FATHER SAID HE THOUGHT his daughter was fine, and the problems were all in her mom's head. When Lara was in session, both parents watched on a video monitor from another room as the child manipulated, swore, lied, and tried to prove to the therapist that she was the boss. "Daddy's little girl" was showing her true colors, and her father admitted, "If I hadn't seen it, I wouldn't have believed it." Lara's mother was vindicated, her father was forgiven, and the family could begin to heal.

ATTACHING DURING THE CRITICAL YEARS

Most professionals who work with and study the process of bonding and attachment agree that a child's first eighteen to thirty-six months are of vital importance. In a healthy situation, this is the period within which the infant is exposed to love, nurturing, and life-sustaining care. It is the time when the bonding cycle is repeated over and over again:

- The child has a need.
- He expresses that need by crying, fussing, or otherwise raging.
- The need is gratified by a caregiver, who provides movement, eye contact, speech, warmth, and/or feeding.
- This gratification leads to the development of the child's trust in others.

When abuse and neglect occur, they can interrupt the attachment cycle—leading to serious problems in the formation of the personality and most likely affecting him throughout adulthood. When the cycle is not completed and repeated, difficulties may arise in critical areas, such as

- Social/behavioral development
- Cognitive development
- Emotional development
- Cause-and-effect thinking
- Conscience development
- Reciprocal relationships
- Parenting
- Accepting responsibility

SYMPTOMS OF REACTIVE ATTACHMENT DISORDER

A child born into a dysfunctional environment that features abuse and neglect as overriding themes will not experience the attachment cycle with any predictability. As a result of this attachment interruption, he may exhibit many—or perhaps all—of the following symptoms:

- Superficially engaging and "charming" behavior
- Indiscriminate affection toward strangers
- Lack of affection with parents on their terms (not cuddly)
- Little eye contact with parents (on parental terms)
- Persistent nonsense questions and incessant chatter
- Inappropriate demanding and clingy behavior
- Lying about the obvious
- Stealing
- Destructive behavior to self, to others, and to material things (accident-prone)

- Abnormal eating patterns
- No impulse controls (frequently acts hyperactive)
- Lags in learning
- Abnormal speech patterns
- Poor peer relationships
- Lack of cause-and-effect thinking
- Lack of conscience
- Cruelty to animals
- Preoccupation with fire

When faced with these behaviors, the pain and heartache experienced by the adoptive parents cannot be underestimated, nor can the hope that comes with identifying this disorder. From identification comes treatment that can fill in the child's developmental gaps and allow him to grow to maturity.

JASON WAS REMOVED FROM HIS NEGLECTFUL BIRTH MOTHER WHEN HE WAS a year old and was placed in a very nurturing foster home before being adopted at age two and a half. By the time he was six, he was hitting and biting his adoptive mother and other authority figures. His past neglect—coupled with his unexpressed anger and sorrow over leaving his foster home—resulted in his becoming a very troubled child. Even though his history had few moves and much nurturing, he was still a child with unresolved loss issues that impacted his attachment.

EFFECTS OF ABUSE AND NEGLECT

Even before a child is born, the building blocks of development are being laid. During the critical nine months that the child is within his mother's womb, he must receive sufficient nutrition and be free of harmful drugs if he is to develop into a healthy baby.

Many of the children who hurt were born to mothers addicted to drugs and/or alcohol. These children can be viewed as life's earliest abuse victims, because prenatal maltreatment may have prevented some of their physiological systems from developing properly. Oftentimes they are not primed to attach to a caregiver. Impeded by immature neurological systems, they are often hypersensitive to all stimulation. They do not like light and may perceive any touch as pain. In fact, any child in chronic pain, even when nurtured by the most loving caregiver, may develop attachment disorder as the pain short-circuits his ability to attach.

Sadly, a baby born with fetal alcohol syndrome or with drug-induced problems is most often tended to by a substance-addicted mother who is incapable of providing even basic care. The infant's heightened sensitivity and irritability may set him up for further abuse or neglect, because the mother faces the added challenge of parenting a baby who is often fussy and upset.

Children placed into an orphanage shortly after birth receive little one-on-one care. No matter where in the world the orphanage is located, this early placement can affect a child's development and create attachment issues.

Whether the abuse and/or neglect occur in utero or after the child is born, the results may be similar. The attachment cycle breaks, and the likelihood of attachment disorder is great. Without the intervention of proper therapy, this emotional condition can create problems for a lifetime.

MIKE WAS TEN MONTHS OLD WHEN HE ENTERED FOSTER CARE AS A FAIL-ure-to-thrive child. By the time he was adopted at the age of three, the physical traits of failure-to-thrive were gone. But his anger remained. He came to us at fifteen after multiple treatments, including counseling, anger management, day treatment, residential treatment, and in-home therapy. When we showed him a photograph of a failure-to-thrive child and explained where his anger came from and where it belonged, he began to change and join the family.

CHOOSING THE RIGHT KIND OF THERAPY

To maximize the effectiveness of therapy for a child with attachment difficulties, treatment must be directly related to the problems that the family and the child are experiencing. Specific problems warrant specific solutions, and boilerplate methods serve no purpose. In most cases, finding the right therapist to point out the right path is the first step toward family harmony.

We continue to hear complaints from adoptive parents stating that mental health professionals blame them for their children's current problems. It is an unfortunate fact that many of those who attempt to provide treatment to adoptive parents with disturbed children know very little about issues related to adoption and are not well versed in the potential damage that early trauma can cause. This is particularly alarming when we realize that besides failing to provide effective therapy, these well-meaning professionals solidify the child's existing pathology and complicate subsequent therapeutic efforts. It is not unusual for us to work with families who have seen four to six mental health professionals with little or no results.

Bᴇᴛʜ, ᴀᴅᴏᴘᴛᴇᴅ ᴀᴛ ᴀɢᴇ ᴇɪɢʜᴛᴇᴇɴ ᴍᴏɴᴛʜs, ɪs ɴᴏᴡ ᴛᴡᴇɴᴛʏ-ꜰᴏᴜʀ ʏᴇᴀʀs old. She was in treatment with a psychologist to discover why she had such a hard time making commitments—to both other people and to a job. She suspected that her early life had impacted her adult life, and she began to educate her therapist about adoption and attachment issues. Finally, she became frustrated with his comments, such as, "I didn't know that," and "Can I borrow your books?" Ultimately, she grew weary of spending her money to educate her therapist and switched to an adoption-friendly professional who soon had her on the right road.

■

The reason for this ineffectiveness in treatment is startling in its simplicity. While graduate training enables therapists to deal with the neurotic personality, it does not adequately prepare them to deal with children who have not yet made it to a developmental level that is complex enough to be neurotic.

WHAT MAKES THERAPY FAIL

Young people with developmental delays—whether social, psychological, or cognitive—tend to be extremely skilled at figuring out the traditional therapist's goals and style. They effectively assume the role of victim, and the therapist responds with sympathy. Rarely does a clinician challenge a victim child, which is precisely what needs to be done when the child is faking it. When the therapist buys into the victim positioning, his sympathetic response serves to empower the child—and disempower the parent.

To compound the situation, many children who have experienced neglect, abuse, and abandonment have not yet developed an internalized set of values by which they judge themselves and others. They are not able to receive and experience empathy— nor can they develop insight—so they tend to project blame onto others and onto objects. They blame their adoptive parents for causing their anger, and they blame toys for breaking. They blame things that could not possibly be responsible for anything!

Most often, children or adolescents who engage in project- ing blame have not yet developed a conscience. They become adept at engaging others in a superficial manner, amplifying the distorted reality that exists with their therapists. They even man- age to draw teachers and others into their web of delusion, mak- ing these outsiders to the family feel that these "poor children" are quite easy to be around and are truly misunderstood by those who should know them best—their parents.

Many professionals are quick to endorse the helplessness of these children and their lack of social competence. While the young con artists are initially satisfied with their success at hook- ing yet another adult, they will ultimately hold him in contempt for "being so stupid."

Scores of therapists have fallen into this category and will be of little help to the child and his family if they continue to blame the parents or the family system for the child's difficulties. Character-disturbed children and adolescents are highly skilled in engaging the therapist when it should be the other way around.

It is an interesting dichotomy that the same therapists who are easily taken in by disturbed children find it difficult to work with the parents. Because their efforts are focused on helping the parents understand and tolerate the child, the implied— and sometimes direct—message is that the problem is one of parenting.

When parents are influenced to feel that their own issues are to blame, they may assume the "I need to change" role. Even when they objectively know that they were perfectly functional prior to becoming adoptive parents, they may be seduced into identifying themselves as the ones who should change. When their thinking no longer matches their experiences, they can feel crazy.

MARY, A SINGLE MOM, ADOPTED THREE CHILDREN. "IF ONE MORE PERSON says what a saint I am, I may kill them! I feel like I want to kill these children at times, and I'm doing the best I can. When they tell me I'm a saint, I feel like a fraud. No one knows how angry I get at times."

■

Many parents with whom we have worked describe years of nonproductive therapy. At the suggestion of therapists whose empathy focused solely on the child, they kept charts of chores, doled out rewards and stickers, and imposed monetary fines. They compromised their values, altered their expectations, and skewed their rules. They were therapeutically robbed of their parenting roles, resulting in an unexpected shift of power from them to their troubled child. Once this occurred, there was little reason for their child to change.

After many failed attempts at therapy, adoptive parents frequently become defensive, guarded, and overly controlling in their relationships with therapists. Once this happens, the parents are likely to look as if they are, indeed, the ones who need help. We often ask parents, "Did you feel and act this crazy before you adopted Bobby?" When we approach them from a humorously empathic point of view, we generally get a response such as, "Finally, we've found someone who understands!"

WHAT MAKES THERAPY WORK?

In order to help the child with attachment difficulties, it is necessary to provide therapeutic support to his adoptive parents, as well. This serves a twofold benefit:

- To counteract years of minimization and disbelief by mental health professionals, teachers, social workers, and extended family members
- To enable parents to receive, process, and utilize the information the therapist gives them, because it is presented in an atmosphere of support

Let's face it—anyone will listen and respond more positively to an ally than to someone who is placing blame. What's more, they will be more open to making any necessary changes in their parenting techniques.

WHEN THE SMITHS CAME TO OUR CENTER AFTER INTERNATIONALLY ADOPTING two siblings, they were in crisis. Their adoption agency was bankrupt, and their extended family was uninterested in the children who weren't, after all, "real Smiths." The mom was angry, and the dad was in denial. As part of their treatment, we suggested that they join our support group for parents of children with attachment disorder. The other mothers rallied around the new mom, while the fathers quickly nudged the dad into reality. Soon they were able to laugh about the antics of their children and could hardly wait to share stories and solutions, and get advice from others in the group.

■

When working with adoptive parents, we always make it clear to them that they are not responsible for the problems their children have. They are, however, responsible for doing what they can to help alleviate them. While we don't blame them, we do expect them to assume a role that is strong, committed, resilient, and persevering.

The support we give is not *carte blanche*. While it is the parents' right and responsibility to call the shots in their families, it is our responsibility to help them make appropriate changes in their interactions with their children that coincide with our therapeutic work.

We are constantly amazed at the reports we hear about therapists who treat children without informing the parents of what happens in therapy. The parents of our young clients are always involved—either by their presence in the treatment room or in the observation room. Although we have high regard for the confidential nature of some therapy, we firmly believe that parents of character-disturbed children must be aware of what we are doing.

We are honest with the child, as well, and our openness has always proved effective. The hurt children with whom we have worked respond well to a contract that states, "Your parents are important people in your life. Because we believe they are the best people to help you, we want them to know everything that goes on in our work. There are no secrets here, and there will be no secrets about what goes on at home."

TO MEDICATE OR NOT

A question that frequently arises during therapy is whether or not medications should be used. Some parents summarily reject information about medication with the common arguments, "I don't want my child to use drugs." "I'm not much of a medicine person—I don't even like to give my child aspirin." However, the fact remains that there are mental disorders that have a clear biogenic component and therefore respond well to appropriate medication. It would be as foolish to ignore the role of prescription drugs for some children and adolescents as it would be to ignore the use of insulin for diabetics.

Parents need to rely on the health care professionals with whom they are working for guidance and expertise. In addition, the behavior of a child on medication should be monitored carefully. We have seen dramatic improvements in those on medication . . . we have witnessed those who experience little or no change . . . we have even seen children who exhibit worse behavior after taking medication. Parents should never attempt to alter dosages without first consulting the prescribing physician. Such alterations are unhelpful—at the very least—and can be downright harmful. Medication probably serves its most beneficial purpose when used in combination with supportive services and appropriate therapy.

THE ROLE OF PARENTS IN THERAPY

When children have developmental delays and attachment issues—and therefore exhibit significant behavioral problems—their parents often become much too serious about everything. While the children tend to take nothing seriously, their parents become just the opposite. They allow themselves no levity and take nothing in stride. Instead, even small issues become major issues in their eyes. Their problems and miseries lead to the loss of support of family and friends, and they drift in a sea of isolation.

Like most people, adoptive parents may have unresolved psychological issues. Because hurt children seem to have a "button-locating radar," their parents' issues are generally targeted for exposure, aggravation, and agitation. If there's a button that can be pushed, these children will find it. And once they zero in on it, they push mercilessly.

Every day spent with a disturbed child heightens parents' awareness of their own issues. Most often, their unresolved struggles are reduced to power-and-control battles with the child. And once they are engaged in a battle initiated by the child, they have a difficult time pulling out.

Treatment efforts must therefore be focused on at least two dimensions. First, the parents' issues need to be explored and resolved. Simultaneously, parents must be given the practical strategies and tools for correcting the emotional imbalance in their homes. As a result, the therapist often assumes a multidimensional role with the parents, serving as mentor, adviser, psycho-educator, supporter, confronter, and guide.

The intake process includes a complete assessment involving a structured, written autobiography by each parent; child history; a marital assessment for couples or an individual one for single parents; and a family assessment completed in conjunction with the child's assessment.

TAKING A BREAK TO GET IT RIGHT

As the child's therapy progresses, it is imperative for parents to take breaks from counseling sessions, school problems, court problems, and any other unpleasant issues that are part of the package of raising a difficult child. When parents take good care of themselves, they continue to grow and develop. They become stronger and more comfortable, and can laugh at things that used to send them rushing to the therapist. They become aware that there are more good times than bad ones at home, and that awareness is a source of pure joy.

There is no denying the excitement we feel each time we see parents change from reactive to proactive. It is precisely at this point that we know significant progress is in the making. The child has begun to grow, and the parents are just far enough ahead of him to encourage and celebrate his ongoing journey.

CHAPTER 2

DARE TO PARENT:
Claiming Your Role in
Your Child's Life

Parenting is a truly awesome task. Many otherwise confident individuals are intimidated by the challenge, feeling undermined by all the systems that come into play, such as schools, child welfare workers, and mental health professionals. Even the glut of parenting books on the market today poses a subtle threat—making parents feel that if they haven't read the latest book on the latest way to raise a child, they have failed.

But the bottom line is this: despite the positive intentions of our society's systems and despite the valuable guidance and insights that might be found in books, only parents can raise their children. Only parents can build the foundations for moral thinking by setting day-to-day examples and expectations.

If we, as a society, expect to have strong children who embrace strong qualities and values, we must recognize the need to start this pattern with strong parents. Although the hottest best seller on parenting might have us believe that new trends are emerging all the time, the truth is that most of us already know how to parent.

Let's face it—some of what our parents did must have been right. Some of it must be worth replicating. Even if we want to avoid some of the techniques our parents used, most of us will find that it is nearly impossible to avoid falling back on the lessons we learned experientially as children. After all, isn't that the purpose of parenthood—to teach children how to "do life" so they can internalize what they learn, experience it, and ultimately transform it into their future?

The concept of the dysfunctional family really took off in the late-'70s and the '80s, when everyone suddenly became the "adult child" of some disorder or another. We once saw a cartoon depicting a meeting in a large auditorium, with only one person in attendance. The caption read, "A Meeting for Adult Children of Normal Parents." While it was certainly funny, it also captured the tone of the times—suggesting that everyone has a disorder that can be blamed on parents.

The real truth is more like this: *All* parents make some mistakes. *Some* parents make more mistakes than others. *A few* parents do almost nothing but make mistakes. This final group is most often found among the birth families of hurt children—those individuals whose parenting skills are so poor that their children have been removed from them.

The readers of this book, we assume, are found among the first two groups of parents. Unfortunately, these mostly healthy parents are held to a much higher standard than the parents who impose horrible atrocities on their children. To make matters worse, parents who are raising a hurt child are often misunderstood by others. Most people do not comprehend the dynamic that these wounded children bring into the family environment; and, consequently, they judge, blame, and often undermine the parents. Too often, the accusation of emotional abuse comes up long before there is a clear understanding of the context.

TAMMY WAS A SERIOUSLY DISTURBED FIFTEEN-YEAR-OLD GIRL WITH A HISTORY of self-abuse and self-injury. Her parents had to monitor everything in their home that was potentially dangerous to her—a daunting task when a child is intent on harming herself. They had prohibited her from using razors for shaving, because she always purposefully cut her body. When they allowed her to use an electric shaver, she managed to turn it into a weapon against her already scarred legs, so they removed that, as well.

Tearfully, Tammy appeared before her school guidance counselor, lamenting, "My parents won't let me shave, and all the kids are making fun of me." Outraged that Tammy's parents could be so insensitive and emotionally abusive, the counselor took it upon herself to buy the girl some safety razors. Tammy promptly took them home and inflicted cuts all over her legs and underarms.

Her parents were not considered in the guidance counselor's decision making. The woman didn't think to check with them to find out why Tammy wasn't allowed to shave. Tammy had succeeded in luring yet another person into her damaged world.

■

Professionals who work with children who are disturbed at any level must keep parents in the loop. Similarly, parents must demand that they have a role in the child's life. The concept of privacy and confidentiality for children and adolescents must be reevaluated when there are issues that parents need to know about.

Too often, confidentiality is maintained for everything except overt suicidal thinking or other safety-related areas. Well-meaning professionals need to remember that parents are ultimately responsible for their child's well-being and therefore need to be informed of anything that requires their attention. How can parents possibly help change a child's negative behavior if they don't know about it in the first place?

It is interesting to note that children in this country cannot go on a local field trip without signed permission slips and emergency medical forms; yet in some places people outside the family can arrange for contraception—even abortion—without parental consent. This sabotage of parents is both absurd and ultimately destructive, and must be changed if the family is to survive as a strong unit.

THE FEARS OF HURT CHILDREN

Children who have been hurt—either emotionally or physically—have fears that differ from those of other children. They are particularly sensitive to their own vulnerability and perceived weaknesses. They are terrified of losing control and are fearful of control by others. They are afraid of anything they think might hurt them and are threatened by anyone they think might not protect them. Determining the best type of parenting for these children can be accomplished by examining their individual fears.

Healthy Versus Unhealthy Fears
The paradox for children who have been severely hurt is this: because someone has repeatedly tried to kill them either through persistent neglect or outright assault, they develop a survivor's mentality. They begin to think that because they beat the odds, they are the strong ones. They vehemently deny their own vulnerability and have an unnatural sense of power. In essence, they fear nothing.

Tommy, AGE FOUR, WANDERS OFF IN THE MALL ALL THE TIME. HE approaches complete strangers, hits them, or tries to touch them in sexual ways. His parents claim he has absolutely no fear and will do whatever he wants to do—anytime and anyplace. The only thing he seems terrified of is allowing his mother and father to have any direction over him. He emphatically resists bathing, combing his hair, and getting dressed. In their words, "He is an absolute control freak!"

Tommy's fear, of course, is unhealthy. But healthy fear eventually expands to include respect, and, over time, leads to empathy and love. It is a developmental progression that needs to be experienced sequentially. A child cannot arrive at one level without going through the prior stages.

Early in life, fear is constructive. It is one of life's first inhibiting dimensions, because children often make proper choices based on what they perceive their parents might do to them. If this keeps them on the right track—doing the right things until their internal guide/conscience takes over—then what's the problem with it?

What's more, we sometimes tend to forget that negative events or processes often yield positive outcomes. Most of us have learned as much from our failures as we have from our successes. Michael Jordan has captured this concept in one of his posters, which reads, "I've missed more than 9,000 shots in my career. I've lost almost 300 games. Twenty-six times, I've been trusted to take the game-winning shot and missed. *I've failed over and over and over again in my life. And that is why I succeed.*" This wisdom speaks for itself.

Vulnerability and Perceived Weakness

Traumatized children are afraid to be cooperative, compliant, and receptive. To them, such behavior represents giving in, which translates to losing. They have learned to oppose anything that is suggested by others . . . they are experts at counteracting anything directed by others . . . they refuse to respond to anything that someone else wants. Consequently, they choreograph battles over the most insignificant issues.

The struggle, however, represents something completely different for parents than it does for children. While the parents are simply trying to get the child to accomplish a simple task—such as dressing for school, getting ready for dinner, or picking up his toys—the child is involved in a struggle to survive. He resists the intrusion and direction by others and perceives it as a fight for his life. As a result, his behavior becomes stubborn, tenacious, and intense. Think about it—how hard would you struggle if you thought that giving up or giving in would mean certain death?

Abused children learn to rely on control as a means to survive, and it is, indeed, an effective technique. However, once a child leaves the abusive environment, the behavior is no longer necessary or appropriate. In fact, he must learn to abandon his control issues if he is to survive in his new environment. The very things that kept him alive in the past will ultimately result in a very difficult life—perhaps even death. He must reverse his thinking if he is truly to survive and become a productive member of society. Helping him accomplish this shift in perspective becomes the parents' job.

Loss of Control, or Control by Others

For children who have experienced negative control by others, control issues abound. They associate control with hurt and, therefore, are internally mandated to resist control by their parents.

The word "control" generates a lot of negative response in the mental health field. We are never quite sure why, because every infant is completely under the control of his parents, is completely vulnerable, and, in healthy families, is completely safe. Children get the message very early in life that to be taken care of and nurtured equals being safe and comfortable. Quite simply, their very vulnerability ensures their safety.

They learn to rely on others throughout their lives without feeling that they will be hurt or taken advantage of. Control for infants and children translates to love—how else could it be expressed early in life? A parent certainly couldn't say "I love you" to an infant and have the message understood. Control doesn't have to be a dirty word—at any point in life.

In addition to accepting control, healthy children also develop a level of fear. Now here's where both traditional psychological thought and trendy parenting beliefs might jump in and say that fear in children is unnecessary. But the truth is, there's probably not a healthy adult among us who hasn't said something during childhood like, "If my mother knew I went out with Danny, she'd *kill* me!" This kind of comment reveals the belief that parents are powerful—powerful enough to fear—and that is a concept that will serve a child well.

Look at it this way: only the parent who is powerful enough to *kill* also has enough power to *love* and *protect*. Children with strong, healthy parents learn that vulnerability is okay—they can be weak without being unsafe. Tolerance of their weaknesses becomes a major strength, and they learn that humility is powerful.

Perceiving parents as big, powerful, and God-like also helps children develop a conscience. While soft love and nurturing contribute to the foundation for conscience, the imposition of discomfort and consequences also plays a part. Well-adjusted children don't want Mommy and Daddy to be unhappy, so they behave accordingly. In the process, they learn that life is not always win-win—they can make mistakes, deal with the consequences, and do better next time.

DEALING WITH YOUR CHILD'S FEARS

Because the fears of hurt children are different, each child's need for nurturing takes on a unique dimension. Parents must be completely present to meet this need—being "busy" does not absolve them of parenting responsibilities.

Life can sometimes be a merry-go-round. As it gets more complex, it's easy to lose sight of priorities. Things begin to change. Social contexts, family roles, and the amount of time parents spend with their children are all subject to change. But one critical factor does not change—the process of child development and the things that children need.

This presents a particular dilemma. With all of the things that have changed, children are expected to accommodate. *They cannot.* Furthermore, why should they? The price for change will be enormously high if children are the ones who have to pay. They have fundamental needs—many have special needs—and it is not fair to expect their needs to work around parents' deadlines, work schedules, divorces, and more.

When adult lives become too consuming, too busy, too involved for children, it is imperative to consider whose needs come first. For those of you adopting children who have experienced trauma as the result of neglect, abuse, or abandonment, please note that your kids need to be with you. They need to experience you as the parent, the guide, the teacher. Others cannot do this for you. If you are going to another country to adopt a child who has been institutionalized, do not bring him home and put him in day care. He needs to be with a family, and we can only assume that if you are adopting him, you want to be with him, too. Too many people are fulfilling only their half of the dream—to have a child. You must remember that it is equally critical to fulfill the child's half of the dream—to have parents. Only in this way can the arrangement be complete.

PARENT-CENTERED FAMILIES

By now, you may be asking yourself: why is a book about hurt children dedicating so much space to parents? The answer is a simple one: because without good parents, hurt children will stay stuck in their developmental quagmire.

Parent-centered families are better able to be child-focused than are child-centered families. The difficulty in child-centered situations is that nothing ends up focused at all—the child runs circles around his environment, while the parents frantically struggle to keep pace. However, when a parent is the central figure in the family, he or she is in the best position to watch the child, protect the child, contain the child, capture the child's attention, and, therefore, model for and teach the child.

Here's where we can take some cues from the animal kingdom, which is *parent-centered* and *child-focused*. Next time you're in a position to observe a mother animal and her young, you'll notice that while she knows where they are and what they are doing at all times, they are still responsible for keeping up with her . . . for initiating nursing . . . for staying where they are supposed to be. This arrangement helps ensure that the baby will be safe and close to the mother. If it lags too far behind, harm may come its way. Check out the ducks on the pond—who's leading and who's following. Watch the calf run to keep up with its mother. Then go to the supermarket . . . to the playground. Look at the people. Are the little ones following or being followed?

Obviously, we are a bit different from ducks on a pond. But as we watch families today, we see exhausted parents chasing their kids around—bargaining with them just to get through the checkout line at the grocery store or to make it through a department store with some remaining dignity.

While walking through a store one Saturday morning, there was an opportunity to watch a father handle his children quite well. He was walking a few steps in front of his two sons, whose ages were about five and seven. Their little legs had to do two to three steps for every one of his—they were keeping up with him! One boy asked, "Daddy, what do we get if we're good in the store?" Still keeping his pace, the father replied nonchalantly, "A happy dad."

What a perfect answer! From that one response, as well as from the father's demeanor, both kids seemed to get the message: it was their job to stay close to Dad, it was their job to act in a certain manner, and at the end of this trip they would have a happy father. Clearly, this was a lesson that must have been reinforced hundreds of times in their lives. They didn't need rewards or promises of treats to get them through the store. Nor did they need warnings, threats, or reminders about how to act. After all, what's the point of rewarding children for doing what they should be doing anyway?

Most hurt children have come from families where nothing was this clear-cut. If they were, in fact, the focus, it likely translated to being the target—the target for anger and abuse or for sexual activity. Without a parent leader, these children learn to rely on themselves. They learn nothing about reciprocity, cause-and-effect thinking, being valued, being contained, being safe, or being directed constructively. And they learn nothing about being nurtured.

As a result, these children need even more of a parent-centered family than a child who has not experienced trauma. After years of negative torment and multiple placements, they need to have corrective emotional experiences. They need to know that their parents can—and will—control and guide their lives. They need to learn that to follow their parents is safe, because these parents will not lead them into chaos and turmoil.

They need to know—both for their childhood and later on in life—that to yield, to cooperate, to surrender, to follow does not signify weakness. Instead, these things may signify wisdom and strength. Eventually, these children may develop the capacity to lead. And they can lead only if they have significant opportunity to follow.

DEMOCRACY AND THE FAMILY

One fundamental component of a democratic government is the assumption of equality among the participating members. Therein lies one answer as to why democracy in families simply isn't helpful or productive for the children or for the family as a whole. Children are not—and cannot be—equally participating members. They are not developmentally equivalent to their parents.

Parents who try to follow their children's lead as their major style of parenting are bound to lose—lose the trust and faith of their children, lose the strength they need to demonstrate for their children, and lose the sense of their true responsibilities as adults.

Children in these kinds of families also lose. They lose a sense of confidence and security in adults. They may lose a sense of safeness—the feeling that their parents know what to do and how to do it. They lose the comfort of knowing that their parents can protect them because they are strong.

Think about going on an extreme adventure—whitewater rafting down the rapids or rappelling down the side of a mountain. Would you feel safer with a guide who seemed confident that he knew more than you and didn't ask for your help in making decisions? Or would you prefer to venture out with someone who seemed more interested in how *you* might rig the safety harness? Obviously, most people would want to follow someone who appears prepared to lead and keep them safe.

Hurt children are no different. While they say they want to be in charge—and often demonstrate that stance in unbeliev-able ways—they know, on some level, that their being in charge places their entire world in jeopardy. Conversely, when they know unequivocally that someone else is in charge, they are freed from the responsibility of thinking, feeling, believing, and acting as if they *have* to be in charge. In helping them heal, we must allow them to be children. Part of allowing that to happen is *making* it happen. Parents need to parent actively, centrally, demonstratively, emotionally, competently, and securely if they want their kids to *get it*.

By now, the reader may be getting the false impression that this kind of parenting has to be rigid, controlling, inflexible, and perhaps even mean. In truth, it can't be any of these things if the child is to engage with the parent and family. "Dare to Parent" parents can do what they need to do without doing too much *work*. After all, kids work hard through their developmental processes, and their parents are there as support beams—strong, firm, and, yes, supportive.

This is not to suggest that the parents do not have to be involved. On the contrary, they must be involved a lot. They must help the child redo his life, get him unstuck, and then show him the way. Parents must be prepared to lead—especially for those children who find it difficult to follow. Other people can help, but it is the parents' responsibility to be primary in the child's life.

It should be assumed that this primary role is necessary until otherwise noted by the parent. Remember—hurt children have been off track for as many years as they have been alive. Do not assume that they know something until you find out for certain. Do not think a fifteen-year-old is an intact adolescent. (If, in fact, there even *is* such a thing!)

These children will have unmet needs from an earlier time—needs that must be addressed if they are to grow into their chronological ages. If they are to move forward, it will likely be necessary to first go backward. And going back means that the parents will have to operate as the parents of a younger person, which translates to performing a more central role than would be deemed necessary when parenting an adolescent. While it might sound unusual, it can be fun and exciting—at least, most of the time.

In summary, people who dare to parent need to believe:

- Parents have the right to parent.
- Parents know more than their children do.
- Adoptive parents must claim their children by moving into the parent role quickly.
- Only parents can give children the basic foundation upon which all other human development occurs.
- Children and adolescents are never too old to have, or to get, parents.
- Character building begins anew in adoptive families.
- Not only is it okay for parents to impose values upon children, it is mandatory that they do so.
- Parental expectations will encourage children to reach those expectations.
- Children and adolescents want parental involvement in their lives.

As stated at the beginning of this chapter, parenting is an awesome task. And parenting a hurt child poses an even greater challenge. To succeed, it is necessary to claim your role as a parent—with all of its dimensions and responsibilities. Claim your child, so you can teach him to claim you . . . and your values.

CHAPTER 3

WHAT DOESN'T WORK:
Parenting Techniques
Doomed to Failure

Many parents who are raising hurt children are good, loving people who possess skills that have worked with other birth, foster, or adopted children. In the case of those who are parenting for the first time, it is likely that they have sorted out effective and ineffective techniques from their own childhood and by observation. After all the work they've done to get a child, they want to be great parents. Many have even attended pre-service adoption or foster classes and have certificates to prove that they are qualified. They are confident that their love, consistency, and quality parenting will make the child whole and emotionally healthy.

But something goes wrong. They try the same things over and over, and nothing works. The child's behaviors do not change. In fact, the child is in control of the parent, the home, and seemingly everything else in his path. Instead of feeling like a family, the parents begin to feel as if they are being held hostage by the child. Everything revolves around what little Johnny or Susie will do. It's not long before they feel that there must be something wrong with them as parents.

In the support group at our office, one mother summed it up: "I'm sure I am the only one in this group who adopted because of infertility, and I think I know what's wrong. God thought that I would be a bad mother, so He made me infertile. I laughed in God's face and said, 'Watch this!' and adopted three kids. God replied, 'Watch *this*—see who I send you!'" The room was silent, and finally people spoke up and agreed that they all felt like terrible people and undeserving parents.

How sad that parents feel responsible for their children's problems—that they can't even turn to their faith for help. To compound the issue, society, school, family, and adoption agencies often condemn rather than help parents. They offer solutions that simply don't work, because the solutions don't match the problem. When these solutions fail, they blame the parents—who already feel that they are incompetent because their parenting and love do not have any effect on the child. While it is not the parents' fault that the child has problems, it is their responsibility to do everything they can to fix those problems.

In this chapter, we will review traditional parenting techniques that most often do not work for hurt children. It is very frustrating to parents when they employ the techniques that work with a securely attached child—and that fail miserably with a hurt child. But when parents understand *why* typically effective strategies don't work, they can learn to discard them and try something new.

Let's take a look at a parallel. If you were trying to lose weight, and someone suggested a great diet that worked for him but made you gain ten pounds, you'd get off that diet in a hurry. Similarly, if giving your child a time out doesn't change his negative behavior, stop putting him in the corner.

Chances are, we might mention a technique that typically fails but works for you. If that's the case, by all means keep doing it. After all, parents know their children best.

REWARDS

There is a chapter in this book that addresses nurturing, which could be perceived by some as "rewarding." But there is a difference. Nurturing needs to take place in order to complete the attachment cycle and should happen whether or not the child is "good." It must be initiated by the parents—not earned by the child—and employed as a way to promote and enhance attachment. Reward, on the other hand, is an offering to a child as an incentive to behave. In essence, it can be redefined as bribery. The problem occurs when rewards work—when the child becomes the blackmailer, and the stakes get higher and higher.

Children should not be rewarded for doing what they are expected to do. This is not the way the world works. After all, when was the last time a police officer pulled you over and gave you one hundred dollars for being a good driver?

Many parents use behavior charts with their children. If the child earns so many stars for being good, he gets a treat. This technique does not usually work for hurt children. To them, time has little meaning, and they often say, "If I'm good for awhile, or if I get good grades, Mom and Dad will want me to be that way all the time." While there is truth to this belief, the expectations are skewed.

Because the child cannot gauge a week in terms of time, he chooses to maintain control *his* way—thus guaranteeing that his parents won't win by "making" him do what they want. He defines his own reward, and most often, that reward is pushing his parents' buttons and watching them go crazy. An angry kid likes angry parents. He likes the energy and the stimulation. He likes the resulting chaos that was such a familiar part of his birth home. Creating interpersonal distance is his goal, and he doesn't care a bit about stickers on a behavior chart. He cares about making his parents mad.

To be good for a week is perceived by the hurt child as being perfect forever. He knows he can't do it, so he makes sure he's in control. It is more fun to pervert his parent's system than it is to earn the reward.

MARIANNE CAME TO OUR OFFICE FOR TREATMENT WITH HER FIVE-YEAR-OLD son. She had been given a star-chart kit by another therapist and was certain it wouldn't work. Instead of using it for the child, she hung it up in the kitchen and wrote "Mom's Behavior Chart" on it. When her son misbehaved, she would smile and add a star to the chart. "Why did you do that?" asked the little boy. "Because," she replied, "I was being a good mom and didn't get angry." It wasn't long before she earned a treat—a new blouse—which she happily showed her son.

∎

Of course the child was puzzled, because it seemed absurd that his mother would get a reward simply for being a good mom. So why do we think such a policy will work for children?

ALEXI WAS FOUR WHEN HE WAS REMOVED FROM AN ABUSIVE HOME IN Russia, six when he came to the United States, and eight when he started treatment. When we suggested to his parents that the use of a behavior chart was ineffective, they vehemently resisted. "You're wrong!" they claimed. "The chart works great. Alexi gets a sticker for good behavior at school and an X if he has a bad day. He brings the chart home to show us, and he hasn't received a single X. Every day he gets a sticker."

The parents later found out that when Alexi didn't get a sticker, he cut a little picture out of a book and fastened it to the chart with tape. When he showed it to his mom, it looked like a sticker. When he took the chart back to school, he removed the picture and revealed the X. He had figured out an effective way to control and lie to all the adults.

WITHHOLDING PARENTAL LOVE

Sometimes a parent will withhold herself from a hurt child to keep him at a distance. After all, why would anyone want to risk loving a child who may never love back? But this is precisely what we are asking the child to do—to trust that the new parent will stay around, unlike the parents of the past.

The hurt child has been given away, "tooken away," or abandoned by his birth parents. He has been abused (sometimes prenatally), neglected, left alone in an orphanage, or dumped by a drug-addicted mom. His siblings have disappeared, he has been sexually abused, and he has lost his primary language and the smells and tastes of home. What's more, his babyhood is in shambles. Why on earth should the punishment of withholding love be added to this tragic list? These children have endured more in their short lives than anyone should ever have to face.

Fear of rejection should not prevent a parent from trying to connect with a hurt child.

Many of us have seen Walt Disney's *Dumbo*. The little elephant's mother is put in jail for defending her baby's massive ears, and Dumbo puts on his best hat and trots off to visit her. Mom sings him a lullaby, caressing him through the bars. This scene invariably causes grown-ups to get misty-eyed—poor Dumbo, separated from his mom. The truth is, Dumbo is an elephant. He's not a child. He's a pretend elephant, at that, and because this is Disney, it's a pretty safe bet that he gets his mother back. We would be wise to extend some of this sympathy to the hurt child, who has endured the greatest loss a child can have—the loss of his birth mom.

Okay . . . she may have been a bad mom, a poor mom, a mean mom, an abusive mom, a drug-addicted mom, or a drunken mom. But children do not differentiate quality and know only the familiar. There is no loss on earth that is worse than what they have endured. Quite frankly, it is impossible to make them feel any worse than they already do. If a parent tries to out-wait a child by withholding herself until he wants her, it won't work. He has already lost too much.

PUNISHMENTS

In *Parenting with Love and Logic,* Foster Cline, M.D.—the renowned pioneer of attachment therapy—defines punishment as "the application of consequences *plus* anger." This definition is helpful in differentiating logical and/or natural consequences from the angry imposition of punitive consequences. When a consequence is given in anger, the child's focus is on the parent and the parent's anger. It is *not* on the behavior that caused the consequence.

The hurt child is familiar with anger and rage and has experienced much of it throughout his life with his birth family. If loud and chaotic ranting and raving occurs in his adoptive home, he gets the message that the "same old thing" is about to occur. It keeps his mindset in the past and does not allow him to have a learning or corrective experience.

When parents are angry and the child is in a heightened state of arousal, he is not in an optimal state for learning. Most likely, he's talking to himself and saying something like, *Yeah, yeah, yeah . . . are you about done yet? I really got to you this time!*

The techniques presented in *Parenting with Love and Logic* clearly suggest letting the consequences do the teaching. Empathy and consequences are more effective in helping the child have a corrective experience than a rage-driven lecture followed by an impulsive removal of television privileges.

There are times when many parents experience what feels like hatred toward their children. When this happens, it is best *not* to make a disciplinary decision.

TIME OUTS

Picture it. A child is standing in a corner, and he keeps yelling, "Is it time, yet?" His mother replies, "No! And every time you ask me, I'm going to add another minute!" And the pattern repeats itself, over and over.

In this scenario, nobody is really timed out, because there's an ongoing interaction. As a concept, time outs may have merit for some. As a practice, they are not only useless for hurt children, they are also contraindicated.

Children who have had so much loneliness and separation from their birth parents need to be with their new parents. Quite simply, they need time ins. Even when they misbehave, the consequence should be something that brings them close to a parent—helping to scrub the bathtub or wash the car. Because separations bring about disconnections, it is critical to *create* connections to help hurt children heal. In a very real sense, the children we are discussing are in a permanent time out.

Children who are sent to their bedrooms to "reflect on their behavior" are not doing that. Were you ever sent to *your* room? Did you spend the time reflecting on what *you* did?

When we presented the bonding cycle in chapter 1, we talked about *gratifying* a child's need to help him learn to *trust*. And that just doesn't happen when we banish him to his room. Take a look . . .

A child is in an agitated state, and his mother doesn't like it. She says, "I want you to go to your room until you can be calm and act like the rest of us." In other words, "Go to your room until you calm yourself down . . . until you engage in whatever *self-gratification* it takes to get you calm . . . and then you will have reinforced the *trust* you have in yourself."

This is *not* the message we want him to keep. We do *not* want him to believe that he can rely on himself. He already believes this, and what he needs to believe is that he can trust his mother.

GROUNDING

Whenever a child is grounded, so are his parents. After all, they have to make sure he doesn't do what he's not supposed to do. In fact, the concept of grounding an adolescent gives him the idea that he is completely free to do whatever he wants to do *unless* he is grounded.

It is far more effective for the adolescent to know that he needs to get permission to do *anything*. In a way, he is permanently grounded until otherwise arranged. As a result, he isn't compelled to do things based on his assumption that he can do whatever he wants without parental consultation. Kids who haven't been raised by good families need to know that their current parents care enough about them to keep track of them.

Think about it for a minute. What is the purpose of the grounding? Is it punishment? Will it be corrective? Will it be a connecting opportunity for the adolescent and the parent? Permission to do certain things should be assumed to be necessary. If this is the case, the length of the "leash" can be changed as the parents determine.

Many children and adolescents are involved in structured activities, such as sports, scouts, band, and church youth group. These kinds of activities are valuable, and depriving a child of them as a means of grounding him can be counterproductive.

For example, if a child's grades are sufficient to meet the school's eligibility requirement for the soccer team, we suggest that he be allowed to play. His grades may not meet parental expectations, but we feel that the school's rules should supersede the parents' rules in this kind of situation. What he will gain from organized activity can be very helpful.

Such activities help him to develop "normal" peer relationships . . . to learn to follow rules . . . to cooperate with adults and peers. If he is not managing the activity well, the adults in charge will have to deal with the situation. And the logical consequences of any negative behavior will fall naturally into place.

DEPRIVATION

Hurt children, almost by definition, have been deprived of just about everything. They have lost their birth parents, siblings, familiar surroundings, schoolmates, grandparents, and foster parents. In many cases, they have even been moved without their toys or clothes ... without anything that is familiar to them. So under the circumstances, taking *things* away from kids who have already lost about everything is pointless.

Unfortunately, frustrated parents, teachers, and others involved with hurt kids tend to rely on taking things away as a means to get some sort of message across. They take away toys, dolls, scooters, skateboards, computers, video games. And nothing has any effect. Most often, the child says, "Go ahead. Take it. I don't need it anyway." As soon as this kind of comment comes out of his mouth, he has already begun to look for something else to play with, break, or take away from a sibling.

Parents who frequently take things away—then give them back—reinforce the child's knowledge that it won't be long before the item is returned. We therefore suggest that if parents feel the need to take something away, it should be something they will never return. Then, at least, the child has the opportunity to know that a confiscated item is gone forever.

> PARENT: "Nicolai, I've noticed that you're not taking very good care of your video games. I keep finding them on the floor, under the furniture, and even outside in the yard. Because they cost a lot of money, I'm going to give some of them to a child who doesn't have any. If you don't really like them, then I can make your life easier by getting rid of them."
>
> CHILD: "I *do* like them. How will getting rid of them make my life easier?"
>
> PARENT: "Well, you'll have less to look after, and you have so many things to pick up."
>
> CHILD: "That sucks."
>
> PARENT: "I guess it does. Would you like to come with me while I take them to Goodwill?"

CHILD: "No!"
PARENT: "Okay. I'll be right back, and then we'll go outside and play catch."

In this interchange, the child can clearly see who is in
charge. The parent is not displaying any anger, yet he is demon-
strating that he says what he means and means what he says. He
also lets the child know that as soon as he returns, the two of
them can have some fun. In this kind of "taking away," the child
just might get the point that he'd be better off taking care of his
things. He just might learn to care about *something*. And the
bonus is that even though he loses an *object,* he gets to interact
with a *person*. This is far more valuable than sitting around star-
ing at something electronic.

In summary, you cannot deprive the deprived. It just doesn't
make sense to them.

ANGER

When we were children, most of us could recognize when our
parents were angry, and we learned to stop short of unleashing
that anger. If we had a very good mom, her "look" alone could
freeze us in our tracks. We didn't want our mom or dad to be
mad at us, because angry parents didn't give us as much time,
attention, or love. For a securely attached child, losing a parent's
love is the most terrible thing in the world.

Most children who have experienced abuse are familiar with
anger. And angry children love to cause others to be as angry as
they are. Many adoptive parents report that their child is most
unhappy when the parents are joyful and smiling. Conversely,
they also report that when they are furious and acting completely crazy, the child seems almost content—which makes the
parent even angrier!

We must remember that anger is the hurt child's friend. It
keeps him safe and distant, and when he sees it in others, he
feels powerful. It also brings the level of energy in the family up
to a level that the child undoubtedly had grown accustomed to
in his birth family.

We are not suggesting that parents should never get angry.
But we believe that if anger is ever going to be effective, it must

be relatively rare. Daily anger is quickly ignored by the child. As the child feels less able to get the parents to respond with anger, he takes notice.

Remember—anger generates distance, and the parents' goal with a new child is to bring about closeness.

EQUALITY

Every child in a family has individual needs, and each requires different responses from the parents. Don't buy into claims such as, "That's not fair! You let Robert ride his bike to the mall . . . why not me?" It is better to respond with a comment suggested in the *Love and Logic* material, "We're all different, and the world doesn't always treat us fairly or equally. It's much better to learn this at a young age than on your first job assignment."

Many parents wonder if they have to parent all the children in the family in the same way, and the answer is no. The child with attachment issues has a special need, and it isn't visible to most people. It is critical for parents to recognize this need and to respond accordingly.

If rewards and time outs work with one child, continue to use them. If they fail with another child, try something else. There's a treasury of parenting techniques out there, so your options are extensive.

Just remember not to lose heart. The next chapter addresses many strategies that *do* work, and they may even inspire you to come up with a few of your own. Also, keep in mind that, in some cases, good parenting is not enough. Attachment therapy, occupational therapy, physical therapy, and other interventions may be needed to help the family heal.

CHAPTER 4

WHAT WORKS:
Cycling Your Way to Health and Happiness

Parents, therapists, and social workers often understand the attachment cycle when it is presented—the cycle of a child's need, arousal, gratification, and ultimate trust. The difficulty they face is treating and parenting the child in a manner that is congruent to the cycle. Children with attachment issues have missed thousands of cycle completions, and it is up to us to make them up. This takes time. Lots of time.

Let's face it—most of us don't know how we became attached to our parents, or how our children might have attached to us. It simply started at birth and progressed over time, with thousands of interactions taking place to complete the cycle.

When a child has not securely attached as an infant, it is critical to give him the opportunity to experience the attachment cycle with his adoptive parents. This should be done over and over again—in ways that build trust, decrease anger, and meet the child's real needs. Most of these children choose to remain distant, but that is their *want,* not their *need*. Parents and professionals need to work with them to help them repeat the cycle, thus enabling them to attach. In our professional experience, the most effective ways are by employing the components of touch, smell, speech, motion, warmth, and eye contact.

Touch is key to attachment, which is why holding therapy (see chapter 11 in *Adopting The Hurt Child*) is so effective for these children. At home, parents can support the positive touch of holding therapy by massage, applying lotion to the child's back, arms, feet, and so on. Whatever the methodology, it is important to remember that holding the child at home is key.

Smells are very important in attachment, so it is wise to use a strongly scented lotion, such as vanilla, for massaging. Apply it to the child's skin and put some on yourself. Comment on how you smell alike.

THE JASPER FAMILY WAS DETERMINED TO DO EVERYTHING TO HELP THEIR adopted sibling group attach. They used vanilla lotion every day, burned vanilla candles, and used vanilla potpourri. One day, they entered a gift shop. Their eight-year-old stopped to exclaim, "It smells just like home!" Sure enough, there was a vanilla scent in the store. He beamed up at the astonished clerk and announced, "That's the smell of a good mom!"

■

Eye contact is also critical and can be strengthened by verbal cues, touching the face, and refusing to respond without it. Younger children can be helped to increase their eye contact when parents get down to their level or bring them up to theirs. Let's take a look at how this works.

Normally, when a parent hands something to a child, it's delivered from the hip—so that's where the child's eyes land. Instead, try holding the desired item—be it a drink, a cookie, a toy, or a book—at eye level and incorporate a verbal cue: "Do you want the cookie? Please look at Mommy. Good girl." Then hand the cookie from the eyes to the child. Because small children need things all day long, this is an easy way to increase eye contact without burdening the parent.

Motion is equally important. Crabby babies love to be held, walked, rocked, or driven around in the car. Rock your child (no matter how old), twirl him around the room, wrestle, dance, ask him to move with you following your lead, hold hands and walk in circles. Simply move together.

Babies get warm when they are fed, changed, and held—proving that warmth is a way to demonstrate love. Talk to your child when he is warm and cozy in bed, after a meal, or after a bath. At these times, he will be more relaxed.

When we talk to babies and toddlers, we tend to change our tone and speak in a different rhythm. We also use lots of rhymes, which children love. Think about it—how many nursery rhymes has your hurt child missed in his lifetime? Make up for it by repeating rhymes and rhyming songs with him. Not only is this key to language development, it's also an activity that your child may enjoy at any age.

These suggestions and the ones that follow in subsequent chapters are not necessarily easy, and they may even seem absurd. While they might appear developmentally out of sync with the child's chronological age, they just might match his emotional age. After all, your intent is to parent the hurt little one inside your child.

There is no magic recipe to "fix" these children. These suggestions are ingredients for the parent/cook to use in the crock pot . . . to put the children on simmer. It doesn't matter how quickly the recipe is finished. It just matters that the final dish is completely cooked and not half-baked.

PARENTING TECHNIQUES

By the time we see parents in our practice, they are usually very discouraged. They feel helpless, because nothing they have done has enabled their children to attach. Or so it feels. They are exhausted, angry, and devoid of hope. Yet once we teach them new techniques—and they begin to understand *why* these interventions work—they see definitive results that the family is beginning to heal. The parents are once again in control, which empowers them and allows the child to trust. After all, who would trust a parent who can't control a child?

Just as all families are different because of each member's personality, all children with attachment problems are uniquely different. Some children have severe problems, while others' issues are milder. Therefore, not all techniques are useful in all families. Parents, therapists, and others who look for a magic solution—a one-size-fits-all approach to helping these children—will be doomed to disappointment.

Here are some ideas to try. Keep the ones that work and discard the others. Remember—as the child changes, develops, and gets well, some of the techniques may need to be altered.

Don't lose sight of the fact that you know your child best, and what works with one won't necessarily work with another. Also, when deciding how to handle a particular problem, keep in mind the child's *emotional* age. A technique that's appropriate for a four-year-old can work wonders with a ten-year-old who's stuck at a younger age.

Mixing up your parenting styles can also be an effective tool. It adds an element of unpredictability, which helps keep you—not the child—in charge. Sometimes, catching your child a bit off guard can be all it takes to regain control of a situation that's getting out of hand.

Keep in mind that safety is key, and be certain never to do anything that will hurt a child or place him in danger. For example, let's say you're trying to teach a twelve-year-old to do what you tell him to do. It's a sixty-degree day, and you remind him to wear a jacket when he goes out to play. He balks, so you let him go out without one. When he comes right back home with goose bumps, it's likely that he's learned his lesson, and he wasn't harmed in the process. Clearly, initiating this lesson in below-zero weather would be downright dangerous.

Many of these ideas might sound contrary to good parenting. In fact, they *would* be if you were parenting a securely attached child. But if you're reading this book, odds are your child has special needs. Certainly, if there are other children in your family who have not been hurt, parent them in the ways that work. Just don't fall victim to the myth that all children need to be treated the same or that it won't be fair.

Believe me—if life were fair, there would be no neglect, no abuse, no foster care, and no adoption. All children would be born to parents who meet their needs, and only those parents who want children would be allowed to give birth. Don't make the mistake of trying to teach any child that life is fair. It isn't.

CONTROL ISSUES

There are some simple rules to remember with children who are overly controlling. First, they learned to control adults early on—when abuse, neglect, or the limitations of an orphanage taught them that adults could not be trusted. To quote Kay Donley Ziegler, an early pioneer in the world of older adopted children, "We live in a world where big people take care of little people. They live in a world where big people *hurt* little people." Asking these children to give up control and hand it over is very difficult, because to them, it is a matter of life and death.

This may seem strange to parents, but think about it for a minute. When infants are well taken care of, the parents are in complete control—dressing them, feeding them, moving them around, and making all the choices. Many of these choices are ones that the infant doesn't like—getting shots, being in a car seat, wearing a snow suit—but the infant learns to trust the parents who make the choices, because in the process, his needs are being met.

Children with attachment issues have learned *not* to trust adults, and that is the lesson they need to unlearn. The only way for them to learn to trust is to give up control, thus getting the message that they won't be hurt if the parent is in charge. This is not an easy concept for the child to learn.

Because control is directly linked to the child's concept of survival, he will often initiate control battles unnecessarily. Don't worry about the battles you can't win or the ones you don't know about. After all, if you try to control everything, you'll end up the loser. The child needs to have some control, and you can decide how much and how it is to be experienced. The more control battles you give up, the more likely it is that you'll win the ones you take on.

There are three simple rules to employ when dealing with a controlling child. Developed by Foster Cline, M.D., and Jim Fay, they are presented here with their permission and with our own spin:

1. Avoid control battles whenever you can.
2. Choose your battles carefully.
3. *Win* the ones you take on.

(For additional information on this topic, we suggest that you read their book, *Parenting with Love and Logic*. A catalog of all their published materials can be obtained by calling The Love and Logic Institute at (800) 588-5644 or logging on to www.love-andlogic.com.)

AVOID CONTROL BATTLES

If parents take on one hundred control battles a day and win thirty, they've lost 70 percent. If they're faced with one hundred control battles a day, take on five, and win them all, they've won 100 percent. The rest of the battles simply do not count, because the parents didn't engage. The result: the parents become more powerful in the child's eyes, because they are perceived as being in control of the family.

One way to help a child relinquish control more easily is to give him the opportunity to make choices.

WHENEVER SEVEN-YEAR-OLD ALEX WAS ASKED BY HER MOM TO TIE HER shoes, comb her hair, and put on a jacket, she would alter the order—first combing her hair, putting on a jacket, and then tying her shoes. Although her mom didn't care, Alex thought she was scoring an enormous control coup. However, when mom started restating her directions—"Honey, get ready by tying your shoes, combing your hair, and putting on your jacket . . . in any order you want."—she took the child completely by surprise. While Alex had been convinced that she was powerful by doing it "her way," she was knocked down a peg or two when she realized that her mom had taken control by not caring. In this case, the parent completely avoided the battle by eliminating the choice of doing things "Mom's way."

Choose Battles Carefully
Although we might not want to acknowledge it, adults are not in charge of everything. What's more, there are some battles they simply cannot win. When dealing with hurt children, parents must be sure to avoid battles involving food, bedwetting, and what comes out of a child's mouth, because no one can control these issues.

It is important to choose the timing of the battles you take on. For example, if the child won't get ready for school and makes the whole family late, you can plan ahead. Because hurt children often repeat the same behaviors, it's easy to plan around them. Call the school and explain the problem. Find out if it's okay for the child to show up partially dressed and finish getting ready at school. This usually doesn't have to happen very often for the child to get the message.

WHEN TESS, AGE SIX, TOOK TWO HOURS TO DRESS FOR SCHOOL, THE ENTIRE family was late. If anyone tried to help her speed things along, the battles raged. Tess's mother eventually called the school, and with the support of the principal and the child's social worker, announced to the family that there was a new plan. The car would be leaving at 7:00 A.M., regardless of how anyone was dressed. The next morning, at the appointed departure hour, Tess was wearing a pajama top, a skirt, and no shoes. Her mother ushered her into the car, packing along the child's shoes and shirt. Tess finished dressing at school. The battle was over. It took only once.

■

Of course, it's possible that the school will refuse to allow the child to show up in such a state of disarray and will report you to Children's Services if you dare to attempt it. If this is the case, try another plan. Take a personal day from work, but *don't* tell the child. When he isn't ready for school, simply stay at home and busy yourself with household chores. He'll wonder why you aren't fussing at him, and that will put you firmly in control.

Another option is to wait until the child wants to be some-where—like a birthday party—at a particular time, and don't be ready. Imitate his slowness, but *do not* say anything like, "Now you know what it feels like." (This may be difficult, but it's a vital component of the plan.) He'll eventually get the message when he's late for the party, and talking about it beforehand ruins the lesson.

Once parents realize there is no "right" way to handle a problem, control becomes easier. They can think about how best to take on the selected issues and leave the rest alone.

WHEN SAM, AGE NINE, CAME INTO OUR OFFICE FOR THE START OF A TWO-week intensive, we told him to take off his shoes and put them against the wall, with the toes pointed toward the wall. Forty-five minutes later, his shoes were still in the middle of the room. We had experienced his oppositional behavior as he placed the toes of his foot on the wall, and the heels of his shoes on the wall. He clearly demonstrated that he did, indeed, understand the meaning of "toes of the shoes" and "walls," but steadfastly refused to comply and do things our way.

His observing parent was able to witness just how controlling her son was. Once she was clear on that, we did a very powerful thing—we changed our minds. We told Sam that we didn't want his shoes by the wall; we wanted them in the hall, and we placed them there. Needless to say, Sam was very surprised when instead of getting mad, we laughed and said, "That was fun! You're good at this game, Sam." The next day, when Sam placed his shoes in the middle of the floor, our comment was, "Good! We knew you'd put them there. Thanks for making us right!" We repeated this exercise for the rest of the two weeks— wherever Sam put his shoes, we said we wanted them precisely there. We won the battle of the shoes simply by changing our minds. He was "obeying" no matter how hard he tried not to.

Because every family is different, you need to decide for yourself the when, why, and how of taking on a battle. And remember—the battle you can win today may not be so easy to control tomorrow.

Win Your Battles
Parents must win the battles they take on. This is usually quite simple, because they can choose the ones in which they want to engage.

Jonathan, age six, flatly refused to put his cereal bowl in the dishwasher. Morning after morning, his mom would remind him to do it; morning after morning, he would not comply. Because his mom wasn't prepared to stay home from work and battle with her son until the cereal bowl landed in the dishwasher, she changed her mind. And as with Sam, it worked.

"Jonathan, how did you know that today I didn't want your bowl in the dishwasher? I want to rinse the dishes in a special way, and you're making it easier for me to do that. Thanks! We must be getting closer, because you can read my mind." Mom avoided the battle . . . she took control . . . she won.

■

To many parents, this scenario may seem as if Jonathan's mom gave in to him. What she actually did was help jump-start the attachment cycle. If they had continued to battle day after day, she would have relinquished control. Jonathan would have been in constant trouble. And if the child is always in the hot seat—if parent and child are always angry at one another—no attachment can occur. The cycle cannot progress to gratification and trust, so everyone loses.

The point is for the family to move to a win-win situation, where the child learns that if the parent wins, so does he. This is a foreign concept to the hurt child, who often feels that if the parent wins, he will lose or be hurt. There are also many times when the child will lose, and that should be okay, too. We have all lost battles and arguments, and losing is good preparation for what happens in life.

CONSISTENCY

It is not necessary to be consistent with hurt children. Of course, that statement sounds radical to parents who have used consistency with birth children with great success. After all, most children do well with consistency, and most parents try very hard to explain consequences and give their children the same ones every time.

But hurt children do not have good cause-and-effect thinking. Even when faced with natural consequences, they truly do not comprehend that their actions caused their predicament.

We teach children lessons like, if you don't do your homework, you get a time out. The securely attached child doesn't want a time out, so he does his math. Hurt children, on the other hand, view this scenario as a choice. They hear: Either do your homework, or get a time out. *So,* the child might think, *that isn't such a bad choice. I've been neglected, starved, and beaten. Sitting quietly for awhile sounds pretty good to me. I choose not to do my homework and will take the time out instead.* Having made what he perceives to be a choice, he can't figure out why his parents are mad at him.

As a result, it is better for children with attachment disorder not to be told what the consequences of their behaviors will be. Instead, the parents should alternate their responses—sometimes ignoring the child's negative behavior, other times commenting on it, other times imposing a consequence. The child needs to be guessing what the parents are going to do, as opposed to the parents guessing what the child will do.

The state of Pennsylvania used to have large posters that pictured a finger-pointing highway patrolman above a caption that read, "Don't Speed." The posters also featured a list of fines for each mile over the speed limit. Now, we Ohio folks know that Pennsylvania patrolmen give tickets, so we would choose the fine we could afford, speed that much, and hope to avoid getting caught. Think how much more impact the sign would have had if it read, "We have new plans for people who speed in Pennsylvania. So speed . . . and find out what they are." We would definitely have driven within the speed limit, and let somebody else find out what the new plans were. The unknown is powerful.

Consistency works well with securely attached children because they don't like being in their parents' bad graces. They seek parental approval and like to know the rules so they can obey them. Children with attachment issues want their parents to be angry and distant, so they often view the rules as a roadmap. They know exactly what to do to make Mom and Dad angry . . . to stay outside the family and avoid compliance. While these goals are what they want in the short term, they are not goals that will afford them a happy life. If their parents are less consistent with consequences, the child's map no longer works. He needs to find a new path, one that will move him closer to the family.

PRAISE

Most children do well with praise. They want to please their parents, so they repeat behaviors that their parents like. When a securely attached child's father says something like, "You've been a great kid for a week," the child blossoms with pride. Say the same thing to a hurt child, and the message he gets is that he's given up power, lost control, and had better get back to avoiding his father at all costs. Such a comment is almost a guarantee that the child will start a new cycle of difficult behavior.

Praise needs to be specific, short, and enthusiastic. A quick touch, a smile, eye contact, and a cheerful "Good job!" recreate the attachment cycle of touch, talk, and eye contact, and indicate to the child that his good behavior has been noticed.

Offering intense praise or treats for normal behavior—such as telling the truth—is counterproductive. It tells the child that acting nicely is difficult and therefore should be rewarded. This is not the way of the world. The police don't give rewards for not stealing—they send thieves to jail. A child's reward for behaving well is having a happy life and happy parents.

Sometimes it is good for hurt children to overhear praise instead of receiving it directly. This methodology is less threatening and can have a positive effect. A parent can call a friend—or simply dial up the weather recording—and talk about something that the child did well. The hypervigilance of most hurt children almost guarantees that they'll hear every conversation. And because most of these children are used to hearing their parents report their negative behaviors to social workers, relatives, and therapists, they're surprised and pleased to hear their parents say something good about them.

Another indirect way is to mail the child a card with a short complimentary message. The fact that you bothered with the mail makes the praise seem great, yet the child isn't required to have direct contact and risk "losing face" with you by acknowledging compliance.

FLEXIBILITY

If you can't make the child change his behavior, make his behavior what you want. Sound confusing? It's not. If your child is having a temper tantrum, telling him to stop is pointless. Instead, say something like, "Oh, a tantrum. I think I'll get some iced tea and make myself comfortable while I watch." Or, if you're feeling particularly brave, say something like, "You can do better than that, can't you? I'll bet you can scream louder."

If the tantrum continues, it seems like compliance. The child now has two choices—to stop or to keep going and do what you want.

ONE FAMILY, INSPIRED BY THE OLYMPICS, HAD CARDS PRINTED WITH THE numbers 1 to 5 on them. When their child's tantrum started, everyone in the family held up a card to judge it. The rest of the family had fun, and the power of the tantrum was decreased.

■

When working in therapy with a child who is a chronic liar, we'll often ask a question that's met with an "I don't know" answer. When this happens, we ask the child to lie. He tends to be speechless and then protests, "I can't do that!" He just doesn't like it when the adult plays the game in a new way . . . when the adult is in control.

GOOD VERSUS BAD

Hurt children are frequently stuck at a very young age—an age when things are big or little, good or bad, cold or hot. This is the world of fairy tales, where there's a good witch and a bad witch, not a witch trying to decide on her behavior.

We need to help children differentiate between degrees of good and bad. Simply "being good" is a concept that's difficult for them to grasp. When asked what they are supposed to do, they often reply, "Behave." But when asked to define "behave," they respond with a blank look. They view "behave" as perfect, and because no one can be perfect, they might as well give up. Because they cannot comprehend degrees of behavior, they perceive both spilling their milk and smacking their little brother as "bad."

We often use the child's body to demonstrate the difference. The head represents perfect behavior; the toes stand for horrible behavior. When initially asked to define behaviors along this body line, most children put everything directly at the head or toes. So not doing homework and yanking on the cat's tail both are placed at the toes.

Over time, we help the child realize that there are degrees of behavior. Hurting the cat is at the toes, but not doing homework might be at the waist . . . listening carefully to a direction is at the neck . . . helping Dad wash the car is at the head. We then ask the child to try giving up behaviors below the belt. These include things that hurt others or take away trust, such as stealing and lying. The parent then has a verbal cue—"That was below the belt"—to help the child sort behaviors. If the child can understand a system of 1 to 10, that's another way to explain it.

Paul WAS ELEVEN WHEN WE BEGAN WORKING WITH HIM. AS HIS BEHAVIORS improved, he would often ask his parents, "What would a normal kid do in this situation?" He knew he was different and didn't want to be. Yet he wasn't completely clear on what constitutes acceptable behavior.

■

Asking these children to give up past behaviors without telling them what to do is fruitless. No one will give up a familiar way of life without knowing what he'll get in return. Instead of telling a child to stop lying, it is much more effective to advise him to become a "truth-teller."

AARON WAS A CHRONIC LIAR. TO DEAL WITH THE PROBLEM, HIS MOM MADE two shadow boxes out of shoe-box lids. One represented the liars' club—a place of black clouds, lightning, and dismal colors. The truth-tellers' club was a lid with a rainbow, sunshine, and a picture of Aaron's parents. Mom mounted a picture of Aaron on cardboard, cut it out, and placed him in the truth-tellers' club. When he would begin to tell a lie, she would sigh and move the photo into the liars' club. This immediately interrupted his automatic lies, and he would tell the truth. It was a great, simple, nonverbal cue about winning for the child . . . and joining the family.

■

Telling a healthy child who is misbehaving that "Smiths don't act that way" will likely have a positive effect. But children who have been through multiple placements probably don't know what the Smiths expect. Those who have been raised in orphanages know about group living, not about family life. Most of us figured out how our families behave and what they expect from us simply by living with them and observing them. Hurt children do not get these subtle cues. The "mother looks" that freeze healthy children roll off the backs of children who are not securely attached. In fact, they often do not even see that piercing gaze.

TOUGH PAYBACKS

Reciprocity is a task that well-cared-for infants learn early in life. They smile . . . Mom smiles. Dad tickles . . . they laugh . . . Dad laughs. Now think about the infancy of abused and neglected children—what reciprocity did they learn?

Neglected children—whether raised in an orphanage or in the birth home—do not have adults holding them, making faces, and talking to them. They do not learn reciprocity. Instead, they learn uncertainty, because they never know when they will be hurt. To make matters worse, the hurt is not in response to anything they do.

Most people know how to get out of trouble with friends, relatives, and loved ones. When they annoy or offend someone, they can usually make amends by doing something like sending flowers, apologizing, offering a kiss, or writing a letter. Because hurt children have not learned reciprocity, they do not know how to make amends when they offend someone. They don't understand why Mom is angry about Monday's offense on Tuesday. After all, that was in the past.

Parents must artificially teach this skill until the child understands it and can be sincere about it. This will not happen spontaneously until the child does it many times at the insistence of the parent.

Brian kicked his sister so hard that he bruised her kidney. She had to rest on the couch for a week, so Brian became her servant— getting her tissues, water, lunch, a book, or whatever she wanted. He knew he was in big trouble, so he complied and waited on her hand and foot. On the third day, he commented that he would never hurt her again. The payback was too painful.

∎

Some paybacks can be quick. A parent can say, "I was going to wipe off the kitchen counter, but instead I had to spend my time talking on the phone with your teacher. Now you get to wipe off the counter for me." The call may have taken twenty minutes . . . the wipedown two minutes . . . but the principle is the same. Payback. The other good news is that it ends in a win-win situation, because the parent can compliment the child on a job well done.

Parents may have difficulty with this insincere reciprocity because it feels phony and the emotion is not real. Although that's true, we embrace a philosophy of "Fake it until you make it." When you say "I'm sorry" to a stranger when you accidentally walk in front of him in the supermarket, it's not all that heartfelt either. The child must learn to fake it until it becomes real. Reading *The Velveteen Rabbit* by Margery Williams either by yourself or with your child will help you remember how hard it is to be real.

SINGING

For whatever reason, children hate to hear their parents sing in public. In truth, they aren't too crazy about it in private either. When you feel angry and have a desire to *talk* and *talk* and *lecture,* try breaking into song instead. Show tunes work particularly well. The child is astonished, because it's impossible for you to sound angry when you're singing. It gives you an opportunity to vent in a fun, engaging, and safe way—you can even make up your own words.

IN AND OUT OF THE BODY

Food issues, peeing, pooping, and swearing are all activities that are completely within the child's control. While that may be difficult for parents to accept, it's a simple fact of life.

Food issues, in particular, can be powerful. Many people pack a snack for a trip—do they really think they will not be able to buy food along the way? People confined to hospitals hoard food in their top drawer. And heaven forbid people show up at an early meeting where there is no coffee!

If a child won't eat or eats too much, a parent needs to keep him healthy. However, one skipped meal or one overeaten meal won't harm anyone. If your child likes only green beans, is it worth the struggle to force him to eat peas? Wouldn't it make more sense to simply cook green beans? We are not suggesting a separate meal for each member of the family, but some accommodations can be made for individual tastes.

If your child wets or soils the bed or himself, he should be responsible for cleaning it up. The job needs to be assigned by the parents' rules and determined by the child's ability. Anger, threats, and punishments will not help solve this problem.

Although parents cannot control these behaviors, the behaviors become a source of anger. What's more, they keep the child at a distance, which is precisely what he wants. When a parent is angry and distant, the child perceives himself as in control. Once again—it's what he *wants,* but not what he *needs.* Instead of getting upset, try to be matter-of-fact and avoid giving the child the anger and distance he wants. Offer a smile, some sympathy, and help with the cleanup. This will give him what he doesn't want and will be more likely to extinguish the behavior.

EXPECTATIONS

Parents must keep their expectations reasonable. This means that they need to understand normal child development and figure out the emotional age of their child. There are many resources about development, so find one you like at the library or bookstore.

A parent can normally expect that a ten-year-old child will play with toys. If your child won't play with his toys, perhaps they are the wrong ones for him. When a mother gives building blocks to a toddler, she shows him how to stack them and smiles when he knocks them down. This happens repeatedly and is an age-appropriate activity. But if your ten-year-old is stuck at a younger emotional age, you might need to replace those video games with shape sorters or building blocks. Go to a yard sale, and look for toddler toys that just may capture the attention of your older child.

ANNE WAS TEN YEARS OLD AND NEVER PLAYED WITH TOYS. HER ROOM WAS a disaster area, and there were parts and pieces of toys everywhere. To compound the situation, she never cleaned her room. Finally, her mother took our advice and cleaned and organized her daughter's room. This was a task that a ten-year-old could easily do, but emotionally, Anne was about four. Mom purchased large, plastic bins, and put all the blocks in one, the doll clothes in another, toy cars in another, and so on. She would announce to Anne, "It's doll time," and sit her down. It wasn't long before Anne began to play with her toys. When she had organization, outside cues, and order, she was able to play. Her favorites turned out to be the baby toys her mom bought her. Eventually, she moved on to learn to be a good mom to her baby dolls.

Anne could no more clean and organize her room than any four-year-old. Yet once it was done by her mom, she was able to pick up after herself. The directions were clear and concise, so Anne could follow them. Reasonable expectations ended the problem and made both mother and child happy.

■

Another reasonable expectation is chores. Parents often think they can give a list of chores to a child and he'll do them. Wrong. Especially wrong for a hurt child. It is better to have a chore such as "Do what I say when I say it." It's simple, direct, and easy to follow.

It is also best to remember that most hurt children do better with your help. Just as a four-year-old likes to dust the furniture with you, so does a hurt child like to work by your side. If the child's chore is to fold the towels, lean against the door and chat with him . . . maybe even lend a hand. A moment spent completing a job together is another chance to attach. Punishing and screaming at a child for chores left undone just keeps the child at a distance.

WIN-WIN

Many hurt children think that if they are compliant and you win, they lose big time. As a result, the family must work hard to make everyone win. It is critical for the child to learn that both can win . . . and he can remain safe. If your child stops wetting the bed, you win because the bed is dry . . . he wins because the bed is dry. If he keeps wetting the bed, you win because you act like you don't care . . . he loses because he has to clean it up. If he decides to join the family, you win a son . . . he wins happy parents. This should not be a battle of wills, but the parents should be the coaches—encouraging and challenging the child to reach the goal of a happy family.

MANAGING ANGER

If parents stay angry, the child will not get well. They can redirect their anger from the child to the adoption agency, to the government, or to the birth parents. This may help somewhat, but the best solution is to stop being angry.

It is not good for the parent, the marriage, or the child to hold onto anger. It is amazing how many angry parents have said, "But how can I do that? I'm not a saint!" The irony is that these same parents expect their hurt children to give up their anger at past neglect and abuse.

There's no surefire way to help angry parents let go. Some try personal counseling or support groups. Others look to religion or journaling. Each parent must find his own path that helps him release the anger.

If the parent is always and equally angry—whether the child lied, didn't eat lunch, cut huge clumps out of his hair, or kicked the dog—the child cannot differentiate between naughty, bad, and horrible. What's more, he will not attach to an angry parent. Why would he want to?

There is a place for righteous anger. Even Jesus got angry in the temple. If the situation is serious, a parent needs to be angry in a direct, close way—inches from the child's face. The expression on the parent's face should match his anger . . . the words clear, concise, and loud. This should not be done often but should be used when a critical offense warrants it.

NURTURING AND FUN

When good parents nurture small children, they do it no matter what. Whether a baby has soiled his diaper, burped up formula, or screamed in Daddy's ear, he coos and comforts him. Hurt children need this kind of unconditional nurturing. It's not always easy to nurture them, but they need it.

Because these children reject nurturing, it is easy for parents to stop nurturing them or to wait until they deserve it. This is self-defeating because children cannot become whole without nurturing, and hurt children will do just about everything they can to avoid it. For example, don't put the power in the child's hands by saying, "We'll all go on a picnic on Saturday if you're good all week." This is the equivalent of saying, "You're completely in charge of the family fun. You get to decide if we go on a picnic." Instead, live out the week, see how things go, and decide for yourself if the picnic will take place.

Nurturing is so important that we have devoted chapter 5, "Cinnamon on Applesauce," to it. It needs to be done over and over for the cycle of attachment to be completed. It can be brief or lengthy, simple or intricate. But it has to happen.

If your child always acts up after having a good time, make that part of the behavior you prescribe. Say something like, "We had such a good time that I know you'll go home and be horrible. That's okay with me." The child will either act up (thereby being compliant) or he won't (just to be noncompliant). In either case, you win. Just remember that he misbehaves because he realizes he has given up control by having fun, and the perceived loss of control frightens him.

Parenting hurt children is never easy. When you can begin to understand their inner world, their reason for behaving as they do, it may decrease your anger and make it easier to parent. It is not that you are a bad parent; the child would act the same with *any* parent. It is not that the old techniques aren't good; they are designed for securely attached children. The techniques we recommend will help you parent the child with special needs, and that's what's important. When you have solutions, control, and fun, the family dynamics will begin to shift. Parents regain a feeling of competency, and the child feels safer. Now go out there and try something new!

CHAPTER 5

CINNAMON ON APPLESAUCE:
Nurturing the Hurt Child

Busy families, sapped by everyday stress and exhausted by the demands of the hurt child, can often feel as if they are under siege. School, therapy, new ways of parenting, e-mail, cell phones, demanding jobs, demanding families, marriage, long commutes, daily stress—wasn't parenting supposed to be fun? No wonder there's no time left to nurture.

But nurturing doesn't have to be a two-week vacation that breaks the bank and leaves everyone exhausted. Sometimes it can be as simple as spending a few extra minutes to take the applesauce out of the jar, put it in a serving bowl, and sprinkle a little cinnamon on top. Simple? Yes. A quick fix? No! But if we don't take time to nurture these special children, the family condemns itself to a bleak, barren life.

WHEN JOE AND LINDA ADOPTED THEIR EIGHT-YEAR-OLD SON, HE LOVED baseball and did okay in school, but he was very cool to them. They opted to remain distant, waiting for him to come to them. Eventually, with encouragement from a professional, they bought bathtub toys, began rocking him to sleep, and taught him nursery rhymes. The more they reached out to nurture him on a younger level, the more open and loving he became.

For the most severely disturbed children, simply changing parenting techniques may not be enough. But by combining good parenting with the right therapy, children can heal and become whole.

The attachment cycle is really as simple as it is profound. When it goes the way it's supposed to go, most parents simply do their job of parenting—and the child thrives. Over and over again, there is a pattern of need, arousal, gratification, and trust. Like drops of water on a tender baby plant, this constant cycle eventually makes a sturdy plant with beautiful flowers.

Unfortunately, hurt children are not always tender plants waiting to be watered. Instead, they are often prickly cacti with needles sharp enough to keep parents away. But even a cactus needs some water, just as a hurt child needs to experience the attachment cycle—including gratification—if he is to build trust.

Attachment is not an event—it is a process. Any activity that completes the cycle adds to attachment. When the cycle does not include gratification, the cycle is not complete. How many times the cycle needs to be experienced before the attachment is solid depends on several factors:

- The genetics of the child
- His past history
- The amount of damage he sustained
- The personalities of the people involved

In any event, if attachment is going to happen, the cycle needs to occur repeatedly. When it doesn't—when the attachment cycle goes wrong—the child may not allow nurturing to happen. Parents pour the love on, but like a cactus in a flood, the child does not flourish. There is nothing wrong with the love; the child simply will not receive it. Parents who have been rejected by their children often feel hurt or angry, give up, and unwittingly interrupt the cycle.

FINDING THE WAY IN

The skill is in knowing when and how much water your little cactus needs. Otherwise, both parents and children get stuck in the arousal phase of the cycle—the child provokes, the parent and child get angry, there is no gratification, and therefore there is no trust.

It is difficult for most people to understand why these children reject what all children need so much—love and nurturing. The answer is simple: They learned early in life to trust no one. They learned that people leave you if you love them. They learned that the ones who are supposed to nurture them do not. And most important, they learned that parents—the very people you are supposed to trust with your life—are capable of hurting you and are not worthy of trust. As a result, they learn a new cycle that goes something like this: I have a need, I am aroused, I make you aroused, we push each other away.

MARILYN SPENT MOST OF HER LIFE IN HER ROOM. SHE WOULD MISBEHAVE, her adoptive mom would get angry, and she would be grounded. She didn't really mind this, because she was used to being alone. She was locked in cupboards in her birth home, so being confined to her room was no big deal. Because she fully expected her new parents to give her away, she wanted to stay distant. Whenever her new mom got too close, Marilyn would be sure to retreat. After all, she couldn't give her heart away again.

■

These children are terrified of being hurt again, so they reject nurturing from their new parents. *After all,* they think, *when these new parents get rid of me, hurt me, or neglect me* [their expectations], *it won't hurt so much if I don't love them. Here is something I can control. When they get rid of me, it will be because I made them do it.*

This concept may be easier to understand in adult terms. Let's take the case of an eighteen-month-old child whose adoptive home is his third placement. (Number one was the birth mom, and number two was an orphanage.) Now imagine if you were an adult who had two divorces in eighteen months. How eager would you be to jump into marriage number three? Even if the new spouse seemed wonderful—and had lots of money— would you hesitate at all? Would the new spouse have to prove his trustworthiness? Would you counsel a friend in that situation to wait before entering a new relationship?

The child's rejection of nurturing is not personal. Although it feels that way, it would be directed at anyone trying to be the parent. Hurt children do not know what they need. They just know how to take care of themselves and firmly believe that if they give up control, they may die.

Rita came from an orphanage in South America at the age of two. When her parents brought her into therapy, she was seven. During those five years, she never permitted her adoptive mother to touch, cuddle, or hold her without inflicting some sort of pain on the mom—a pinch, a hit—or pulling away. She preferred strangers and friends to family and never did anything fun with her mother. She treated her new mom as a servant, allowing her only to cook for Rita, clean for Rita, or buy things for Rita. But never did the child allow any nurturing.

In therapy, Rita was capable of expressing what she thought she might have felt when she was two years old. She spoke of the terror she experienced when she was first placed with her new family. "What I wanted to say at the airport was that you people are all too big and too white. I want to go home!" She was also able, for the first time, to express her grief at the death of her birth mother, with whom Rita lived until she was eleven months old. Educated by the child's revelations, the family began to heal. As part of their "homework," Rita and her mom planned something fun to do every day. Soon they began to enjoy themselves, and Rita finally joined the family.

∎

So the challenge becomes how to nurture someone who repels nurturing . . . how to sneak in enough fun so that the little cactus will begin to bloom. When the child is open, the parent can pour in love and the little plant will begin to grow.

THE FINE ART OF GRATIFICATION

As we explained in chapter 4, "What Works," the attachment cycle often includes a combination of touch, smell, speech, motion, warmth, eye contact—even sweets. Nurturing, if it is to contribute to attachment, must include these elements. When a mother gratifies a crying infant, the baby becomes warm from her touch. He recognizes her scent, he experiences the sound of her voice as she talks to him, and he enjoys further contact as she looks into his eyes. Marshall Klaus, M.D., states, "When you allow mothers to be in a room alone with their baby and enjoy the baby in the first hour of life, 80 percent of what they say is related to their eyes."[1]

Babies experience motion when their parents pick them up, rock them, or drive them around in the car (a common act of desperation when faced with a squalling infant). And the early foods most every human prefers are sweet. Babies like peaches before they like peas. In times of stress, people reach for candy or carbohydrates. Let's face it: how often do you hear someone say, "I've had a bad day. I think I'll have some broccoli"? Instead, we head straight for the ice cream, chocolate, or chips.

What's more, nurturing needs to include both parent and child. Playing a game on a computer allows the child to be nurtured by the computer, while playing a board game with Mom or Dad helps the child attach to the parent. If the child cannot play a seemingly age-appropriate board game, choose one for a younger child. Risk® or Monopoly® can be too difficult and create chaos for some preadolescents, while Candyland® or Chutes and Ladders® can be quick, easy, and fun. If the child has a short attention span, set a timer and play for ten minutes. Whoever is ahead when the timer goes off is the winner.

In this chapter, we will provide you with some nurturing ideas that are arbitrarily divided into the elements of gratification. Many of them overlap, and you can choose the ones that resonate for you, or you can add your own. The point is to start having fun. If the family is having fun, the child is more likely to join it.

Many of the suggestions we make include very brief parent/child interactions. Others are more complex, and children who are more open can accept these. Most of the ideas are for parents and children to do together, and a few are meant to be done as a surprise for the child.

---

1. Marshall Klaus, M.D., "Amazing Talents of the Newborn: A Video Guide for Healthcare Professionals and Parents." Johnson & Johnson Pediatric Institute, 1998.

Like a deck of cards that is being shuffled, the nurturing ideas will fit your child in different ways on different days. If an idea works, that's great. If not, try another. One size does not fit all. Our lists are only suggestions, and even a super parent couldn't do them all. Pick and choose carefully.

INCREASING EYE CONTACT

"Eyes so transparent that they permit your soul to be seen."[1]

"The eyes are the windows of the soul."[2]

Eye contact is key to attachment. Once parents begin to get eye contact with a child, attachment builds.

MICKEY WAS FOUR MONTHS OLD WHEN SHE CAME TO HER ADOPTIVE FAMILY, having been abandoned in the hospital by her birth mother and subsequently experiencing two foster placements. She had a history of ear infections and had been in an accident in which her jaw was broken. From the start, she wouldn't cuddle, had tantrums, and never accepted her parents' love. Often, in desperation, they propped up her bottle because she refused to take food from them.

She was brought to us for therapy at the age of eleven. At that time, she refused to ever look in her parents' eyes. In therapy, we played eye games and peek-a-boo to encourage her to make eye contact. During one particular role-playing session, we helped her say what she might have felt as she moved from place to place and endured physical pain. "Don't you people get it?" she cried. "I was a baby. You were in total control of me. You moved me, hurt me. [Even though the ear infections and broken jaw were not abusive, she perceived them as such.] The only thing I could control were my eyes, so I decided I would never look in my parents' eyes."

■

---

1. Theopphile Gautier, on *www.bartleby.com* [October 10, 2001]. Originally in "Two Beautiful Eyes," c. 1860.
2. Author unknown.

There are many nurturing ways to increase eye contact. Here are a few—some encourage direct eye contact, while others emphasize looking at things together. Enjoy!

- Write an "I love you" message in soap on a mirror. Stand behind the child when he reads it. You may get a glance in the mirror. If not, you still said I love you.
- Pick or buy daffodils and put them in a vase with some food coloring in the water. Watch with your child what happens overnight.
- Get a small glass of ginger ale. (A tall glass won't work.) Put a raisin in the glass and watch what happens.
- Dress the same. Match. Wear blue jeans and a red shirt. Tan shorts and a blue T-shirt.
- Get a family photo taken with everyone dressed the same. Hang it prominently in the home and frame one for each child's room. If your child is young (not a teen), buy a key chain in which to insert the picture, and attach it to his backpack or belt. In this way, he will have family with him wherever he goes. Afraid he'll rip it up? It doesn't matter. There are more.
- Play peek-a-boo when you're holding your child. Children as old as thirteen have played this—and enjoyed it.
- Look at pictures of you as a child. Compare them to the child's photos. If he doesn't have any, be sad with him. It's a big loss.
- Give him a disposable camera when attending a family event. See the event through his eyes.
- Paint his face. Let him paint your face. There is bound to be some eye contact.
- Look at each other and name the ways you are alike— you both have noses, freckles, whatever. Explore each other's features.
- At the post office, look at the stamps. Talk about them. Let the child pick which ones to buy.
- Have a candy-kiss hunt. Hide the kisses. For each one the child finds, he must look in your eyes for five seconds, get a kiss from you, then eat the candy kiss. This is a wonderful win-win activity, where everyone gets something.

- Put a sticker on your face right between your eyes. Don't comment on it at all. The child will look at you and laugh—eventually.
- Each of you wears two different shoes when running errands. Sneak peeks at each other when you go into the stores. After all, you are sharing a secret and playing a game, and the peek is the "go" signal that allows you to enter. Wait to see if anyone comments, and give that person a little prize for noticing.
- Play an eye game with both parents when holding the child. Have him look into your eyes—he's allowed to blink. One parent says "go" when the child looks, and the other parent times how long the interaction lasts. Try to beat your time. It is not unusual to start at four seconds and work up to a minute. Cheer when the previous time is broken.
- Watch Shirley Temple's *Captain January,* or Walt Disney's *Stuart Little, Pinocchio,* or *Tarzan.* These are all great adoption movies.
- Let your child put eye shadow on you. Return the favor.
- Make up an eye signal game. The child stands ten steps away from you. He looks in your eyes, you blink once, then he takes one step forward. You blink twice, and he takes one step backward. When he reaches you, he wins. This game builds compliance, as well.
- Play a card game—"Crazy Eights" or "Go Fish"—but no one can take a turn until eye contact is made.
- Buy a wildly colored hair spray, such as blue. Spray a streak in each child's hair to show that he belongs to the family. Look in each child's eyes as you spray.
- Turn off the lights and play with flashlights. When you beam on the child, he has to look at your eyes for two seconds.

MAXIMIZING TOUCH

Affectionate tactile stimulation is clearly, then, a primary need, a need which must be satisfied if the infant is to develop as a healthy human being. And what is a healthy human being? One who is able to love, to work, to play, and to think critically and unprejudicedly.[1]

Even with older children, touch is a vital component of attachment. It is something that they either missed completely or didn't get enough of from their previous caregivers. Many hurt children avoid touch, but without it, they will not join the family and become part of the family's world.

Think about it—we touch our infants so much in the first few years of life. We touch them to feed them, bathe them, diaper them, and take them places. We constantly cuddle them for no reason whatsoever—except that we love them.

Because touch is critical to attachment, it is important that parents repeat the process as often as possible. It is also why holding therapy works so well with hurt children, providing necessary boundaries. Holding your child at home, in a nurturing and nonconfrontational manner, is effective no matter what his age. The more you hold him, the healthier he gets. In essence, you are re-creating the cycle that didn't occur when your child was a baby. For more information on holding therapy, we suggest that you read books by Foster Cline, M.D., *Holding Time* by Martha Welch, M.D., and our first book, *Adopting The Hurt Child*, all of which are listed in Related Readings.

THE SOCIAL WORKER TOLD KRISTI AND KEN NOT TO TOUCH, HUG, OR KISS their new nine-year-old daughter, who had a history of sexual abuse. They complied, and their child became more and more destructive and hateful. Finally, they began to treat her like their other children, hugging her and holding her every day. After about six months, she began to thaw. This was precisely what she wanted—to be touched in a loving way. She no longer had to be bad to get attention, because she received it daily. She even began to ask for holdings on a regular basis.

■

---

1. Ashley Montagu, Touching: The Human Significance of Skin (New York: Harper and Row, 1986), p. 197.

Sometimes parents are so angered by the hurt child's behavior or rejection that they do not touch him at all. In fact, they go so far as to avoid him, and they never initiate or insist on touch. The bottom line is, children will not get healthy without touch—but it can be difficult.

In England, we met parents and professionals associated with Adoption U.K. Two of the parents, Caroline Archer and Joy Hasler, made the hedgehog the official mascot for children with attachment disorder. Prickly on the outside and soft on the inside, the hedgehog is an accurate representation of the hurt child.

So the challenge becomes how to increase touch with a resistant hedgehog in a nurturing way—without being pricked. Following are some ideas.

- Put a delightfully smelling lotion on your child and have him reciprocate. Talk about how you smell alike.
- Get matching temporary tattoos and put them on each other.
- Comb, brush, or braid your child's hair.
- Scratch his back.
- Hold hands while walking.
- Get your hair cut the same way. Touch it frequently as a reminder.
- Hold and cuddle your child every day, even when you're tired or busy.
- Give him a back rub or foot rub.
- Let him stay up an extra fifteen minutes past his bedtime, but make sure he spends the time in your lap.
- Wrestle with the child or teen.
- Allow him to watch television only if he sits beside you and a part of his body touches a part of yours.
- Hold hands while saying grace before a meal.
- Give a group hug before going your separate ways in the morning.
- Go horseback riding together.
- Give butterfly kisses—fluttering your eyelashes on the child's cheek—and let him reciprocate.
- Play hand-holding games like "ring-around-the-rosy" or "London Bridge."

- Teach the child to somersault, in-line skate, or ride a bike. You'll have to touch him as part of the lesson.
- Play a clapping game.
- Give him a horsy ride.
- Go bowling.
- Play tag.
- Tuck him in at night.
- Give a goodnight hug and kiss before bed.
- Get clown makeup and put it on your child. Have him put some on you.
- Tickle him, but be sure to stop when he says so.
- Play "Rock, Paper, Scissors." If you've forgotten, get a game book from your local library.
- Hold him every day. He craves it. He needs it.

MOVING WITH YOUR CHILD

We learn by practice. Whether it means to learn to dance by practicing or learn to live by practicing, the principle is the same . . . one becomes in some area an athlete of God.[1]

These hurt children are often used to moving—from family to family, from placement to placement—but they are not used to moving with the parent. They are good at pushing you away, avoiding you, and dodging you, but they're not very good at moving in sync with you. That's a very new feeling, and like all new feelings, it can be very scary.

JESSICA HAD BEEN IN NINE HOMES IN EIGHT YEARS. SOME OF THEM WERE fine, and some were hurtful. As these multiple caregivers came and went, she learned to avoid intimacy. When she was placed in her latest home, she wouldn't look at her new parents, would take off in a different direction on family walks, and did her best

---

1. Martha Graham, in James Simpson, comp., *Contemporary Quotations* (Boston: Houghton Mifflin, 1988), *www.bartleby.com* [October 10, 2001]. Originally in *ib,* August 5, 1986.

to be in another room rather than occupy the same space as her parents. She was terrified to "surrender" and follow them.

At thirteen, she was a master at avoidance. Her mom took a radical step and enrolled them both in a dance class. Jessica enjoyed the exercise and realized that these brief encounters with her mom were fun. Swinging and swaying in time to the music, the two learned to be in sync in an enjoyable way. With therapy, Jessica was able to become a more integrated member of the family.

■

So here we go . . . ways to move with your child. Some of them offer good exercise for both of you, and others can help if your child has delays in physical development.

- Draw a picture together. If he has small-motor problems or is very young, use the big fat crayons.
- For older children, toss a ball or beanbag.
- Blow bubbles. Chase them around to pop them.
- Surprise! Pop into school and "kidnap" your child. Move swiftly through the halls, and jump into the car as if someone is chasing you. Dash to a fast-food restaurant and have lunch—for no special reason. Dash back to school. (Of course, you'll have to clear this with the school first so you're not reported to the authorities. But remember—you're allowed to pick your child up during the school day for medical appointments, so why not do the same to help him attach?)
- Go fly a kite.
- Rock together, no matter how old your child is. If your child rocks to get to sleep, hold him and do it for him. If he's too big to hold on your lap in a rocking chair, buy a rocker for two and sit together. (Check the garden and porch stores for this item.)
- Teach your child one of the dances you did when you were younger and have him teach you one of his current ones.
- Catch fireflies, then let them go.
- Play jacks.
- Get a pogo stick and take turns jumping.

- Walk like a penguin with your child—in public.
- Buy washable markers and draw on each other.
- See how deep a hole you and your child can dig in the backyard.
- Plant a small vegetable garden, harvest, and eat. Homegrown tomatoes—yum!
- Run under the sprinkler with your child.
- Play miniature golf.
- Turn off the television and go for a walk. See how many animals you spot along the way.
- Play a clapping game.
- Buy sidewalk chalk and help the child draw a mural.
- Buy balloons, even when there's not a birthday party coming up. Blow them up and play a balloon chasing game.
- Build something together—a bird house, a model airplane, or something out of blocks.
- Play badminton.
- Play "Mother, May I?" to increase compliance. When playing this game, the mother must always be the one in charge. The child does not get to give the orders.
- Play "Button, Button, Who's Got the Button?"
- Play croquet.
- Play horseshoes.
- Make a snowman together.
- Make a snow sculpture. Put water in a spray bottle, add food coloring, and spray the sculpture to color it.
- Jump rope together.
- Play "Mommy Says" or "Daddy Says" instead of "Simon Says."
- Play baby. Feed him something good and gooey— such as yogurt, pudding, or ice cream—from a baby spoon. Mom or Dad holds the spoon, the child looks in the parent's eyes, and he gets fed. Parents can set this up as their own need by saying something like, "I never got to feed you as a baby, so I'd really like to do this."
- Make a snow angel.
- Shoot baskets.
- Paint some old flowerpots. Plant something in them.

- Walk to the mailbox with the child and mail a note to someone they miss—a sibling, a former foster parent, a relative.
- Swing together.
- Get a flag. March around the house singing patriotic songs.
- Go for a ride in the country.
- Play hopscotch.
- Sew something together.
- Stand on one foot and recite a nursery rhyme with your child. If he doesn't know any, teach him one.
- Clean out a junk drawer together.
- Sit on the floor foot-to-foot. Hold hands and rock as you sing "Row, Row, Row Your Boat."
- Paint your nails the same color.
- Have an Easter egg hunt in the summer.
- Go to the creek, beach, or lake, and skip stones together.
- Send the child to breakfast on a Saturday with one parent. The other parent stays home and does all the child's chores for one day. This is a terrific surprise for the child and won't ruin his sense of responsibility if it's done occasionally.
- Make something simple and good to eat together, such as a packaged-mix goodie from the baking section of the supermarket.
- Divide the family into teams and go on a scavenger hunt.
- Rent a boat, canoe, or kayak. Sharing an adventure can be fun.
- Teach your adolescent how to drive. Near-death experiences (or those that you think might be) can be funny later.
- Go cross-country or downhill skiing if you're physically up to it.
- Go for a walk in the rain. Get wet. Jump in puddles.
- Tired from all this motion? Get into the car and cruise a main street. Count fast-food places and stop at the fifteenth one to eat.

NURTURING THROUGH FOOD

Onion soup sustains. The process of making it is somewhat like the process of learning to love. It requires commitment, extraordinary effort, time, and it will make you cry.[1]

Food as nurturing? Of course, it is often said that we should never reward children with food and that food should not provide solace. However, we often make a practice of comforting a bereaved family with a cherry pie, following an adoptive-parent support group with coffee and doughnuts, and buying ourselves a chocolate treat because we're feeling stressed.

Nurturing through food is not just about calories. It can be about making dinner fun and eating meals together. Preparing food, enjoying it, and even cleaning up after the feast are all part of the rituals of most families. Whether we like it or not, food is important to most of us—and to our children.

It is not uncommon for hurt children to arrive in their new families with food issues:

- They hoard food.
- They gorge themselves.
- They eat only one or two things.
- They eat everything in sight, including nonfood items.

All of these eating problems are the result of early food deprivation, because children who experience near starvation very often continue to have concerns about food. Their issues are irrational in light of their new living situations, but often persist for years.

In their attempts to change the food problem, parents frequently deprive the child of his favorite foods to get him to eat something more nutritious. However, deprivation will make the child's food issues even more severe. Instead of depriving him, we have found it more effective to allow him to exercise more

---

1. Ronni Lundy, in James Simpson, comp., *Complete Quotations* (Boston: Houghton Mifflin, 1988). *www.bartleby.com* [October 10, 2001]. Originally in "The Seasoned Cook," *Esquire Magazine*, March 1984.

control over what he eats. If he is allowed to do so without interruption, it is much more likely that he will independently
expand his food interests.

After eighteen months in an orphanage, Sally had significant food
issues. Her adoptive mother begged, pleaded, and tried to force
her to eat. When Sally was three, her mom packed a little basket
for her daughter to carry around all day. It was filled with little
snack bags of raisins, cookies, cheese, crackers, nuts, and cereal.
Sally explored the food, ate what and when she wanted, and
actually received considerable nutrition. After about six weeks of
being the "boss of her basket," Sally told her mother she was finished. She began to eat meals with the family.

■

Some children and adolescents prowl around the house
throughout the night looking for food. While many people do
not want to encourage eating in the bedroom—which is where
most kids hide their food anyway—we think it is sometimes
helpful simply to place a container of nonperishable favorite
foods in the child's room. This may serve to resolve his ongoing
quest for food and may reduce his fears about not having
enough. If he awakens with a strong need for food, he can feel
secure in the fact that there is something right there to satisfy his
craving. In fact, he may not even eat the readily available food,
because he knows that it will be there if he needs it or wants it
at a later time. In other words, the child's hoarding need is met
in a way that allows the parent to place boundaries on his prowl-
ing and grazing behaviors.

Ultimately, it is our goal to transfer the comfort the child gets
from food to the comfort he can get from his parents. In the
meantime, indulging his specific food issues will have a more
positive effect than trying to resist them. Food preferences
develop very early in life, and most of us do not alter the kinds
of things we choose to eat. Just think of your own food preferences . . . your own tastes . . . the things you would *never* try . . .
the things you *always* like. Basically, think of it like this: feed
your child what he wants, and he may eventually decide to try
something else.

Does that mean you need to stuff him with sweets? No. But here are some ideas to make food a part of nurturing. Don't worry if it adds calories. All those motion-based nurturings will help burn them up.

- Serve a banana split for dinner. For no reason. Just because. Just once. The nutrition police won't arrest you.
- Buy a fancy plate at a garage sale. Serve the child his meals on it.
- Make cupcakes. A packaged mix and frosting in a can are okay. Have the child choose the pan-liner papers—there are pretty ones in specialty stores—and add sprinkles or other decorations. Brag to everyone about what you made together.
- No time to bake together? No excuse. Try slice-and-bake cookies.
- Buy some M&Ms®. Sort them by color. Eat them together.
- Pack a picnic in the winter. Take the basket into the living room and eat on the floor on a blanket.
- Take turns taking each of your children to the supermarket. That child picks out the cookies and cereal for the week. What a star!
- Make fruit kabobs with your child. They're fun, and they're a great way to get kids to eat more fruit.
- Say yes. "Yes, you may have a cookie after dinner" is so much nicer than "No, you may not have a cookie until after dinner."
- Experiment! Try peanut butter and relish sandwiches, or toast with catsup instead of jelly. (Honest! Regina's mom ate both of these and lived to be eighty years old. Amazingly, they're quite good.)
- Kick back and enjoy a cup of tea or cocoa with your child.
- Have cheeseburgers for breakfast and cereal for dinner. Why? Why not? Don't discuss it. Just do it.
- Make a root beer float for lunch.
- Have an un-birthday cake for dessert. Sing "A Very Merry Un-birthday to You." (If you don't know the words, see Disney's *Alice in Wonderland*.)

- Buy napkin rings. Use terry-cloth fingertip towels for napkins.
- Teach your child to set the table.
- Open a lemonade stand.
- Serve ginger ale with a cherry in it.
- Freeze strawberries in an ice cube tray. Use them in water or lemonade.
- Make pudding in small bowls.
- Have a tea party. Trim the crusts from sandwiches and cut into triangles.
- Eat by candlelight . . . *with* the kids.
- Dress up for dinner just because it's Tuesday. Or Thursday. Or the dog's birthday.
- Drink from canteens.
- Cut a cake or brownies into shapes. When the child names one—triangle, circle, diamond—that's the one he gets to eat.
- Put a spoonful of chocolate chips in the child's oatmeal.
- Give each member of the family three minutes of uninterrupted time to talk at dinner.
- Have canapés for dinner.
- Add a slice of lemon to a glass of water.
- Put some blue food dye in your child's milk once in awhile.
- Let the child sprinkle his pancakes with powdered sugar. Call them crêpes.
- Put the milk in a pitcher instead of pouring it from the carton.
- If your child wants you to, feed him a bottle when holding him, no matter what his age. (Ten is not too old.)
- Use pretty placemats—perhaps the ones you've been saving for a special occasion.
- Get a plain tablecloth and some markers that write on fabric. Design a tablecloth with your child that's used just for your family.
- Serve the child's beverage in a pretty goblet. If your goblets are too expensive, buy some at a resale shop.
- Let the child make dinner or plan the menu.
- Serve raw vegetables with dip instead of a salad at dinnertime.

- Put a love note in his lunchbox.
- If you have assigned seats at the dinner table, change them for a new view.
- Make a rule that there are no headphones, no reading, and no television while the family eats. Ever.
- Help your child make a table centerpiece—flowers, some sort of craft, or just an appropriate knick-knack—even when it's not a holiday.
- Put a sticker on the bottom of one plate before you set the table. The family member who gets the plate helps serve dessert.
- Make a list of love words that are food-related: pumpkin, honey, cupcake, sweetie, and so on. This exercise helps with language development, too.
- Use the good china to celebrate just being a family.
- Have a four-course meal—salad, sherbet (just a taste), soup, the main course.
- Make tomato soup and grilled-cheese sandwiches. Cut the sandwiches into finger-sized strips and dip into the soup.
- Remember finger JELL-O®? You must still have the recipe.
- Make your child's favorite meal for no special reason.
- When your child is sick, be sure to provide extra nurturing with tea, toast, ginger ale, or any food or drink that makes him feel better.
- Go out to dinner with your teen. Create your own special occasion.
- Take him out to dinner with you and your friends.
- Take him out to dinner with his friends.

ENHANCING COMMUNICATION

Humming to the quaintest lullaby
That ever rocked a child.[1]

---

1. Emily Dickinson, on *www.bartleby.com* [October 10, 2001]. Originally in "Part Two: Nature," *The Complete Poems of Emily Dickinson* (Boston: Little, Brown, 1924).

Nonsense questions, chattering, bad words . . . oh, these children know how to talk! But can they carry on a conversation? Do they have anything to say that you are interested in hearing? Many hurt children have poor vocabularies, difficulty in talking in sentences and paragraphs, and poor language skills.

When good parents talk to their babies during the attachment cycle, the baby's ears and brain are flooded with sounds, syntax, and sentences. Babies are programmed by the age of ten months to learn the language their caregivers use. Nursery rhymes help teach them syllables—just recite "Itsy, Bitsy Spider," and you'll see what we mean.

WHEN THE BYRNES FAMILY WAS STOPPED AT A TRAFFIC LIGHT ON THEIR WAY to therapy, they noticed the family in the car beside them doing the motions to "Itsy, Bitsy Spider." They all laughed and started doing it, too—with the exception of their adopted son Jack, age ten. "What are they doing?" he asked. He was blank as his parents told him about nursery rhymes. In his early years, he was in a neglectful home and never heard any. He didn't understand the patterns, rhythms, or rhymes. His adoptive mom picked up a book at the library and began to teach him. He loved it! (As long as his friends didn't find out.)

■

When we talk to a baby, we tend to exaggerate our faces to teach emotions. Our voices change, too, as we sympathetically coo something like, "Oh, poor little baby, do you need a bottle?" Who was talking to your hurt child when he was an infant? What was that person saying? If no one stimulated him, is he behind in language skills? If so, how far behind? And how often do you talk (lectures don't count) *to* your child not *at* him? Here are some ideas to have fun and help your child attach, while assisting with language development.

- Read the funnies together with the child on your lap. Choose cartoons that mirror your family, and make a scrapbook of them for later laughs.
- Listen to and learn to sing one of your child's favorite songs. Teach him one of your favorites.

- Establish a rule that no one is allowed to listen to music in the car through headphones. Talk to each other. Or sing along with the radio.
- Sit with your child and read a book you chose together, chapter by chapter, every day. This also teaches delaying gratification.
- Mail your child a note. On the day it's due to arrive, have him get the mail and read the note out loud.
- Make an audio tape of your family singing. It is especially fun if you can't sing well.
- Read a fairy tale.
- Make a list of something together. (Regina's family and friends named all the famous rabbits they could think of. The list is rather impressive, and you'll find it at the end of this chapter.) Name car models, candy bars, TV shows, or whatever strikes your fancy. This is a great way to pass the time in waiting rooms.
- Discuss where you would go if you could fly.
- Go to the library together and look something up. Not on the Internet—in a book.
- Interview all your helpers—nurse, doctor, therapist, social worker—and see who can name all of Disney's Seven Dwarfs®.
- Teach the family a round song.
- Post a happy note on your child's door.
- Help the child to write to someone famous. See if that person writes back.
- Tell your child you need help with a home repair. Let him hold the flashlight or screw in a screw.
- Make stationery with rubber stamps. Write a letter to someone.
- Choose a song with your child that can be called "our song."
- Order a magazine subscription for the child. Read it together when it comes in the mail.
- Make a life book with the history of the child's current family. Let the child interview relatives about what you were like as a child.

- Collect something together—stamps, baseball cards, coins, pens, buttons—and help the child organize the collection.
- Teach the child nursery rhymes. If you've forgotten them, get a book to help.
- Read the entire set of Oz books together. There are lots of them besides the *Wizard of Oz*.
- Learn a foreign language together.
- Tell the story of your child's adoption—again and again.
- While waiting for an appointment, instead of sitting in silence, make a bet on the color of the professional's tie or shoes. If the parent wins, the child gives him a hug and kiss. If the child wins, the parent gives him a wink. (This, of course, also encourages eye contact.)
- Sing together. Even if it's not in tune.
- Trace a word on your child's back with your finger. If he guesses the word, he gets a point. (And you get to touch the child more, practice spelling with him, and have fun.)
- Look in the mirror and make sad, mad, glad, or scared faces with the child in response to different questions. "How would a child feel if he lost his bike?" "How would a child feel if someone took his favorite toy?" "How would a child feel if he could eat a hot-fudge sundae for breakfast?" "How would a child feel if he heard a ghost story?" You might even sneak in some eye contact during this exercise.
- Have your child teach you something that he's good at—such as a video game.
- If your child can read, let him read you riddles, knock-knock jokes, or funny stories.
- Go to a concert with your adolescent. You don't have to like the music—you just need to be there with him. If it's too loud, you'll get over it . . . and you'll have a story to tell your friends.
- If your child likes to banter, banter with him instead of discussing why it's not nice to talk that way.

GETTING WARM AND COZY

What feeling is so nice as a child's hand in yours? So small, so soft, and warm, like a kitten huddling in the shelter of your clasp.[1]

When we pick up babies, they get warm from our body heat. When we change them, they get warm from a clean, dry diaper. When we feed them, they get warm as their stomachs fill up. They even enjoy containment at times, such as playpens, highchairs, and being held tightly.

Providing containment can be very nurturing, affording a child the opportunity to "play baby" with toys—such as shape sorters, stacking rings, and stuffed animals—to help him meet some of his early needs for containment. It is never to be used as punishment, but rather as a loving, reparenting tool.

If a child did not have a secure early life, the containment can be set up with the words, "You know, I was thinking . . . you didn't have a very safe, loving babyhood, and some kids like to play baby. Here's what we're going to try . . . just for ten minutes." Then guide him to whatever containment you have made available. Make it clear that he can get out anytime he wants. Odds are, he'll stay put for awhile if he needs the confinement. When this practice stops being fun for the child, you'll know he doesn't need it anymore.

Some of the suggestions we make for containment were developed by adoptive parents. The chronological ages of the children on whom these techniques were employed range from five to fifteen, but the need for safe confinement—like a toddler in a playpen or a babe in arms—was the same.

- Set up a card table. Put a blanket over it and play baby underneath. (Do not do this with more than one child at a time if any of the children has issues of sexual or physical abuse.)

---

1. Marjorie Holmes, in James Simpson, comp., *Contemporary Quotations* (Boston: Houghton Mifflin, 1988). *www.bartleby.com* [October 10, 2001]. Originally in *Calendar of Love and Inspiration* (New York: Doubleday, 1981).

- Make a "playpen" by using a corner of a room and two stair gates.
- Set up a pup tent in the living room. Zip the child in to play and zip him out when he wants out—or let him do it himself.
- Buy a cardboard or plastic playhouse and set it up indoors or in the yard.
- Buy a throw rug featuring a child's favorite cartoon or movie character. Unroll it exclusively for baby play.
- Place large floor or couch pillows on end. Tie scarves to the ends of the pillows to make "sides." The result is a "box" with pillow ends and scarf sides. Voila—a crib.
- Turn a daybed around with the opening against the wall. This makes a perfect crib for an older child.

Shelly was fourteen when she came to her adoptive mother. She had been raised from birth to the age of five in a crack house, where she experienced neglect, physical abuse, and sexual abuse. She was in several foster placements before finally arriving in her adoptive home.

It was immediately clear that her infant needs had not been met. After some work in therapy, she and her mom decided that she needed "baby time" every day. They first went to a few garage sales, where they bought several baby toys. Every day, Shelly got into her crib made of pillows and scarves, and played with her toys. During a session, she asked the therapist if she had ever tried this technique herself. "Not as an adult," was the reply. "You should really try it," countered Shelly. "It's so relaxing and so safe. I love it."

■

Besides containment, there are several ways to increase that warm and cozy feeling for your child:

- Make or buy a soft, warm blanket to use while watching television, reading, or engaging in other quiet activities.
- Let your child sleep in a sleeping bag on the bed instead of under a blanket. It's cozier.

- Put his gloves and scarf in the dryer for a few minutes to make them warm. They'll feel wonderful and will send him off to school with a comfy feeling.
- Make a nest for you and your child. A cozy little place—perhaps a card table with a blanket over it, a small tent, or an empty closet.
- Share a lap robe while watching television.
- Live in a hot climate? Go outside with the child and enjoy feeling the heat.
- Serve hot soup as an after-school snack.
- Steam up the bathroom with all of you in it. Draw on the mirror.
- Is your car cold in the morning? Take along a small blanket to tuck around your child's legs.
- Pitch a tent in the backyard or the basement and climb in with your child.

JUST HAVING FUN

Laughter is a form of internal jogging. It moves your internal organs around. It enhances respiration. It is an igniter of great expectations.[1]

Without fun, the world is a barren place. Family memories are usually about funny incidents, and laughter is a great stress reliever. And who would want to attach to a person with no sense of humor anyway? Here are some ideas for just having fun.

- Play hooky. Don't go to work and keep your child home from school. Have fun.
- Buy a plant for your child. Teach him to care for it.
- Treat your child kindly when he has a bad day at school. Be sympathetic, not angry.
- Give everyone a day off from household chores. Get up on Saturday morning, make a list of what needs to

---

1. Norman Cousins, in James Simpson, comp., *Contemporary Quotations,* (Boston: Houghton Mifflin, 1988). *www.bartleby.com* [October 10. 2001]. Originally in *Anatomy of an Illness* (New York: Norton, 1979).

be done, then rip it up and do something fun instead. No one ever died from a dust bunny.

- Get a new, *big* box of crayons and throw away the old shabby ones. Just because.
- Plant something outside. If you live where bulbs grow, plant some in the fall for blooming in the spring.
- Take a picture of the child standing next to the parent(s) on every birthday. Watch him grow.
- Stop by a pet store and look around.
- Rituals can be important to children. What fits your family? Try an Advent calendar or menorah.
- Buy a small treat—a cute eraser, stickers, or a poster—and put it in the child's room as a surprise.
- Get a catalog of free items from the library and order your child loads of merchandise. Help him feel anticipation and learn to delay gratification until all the goodies arrive.
- Blow bubbles in the bathtub with straws.
- Use those fancy soaps—shells, flowers, exotic fragrances. What are you saving them for anyway?
- Take a class together—painting, auto repair, anything.
- Let the girls wear socks with lace to school on a non-special day. They will outgrow them soon enough anyway.
- Go to garage sales and resale shops, and buy loads of dress-up clothes.
- Wear the pin, scarf, or macaroni necklace that the child gave you—even if it's hideous.
- Wear matching T-shirts.
- Buy an initial pin or necklace to remind the child that he is now a (insert your last name), and have him wear it every day.
- Buy a crown. Wear it when you are king or queen of the house. When you wear it, there are no more chores for you.
- Make a magic wand. Use it to make wishes.
- Get a clown nose. Wear it when your child doesn't expect it, such as out to dinner or to a teacher's conference.
- Get a comb, coin, sandpaper, and other textures. Put paper over them and rub with a crayon. Talk with your child about what you see.

- Color with your child.
- Complete a jigsaw puzzle as a family project.
- Buy bathtub toys. Even young teens like a rubber duck.
- Have a pajama party with the family.
- Use pens that write in different colors.
- Collect the child's unused toys and clothes, and have him accompany you when you donate them somewhere.
- Don't make the beds for a whole week. Honestly— nothing bad will happen.
- Buy colored paper clips for everyone to use.
- Attend a different church to see what it's like.
- Tie-dye a shirt for everyone in the family.
- Learn a craft together.
- Do something kind for a neighbor.
- Buy a beautiful candle. Light it for the people you and the child miss.
- Set up an office for the child and equip it with his own paper, pencils, sharpener, tape, stapler, and so on.
- Go to a used bookstore and find a treasure.
- Cheer for the same team.
- Pretend you're a tourist in your town and visit something interesting.
- Create a wall border for his room by dipping his hand in different colored paints and using his hand as a stencil.
- If your college-aged child asks you to join him and his friends for Spring Break, you must go. Greg did this— it is a true eye opener. Be brave!
- Talk with your adolescent as if he were someone else's child. Drop the tutorial/parental comments, and you might find out why other parents really like your kid.
- See school as *one* component of your child's life. Remember—most subjects in school are not *that* important. Just how well did you do in algebra, geometry, or world history? Has your D or D-minus ruined your life? Do your friends know just how poorly you did? Does anyone care now?
- Is the *real world* actually the way we tell our kids it is? Lighten up. People miss deadlines in the real world and . . . they get extensions!

■ Laugh with your adolescent at things that, at first, you may not think you should find amusing. If the teacher fell out of his chair (and wasn't injured), isn't that a little bit funny to you? Come on, you know you would have laughed when you were sixteen!
■ If your teen has a license, go for a drive together and take turns driving.
■ Take a mini-vacation.
■ Go to a movie—one that your child wants to see.
■ Just let go and have fun!

Now, many of you are probably thinking, "Just when would I find the time to do these things?" Well, think about what we tell our kids when they lament, "I don't have time to clean my room!" We usually reply, "If one of your friends called, you'd have time to talk to him or go play with him. You always find time to do what you think is important." So take the time . . . make the time. "Too busy" or "too tired" just won't cut it.

Many parents of hurt children fall into the child's trap. They come to believe that what the child says is true, and they say it, too: "I don't care." While these children almost always resist trying something new, they invariably enjoy it when it happens. If they have never tried something, of course, they don't want to do it because they are afraid. But if you can get them to experiment, you'll add one more thing to their life's repertoire . . . one more thing they can say they've done . . . and yes, one more piece of history with you, the *new* family. In fact, once you start having fun with your kids, you will be less tired, less fed up, and more energized.

More good times with your children should reduce their bad times. Dr. Martha Welch, a psychiatrist and author, makes an excellent point about so-called quality time. She suggests that quality time will never replace quantity, because children need both to flourish and develop. Giving your child only quality time would be like giving him five hundred calories of nutritious food each day—ultimately, he would die from malnutrition due to an insufficient amount of food. Even though the child was getting *quality,* he lacked the necessary *quantity.* The idea of quality time seems to have developed as the result of people feeling too busy to spend the kind of time they need to spend with their children.

Other readers may feel they have enough time to do some of the things mentioned in this chapter, but they find themselves thinking, "Johnny would ruin the cupcake making! He wouldn't enjoy it." We have found that if parents take the lead in a strong assumptive manner, the child will follow. If you, as a parent, do not believe that you can get your child to do something, odds are you will *not* be able to do it. If, on the other hand, you believe that you are going to go to the store, buy the kite, and go fly it with your children, you will probably have a good time. Don't ask them what they want to do; they don't know. They're unaware of life's many options, so it becomes the parent's job to show them — to force them, if you will — to have a good time.

We often find that parents who are the most spontaneous, the most creative, the most unusual, the most unpredictable — and, therefore, the most fun — are the ones whose children finally "get it." The adult must take the lead and demonstrate life. Most healthy parents of infants and very young children have no qualms about "making" their children do things by simply doing them. Think of every mall at Christmas time. There are long lines of parents who are "forcing" their babies and children to sit on a perfect stranger's lap for a photograph. While the kids are sobbing in fear of this strangely dressed man, the parents are thrilled . . . anxiously waiting to see the photo they hope they can use on their Christmas card. Curiously, as the child gets older, he, too, excitedly wants to repeat this adventure because he now understands that something good may come of it. If his parents hadn't "forced" him to see Santa, he may never have wanted to.

With older children, having fun is more of a challenge, and some of them will try to sabotage it. However, their misbehavior does not have to taint the entire family's day of fun. If your child claims that kite flying is stupid, let him sit on the sidelines and watch while everyone else participates in the activity. Most likely, he will choose to join you once he sees that no one is suffering — no one is angry — because of his refusal to play. Remain open to letting him jump in when he's ready. This is not the time to punish him by saying, "You didn't want to join us before, so you can't do it now." Instead, welcome him.

Will our suggested activities always engage every child? Of course not. Will some kids refuse to do anything? Probably. However, the more assumptive the parent is about what's going on, the greater the likelihood of a successful outcome. Remember—if you expect an idea to fail, it most likely will. Fatalism is a death sentence for creativity, and once parents lose sight of what *could* be possible, they are seeing the world as their hurt child sees it: limiting, defeating, and hopeless. It is the job of parents to cut the path . . . to lead the way . . . to show their children what *could* become their truth. They just might come to view the world as a place filled with infinite opportunities for them and a giving, hopeful environment in which to live.

Just for Fun . . .

In our suggestions about enhancing communications, we suggested that you make a list of something. Just for fun, we did rabbits. Special thanks to Regina's brother, Jim Breig; his wife, Mary; their children Jim, Matt, and Carrie; and the staff of the *Albany Evangelist* who helped compile the list. If you think of more, please drop us a line.

1. Peter Cottontail
2. Flopsy
3. Mopsy
4. Bugs Bunny
5. Roger Rabbit
6. Jessica Rabbit
7. Easter Bunny
8. Harvey
9. White Rabbit from *Alice in Wonderland*
10. March Hare from *Alice in Wonderland*
11. Velveteen Rabbit
12. Thumper from Bambi
13. Watership Down rabbits
14. Crusader Rabbit
15. Bugsy (Bugs Bunny as a child)
16. Energizer® bunny
17. Trix® rabbit
18. Nestlé Quik® rabbit
19. Rabbit Maranville (baseball player)
20. Rabbit in the series by John Updike
21. Runaway Bunny
22. Pat the Bunny

23. Uncle Wiggly
24. Brer Rabbit
25. Bunnicula
26. Bunny Rabbit from Captain Kangaroo
27. Hare from "The Tortoise and the Hare"
28. Benny Bunny from *Sesame Street*
29. Little Bunny Foo-Foo
30. Bunny Berrigan (jazz trumpeter)
31. Bunny in *Roger and Me*
32. Buckles the Bunny
33. *Cutie Bunny* (comic book)
34. Hocus-Pocus from *Frosty the Snowman*
35. Irontail from *Here Comes Peter Cottontail*
36. Stuffy from *The First Easter Bunny*
37. Flops from *The First Easter Bunny*
38. Zero from *The First Easter Bunny*
39. Spats from *The First Easter Bunny*
40. Jack Rabbit (we think this is a cartoon character)
41. Bunnykins
42. Babette (Radar's bunny on *M*A*S*H*)

CHAPTER 6

THE SCHOOL DANCE:
Knowing When to Lead
and When to Follow

Contributed by Carol Blatnicky, M.Ed.

Although all children attend school, all children do not have the same school experience. As the young child approaches that first day of kindergarten, emotions range from joy and excitement to dread and fear. Parents also find themselves somewhere on this continuum of feelings, which may or may not be in sync with what their child is experiencing.

That first day marks the beginning of a new phase of parenting that will last a minimum of thirteen years. Parents who have been the most important adults in the child's life will share responsibilities with school personnel. The child who has perceived his parents as the all-knowing ones now has an additional authority in his life. Hurt children who have not yet accepted parents as all-knowing will have difficulty accepting authority from others.

Most parents expect school to "work" for their child, and it usually does. However, children with social immaturity, emotional difficulties, and learning problems discover that school is not often an inviting place. Parents who hoped for relief from the all-encompassing parental role may find themselves unexpectedly embroiled in conflict with a teacher, principal, or school counselor. If some action is not taken, school difficulties escalate and impact the entire household. It is therefore important for families to be proactive so they can create the best possible school situation for their child. Even children who are not experiencing adjustment difficulties can profit from good planning.

WHAT CAN PARENTS DO?

Thinking About Education

Most parents recognize the importance of school and try to prepare for that first day by purchasing the perfect lunch box, the recommended school supplies, and the latest new clothing. If your child is new to the family and from a different culture, every new activity carries an additional stress.

EKMEL STILL HAD NOT ADJUSTED TO SLEEPING IN A BIG BED ALONE. FOR THE first eight years of his life, he had shared a bed with at least four other children. Now he had no one in a room that was almost as large as his previous home. He felt lonely and frightened at night. He was looking forward to school because he knew he would excel there and meet new friends. He had always been at the top of his class and was aware that his peers looked up to him.

He was shocked when he entered the third-grade classroom that was brightly decorated with lots of pictures, labels, and words on every wall. There were even things hanging from the ceiling. He could not decide where to focus his eyes, and he couldn't find the rows of seats that could give a sense of order to this chaos. The children were too loud and did not show the teacher the proper respect. As Ekmel stood there in his brand-new sneakers—purchased by his dad so he could look like everyone else—he longed for the security of his sturdy black school shoes and the structured orderly classroom of his native country. He hated this new school . . . and everything about it.

■

Because there are so many practical issues to worry about, such as after-school care and family schedules, many parents do not spend much time thinking about educational goals for their child. In fact, they may even laugh at such an idea. However, potential difficulties can be lessened or even avoided if families have clear expectations about what they want their child to accomplish. While it may seem obvious that every parent wants the best experience for his child, it helps to be able to verbalize expectations. Hurt children can have so many confused thoughts and feelings about every new activity that they need a loving parent's help in structuring their thinking.

IT WAS THE FIRST DAY OF KINDERGARTEN IN A NEIGHBORHOOD WHERE PARENTS could walk their children to school. Moms and dads stood outside, waving bravely as their little ones entered the large brick building. The boys and girls, chatting happily, skipped and ran to the classroom. After all, they had met the teacher during the previous week and had seen all the wonderful toys and books. They were anxious to get started—all except one little boy.

Tyrone stood hanging onto his mother's hand, screaming that he wanted to go home. The embarrassed mother tried frantically to extricate her hand from little Tyrone's grip, while she unconvincingly told him that he was going to have a lot of fun. Finally, the principal intervened and told the mom that she could leave. She assured her that this was not the first time she had seen a crying child at school and that within a short time, the tears would be gone.

Unlike other children, Tyrone did not stop howling all morning—except for a juice break. During that first week, he screamed from the time he entered the building until the time he arrived at the classroom. The guidance counselor was involved daily and held several meetings with Tyrone and his parents.

It seems that Tyrone's mom had always hated school, and although she thought she was being positive by saying that he would have fun there, he could see that she was skeptical. Because of her bad experiences with teachers, she chose not to attend the pre-kindergarten conference. Tyrone was operating at a disadvantage because he did not know what to expect. Although his mom really wanted Tyrone to like school, and hoped that his school experiences would be better than her own, her fears got in the way. It had never occurred to her to talk with him about her hopes and expectations for him. She simply avoided even thinking about school because of her own painful memories.

◼

One of the first things a parent can do to clarify expectations is to examine his own feelings about school and identify his own belief system. Ask yourself the following questions:

- How do you feel about school and education?
- Is learning something that you value?
- What are your expectations for your child?
- If you had a magic wand and could create the perfect school experience for your child, what would it look like?
- Can you recognize the strengths and weaknesses of your own child as they relate to school?

YOUR FEELINGS ABOUT EDUCATION

If you find that you have some negative feelings or attitudes about school, teachers, and learning, it is time to change your thinking. One of the benefits of parenting is the growth opportunity it provides to stretch and expand your belief system. To help your child, you may have to relinquish some of your negative attitudes. If you want your child to enjoy school, the first step toward this goal begins with your thought process about the value of education.

Embrace the joy of learning new things. Decide to value learning and education. Be strong about this decision, because children know the difference between pretense and reality. You cannot fake it. Look for opportunities when you are doing something new to demonstrate positive approaches to learning. Be careful about the behaviors you exhibit.

For example, if you are trying to decipher directions for some "easy-to-assemble" product that turns into an all-day job, this is the perfect opportunity to model mature learning behavior. If your child is young, you can make statements like, "Mommy has to read this over and over because it is a difficult task, but if I keep trying I will probably catch on." Then if Mommy still does not catch on, you can say something like, "Mommy is going to ask for help. There is always someone to help us when we are learning something new." Your responses to situations can help your child develop a repertoire of behaviors to apply when he is engaged in the learning process.

If the child is older, you can ask him to help you figure it out. Slowing the process by drawing a picture and thinking it through with your child will help him to recognize that effort might be required. Trial and error is a part of learning. If by chance the child helps you figure something out, it is a bonus for both of you. By the same token, if the two of you fail, you can seek help together. Both experiences can contribute positively to the bonding process.

It is your job, however, to monitor your responses. If your older child becomes frustrated during the process, it is the perfect time to use the language of learning and feelings. Give him sentences like, "Mom feels like kicking the box, too, but that would not help us. Let's take a break now and come back to this later. Learning to do new things is hard, but I know we can do it."

It all sounds easy on paper. The difficulty comes in monitoring your own language and providing proper sentences. These are the moments when you must stretch yourself beyond what you thought were your limits. *Do it for your child,* and you will all benefit in many ways.

YOUR EXPECTATIONS FOR YOUR CHILD

Parents hope that their children will adjust to school, find friends, and achieve academically. Often there are additional dreams, such as participation in the areas of fine arts or athletics. Parents who have dreamed for years about having a child and have waded through the adoption maze may have even more of a "dream child" in mind.

Sometimes their expectations are based upon what the parents did or did not accomplish in school. Other times, they are based upon realistic observations of the child. In either event, children are much more likely to succeed if the parents have realistic expectations that they can verbalize. In this way, they can take the necessary steps to help the child move in that direction.

Children who have been hurt may already exhibit behaviors that cause parents to be worried about school participation. It is obvious that the parent who is anxious is less able to help the nervous child. On the other hand, a parent may perceive his child as quite advanced and anticipate seeing him at the top of his class.

Unfortunately, when the child joins with the other "advanced" children in his age group and discovers that he is just one of a group who must share and take turns, both parent and child may experience a sense of defeat. Sometimes children who seem so quick and clever at home—supported by family and friends who provide a responsive audience—find that they are not prepared to share the limelight. They miss all the family attention and soon decide that this school business is not for them.

When a little child who has just started school does not find his place and does not feel as safe and secure as he did at home, the parent suffers with that child. The parent may feel angry, hurt, or helpless because school unhappiness was not part of the plan. It is natural to want to strike out against everyone and to think there must be something wrong with the school, the child's classmates, or the teacher. In addition, a parent may lose faith in his child and start a cram course in rules, playing, and sharing. Once again, the parent must control what is in his thoughts so he can plan proper actions.

A child in foster care who has experienced multiple moves, or one who has been neglected by abuse and inadequate orphanage care, is often subjected to additional trauma by the school system. Many teachers and administrators view these children as nuisances, because they have huge files from many schools and do not easily fit into the admission procedures. It requires effort to bring these children up to par with the class academically, emotionally, and socially.

Teachers may unconsciously feel that it is hardly worth the effort because the child will probably move again. If this child is eventually adopted, he is subject to compounded pressures. He not only has never had a secure home base, but he also knows that school can be a painful place. If the new parents are not cognizant of these factors, they might add to the pressure with lofty, unrealistic expectations.

TAKING CHARGE

Once you have a clearly defined idea of your educational expectations, begin to incorporate sentences into your daily life that will help your child understand your family's beliefs or approaches to learning. With younger children, you can help them see their roles as important by comments such as, "Mommy and Daddy go to work and you go to school. We all have a job to do."

Model responsible behavior by preparing for work the night before or by making a list of what you need for work. Help your child do the same for school. Teach him organizational techniques, such as putting his books, backpack, and other required items near the front door. Talk about responsibility as something that is important in your family. Help him understand what your family does.

"Our family likes to be organized, read, and participate in sports. We are not always perfect, but we always try to do better." Use the same type of sentences with your daily routines. "In our family, we do our homework right after school, so we don't have to worry about it later." Using such sentences not only helps the child understand expectations, but also depersonalizes some of what must be done. Instead of thinking, "Dad is making me do my homework," the child realizes that it is simply a part of what the family does.

All this talk also contributes to feeling part of a family. Some parents might think that all of this planning and structure is unnecessary, but hurt children need a firm base to help them feel protected and secure. Teach your children to use sentences that will help them survive in school and help them develop a positive approach to learning. Statements such as the following are useful.

- I need help.
- I can do difficult things.
- I always have a choice.
- I can learn from my mistakes.
- I like to try new things.
- I like school.
- I can solve this.
- I know I can count on myself.
- I know where to get help.
- I can problem-solve.
- I need your help to understand.

When a child can clearly verbalize his beliefs, he is able to help the teacher gain insight into his behavior.

PATRICK, A THIRD GRADER, HAD A HARD TIME FOLLOWING CLASS RULES. THE teacher tried several different consequences—detentions, time outs, and loss of privileges—but none of them had any effect. One day, Patrick asked his teacher why she didn't like him. The teacher was quite surprised because she found him to be a delightful addition to her class. After questioning Patrick about why he had come to this conclusion, he confidently replied, "I know you don't care about me, because you have never given me a paddling. In our family, when the kids are bad, we get the paddle. Our parents do that because they love and care about us. That's how I know you don't like me, because I keep being bad, and you never hit me even once."

Patrick had a clear understanding of his family's belief system and was able to verbalize his thoughts. The teacher was able to explain that in her classroom, she did not use paddling to help children learn and that the consequences she imposed were done because she cared. From then on, whenever Patrick had a detention, the teacher would explain that this was like paddling to her. Patrick eventually improved his behavior, and the teacher realized the impact of the family's values on a child's perception.

■

With older children and adolescents who may not have been in your family in earlier years, it is not as easy to provide language they will embrace. They often have their own well-developed, colorful statements about school and learning that might be the opposite of your beliefs. You may need to watch for situations where they do exhibit some "love of learning"—such as reciting the lyrics to every CD they own or getting positively passionate about learning a new video game. You can begin to build a bridge with these activities as proof of their ability and interest in learning new things.

Adolescents with histories of school difficulties often perceive themselves as dumb. It has never occurred to them that they are capable of learning, even though a teacher or counselor may have said precisely those words. Even if you convince them that they are intelligent, it is unlikely they will see any connection between their ability and their school work. You are only beginning a very small step toward providing hope. Because you will have a realistic goal for your teenager, you can find words to help him share the goal.

For example, you know that you want him to earn a diploma, so you might use sentences like, "I know school is tough for you, but you must graduate. Although employers might accept a GED, they prefer employees who have earned a high school diploma. A vocational program could help you get a skill." Just the matter-of-fact repetition of the goal will help him know where he's going.

Talk with him about the fact that his previous moves, school difficulties, and other problems were results of his situation. He can change now. You will support him, but he must do his part. Even if you have a long-term dream that your teenager will attend college, concentrate on the short-term goal of a high school diploma. An adolescent who hates school only wants to escape. Other goals can be set later.

PARENTS AND TEACHERS

Parents and teachers share the same children and have similar hopes and expectations for them. Both operate in the gray area where there are no absolutes. What works for one child may not work for another. Children from the same family with the same birth parents do not respond in the same manner. Different students do not react to the teacher and his style in the same way.

Because parents are always "teaching" their child and the teacher is often "parenting" a student, it would seem likely that parents and teachers would automatically form a bond of cooperation. Yet parents and teachers sometimes seem to be working at cross-purposes. Conflicts may arise, and the teacher and parent might appear to be on opposite sides. In some situations, the parent feels that the teacher is holding onto his position and is not listening.

Other parents might feel unsure about contacting a teacher. For a hurt child to get the best education, teamwork and cooperation between parents and teachers is essential. Most of the time, the secret to good parent-teacher relationships lies in frequent, honest communication. You might be surprised about the benefits.

Eunice was determined that her little boy was going to be a good student. She established a time after dinner each night when she and Ian would read or do homework together. Because her husband worked late and traveled a lot, Eunice knew that school help was up to her.

By fourth grade, Ian was working with fractions, and Eunice feared that she would not be able to keep up with the math. She was embarrassed about her lack of elementary skills and finally found the nerve to explain the situation to Ian's teacher. She asked the instructor to suggest some books that she might read to help her improve. Ian's teacher was so impressed with Eunice's determination that she offered to stay after school with her on the night that Ian went to Cub Scouts. In a few months, Eunice was completing the sixth-grade math and wondering why she had never liked it when she was in school.

What You Should Know About Teachers

Most teachers chose their profession because they like school, learning, and children. They want their students to achieve their full potential, just as parents do. They have developed clearly defined objectives for their classes, and they know how to achieve them. They even have their own "bag of tricks" to use with reluctant learners and misbehaving students. Quite simply, they know what they're doing, and they feel confident doing it.

When problems occur that do not respond to any of their usual interventions, teachers can take additional steps to solve the problem: calling the child's parents, talking to the school psychologist, trying new techniques, seeking special education services, and getting input from other teachers. However, with a hurt child, these interventions may not work . . . and might even exacerbate the situation.

Because teachers are used to solving problems, they are caught off guard when their efforts do not work. They may question the parents' role or develop a negative attitude toward the child. Other teachers and professionals may reinforce their position. Just as parents become defensive when they feel helpless in dealing with schools, teachers who are used to being in charge become defensive when they feel helpless. But all of these stressful interactions can be avoided through good communication.

HOW TO COMMUNICATE WITH THE SCHOOL

Elementary level: Good communication is key to ensuring your child's success. To get started, you can make an appointment with the teacher early in the school year and also connect with the principal and guidance counselor before the term begins. Prior to the meeting, make a conscious decision to like the teacher and think of yourself as gaining a partner to help your child reach his potential.

When you meet with the teacher, start by explaining that you are there because you want to do everything you can to help your child have a successful year. Don't worry that revealing information about your child's background will cause the teacher to have a negative attitude. It is important for him to adequately understand the trauma your child has experienced so he is well positioned to help him. Remember—a hurt child is unlikely to be at his best in new situations where additional demands are placed upon him.

Erik's father did not want anyone to know about the circumstances of his son's early life. The biological parents had beaten Erik and thrown him around. They had not fed him when he was hungry, nor had they sought medical help for recurring ear infections. Erik had suffered some brain damage and was academically and emotionally immature. He was large for his age, which accentuated his immaturity. In addition, he constantly had a runny nose, which he wiped on his sleeve or any other fabric near him, such as the teacher's skirt or a peer's jacket. Needless to say, Erik was without friends.

Each year, his adoptive parents would attend school conferences and listen to a long list of complaints about their child's behavior. When he was in the fourth grade, a team of teachers gathered to enumerate the never-ending list of Erik's flaws. As his father listened to the same tiresome descriptions, he became so exasperated that he spoke out in defense of his son, "Well, how do you think you'd be acting if your parents had tried to kill you when you were a baby?" That statement, and the silence that followed, were all the mother needed to follow her husband's lead and begin telling the painful story of Erik's early years.

Fourth grade was the beginning of improvements at school for Erik and his parents. As one of the teachers described the situation, "It wasn't that Erik changed a lot, but it was easier for the staff to accept his odd behaviors once they knew his history." As they demonstrated more compassion, Erik seemed to respond more favorably.

■

When you speak to your child's teacher, describe his situation and explain his unique needs. Help him understand your hopes and dreams for the school year. Share the aspects of your child's story that have relevance for the school. If the teacher gains an understanding of the background and the approaches that have been successful in your home, he will be able to respond similarly in the classroom. If you are working with a therapist, share that information, too. You may want to sign release forms so the teacher and therapist can communicate.

Ask the teacher about his goals and expectations for his class. If some of them seem beyond what your child can manage, express your concerns and try to plan some strategies that will help your child prosper. Request that you work as a team and offer your support to the teacher. If you have shared details of your child's life, be clear about what is confidential and what is known to your child. If there is a school psychologist, you may want to meet with him. The more people you include in your child's success plan, the more likely the plan will work.

Middle school and high school: As children enter the upper grades, especially high school, parents sometimes think it is time to back out of the child's life and let him handle things on his own. But teachers of adolescents need to understand your child's situation and your expectation even more than the elementary teachers do. Preteens and teenagers need to know that their parents and teachers communicate and work together.

While most elementary students are honest about parental expectations, upper-grade students often convincingly misinform their teachers. "My parents don't want to know about school." "It doesn't matter; my mom doesn't care." If, in fact, you do care, you should probably find a way to let someone at the school know this.

If you think it is too time-consuming to meet with your child's teachers on an individual basis, call the guidance department to arrange an appointment with his counselor. Explain your child's unique needs and ask for help in the coming year. Use the counselor as your contact person when you have a question or concern. Ask what services the guidance department can provide. For example, they might send out a progress checklist to teachers for a weekly report about the student's academics and behavior.

The counselor can serve as support for your child at school and as a go-between for teacher problems. The counselor can also set up a meeting with all of your child's teachers and help you convey the messages you want shared. At times, it might be advisable to include the child's therapist in a group meeting. Just as with elementary students, if the teachers know your child's story and understand the best way to work with him, they will be able to alleviate problems.

Most teachers like the idea of working as a team with a child's parents, so don't think you're being too demanding. They want to help, but they need your information and your support to do so effectively. Just remember that the school works for you.

If you feel inadequate about asking for meetings or communicating with a staff member, remember that your child needs all the help he can get. You can ask a friend to accompany you or help you do the talking. If a meeting before the school term begins is more than you can handle, you can wait a few weeks. Then, as soon as your child is attending classes, listen for any positive comment about any teacher. Call that person, and explain that your child seems to like his class and that you need his help. Be honest about your reticence in contacting teachers and request his assistance. A teacher that your child even mildly likes can be a great asset.

Keep in mind that teenagers who know that their parents and teachers are in contact and sharing goals are not as likely to waste their time trying to pit one against the other. The adolescent needs to know that his family and teachers are united to help him—whether he likes it or not.

THE HIGH SCHOOL TEACHERS LOOKED FORWARD TO SEEING PRISCILLA'S mom, Trudy, at their door after school. They had watched Priscilla change from a boy-crazy, note-passing, failing student who hated school into a boy-crazy, solid B student.

Priscilla had been in many foster homes before she ended up with her family when she was in the eighth grade. Her mom assessed her daughter's grades and attitude, and realized that Priscilla had never been required to do school work and was just waiting to drop out. To complicate matters, Trudy worked nights and would not be at home to monitor the situation.

Because Priscilla did not bring any assignments home, Trudy sent notes to all the teachers explaining that she would like to stop by after school at least once a week to find out what Priscilla needed. Some of the teachers thought that this should be Priscilla's job. The mom agreed, but explained that her daughter was just learning about homework and needed help for a while. She wanted to know everything her daughter needed because she would be leaving notes for her husband. She asked for co-operation from the teachers for one grading period.

That first grading period, poor Trudy was at school almost every night because all of her daughter's teachers were not available on the same evening. By the end of that first grading period, Priscilla's grades and attitude had improved dramatically. Priscilla, who had been totally embarrassed about her mother's classroom visits at first, began to like the fact that her mother and teachers were talking, especially because the teachers were always thanking her mother and making positive comments to Priscilla. By the second grading period, Priscilla had learned to write her assignments down and definitely demonstrated a friendlier attitude at school.

COMMUNICATION TIPS

Everyone seems to be obsessed with the idea of communication. Parents and children are told to talk with each other. "Keep the lines of communication open" has become a cliché. Company executives attend workshops on communicating and send their employees to learn the latest methods. Teachers are encouraged to communicate with parents, and parents are told to contact the school. But sometimes, when we think we are communicating, we are doing just the opposite.

Suzy was a very verbal second grader who had three teenaged brothers. She had lost bus privileges for a week because of her obsessive swearing, which showed no signs of diminishing even after several warnings and a detention. Suzy's classroom teacher was puzzled by this defiance, because the one time she had heard Suzy swearing, she had taken her aside for a discussion. Suzy had reported that her brothers swore all the time. After the teacher explained that they did not use swear words in the classroom, that had been the end of it. When the teacher asked Suzy why she kept swearing on the bus, Suzy responded, "Swearing! Why the hell . . . sorry, Miss K . . . didn't they tell me it was about swearing? That driver kept telling me I was using some kind of inappropriate language."

■

Good communication takes time and planning, and it is better to err on the side of too much rather than not enough. Remember that your goal is to help your child, and any efforts you expend will be well worth your time.

During the initial meeting with your child's teacher, have a list of items that you want to cover. Determine the best way to be in contact. Many teachers have e-mail, which can be a convenience for both of you. There is usually a time period during the school day when a teacher can receive messages and make phone calls. Ask for the time that is best, so you will feel comfortable and confident about initiating calls. Let the teacher know the phone numbers where you can be reached during the day and evening, and tell him when you would prefer calls. Also, discuss a plan for emergency communication.

With younger children, you can set up a system of notes that the child carries back and forth. A note that tells the teacher about significant events is a necessity. For example, if the child's dog is sick or if a pet has been lost or has died, the child will be impacted. The teacher needs to know these things so he can make adjustments. If your child has given his best efforts on a homework assignment and was unable to finish because of exhaustion, poor understanding, or a family event, inform the teacher. Likewise, if you think your child is not doing an assignment because he thinks he can get away with it, let the teacher know the facts. The teacher can monitor and adjust his response to the particular situation.

Teachers in the upper grades usually have a planning period when you can call them. If there is something important that you want a teacher to know early in the day, call the office and leave a message with the secretary. Indicate that you want the message delivered immediately. Otherwise the message may be put in the teacher's mailbox, where he will not see it until the end of the day or the next morning. Many miscommunications occur because messages are not received.

You can also communicate through the guidance counselor. Just remember that parents who make their needs known usually have their needs met.

If you do not want your child to know you are contacting a teacher, be sure to include that in the message. If your family has had a lot of open communication with the staff, the teacher may innocently ask his student why the parent has called. On the other hand, if you are not calling with some confidential information, inform your teenager. Give him every opportunity to be in charge, and don't take him by surprise. He might even want to be part of the communication by telling the teacher that his mother is going to call about grades, behavior, or a vacation. The teacher can then be prepared with the information you need, and your adolescent will be advocating for himself.

If your child comes home from school and announces a project or field trip that you know will be traumatic for him, contact the teacher immediately to create a plan for an alternate assignment or activity. For example, if the class is visiting a fire station and your child has lost a family member in a fire, he may not be capable of the visit.

Decide upon a strategy that will work for your child. If you experience resistance from a teacher who erroneously thinks it is time for your child "to get over it," seek assistance from the guidance counselor, the school psychologist, or the principal. Consult your physician or therapist for support. You always have options. It is imperative that teachers learn about these sensitive issues so that they do not keep making the same mistakes in their classroom. As a parent of a hurt child, you may have to teach the teacher.

MONICA, AN ADOPTED CHILD WHO WAS A SOPHOMORE IN HIGH SCHOOL, was angry and upset. Her social studies teacher had assigned a research project entitled "My Family and My Ancestors." While he was explaining the project, Monica felt her heart beating faster and thought she might faint. She was recalling all the previous times she had suffered because of similar assignments. In fourth grade, her class had been asked to bring in their baby pictures. In sixth grade, they had been required to create a family tree. Monica had solved those problems by being absent, but this project was different.

It was a three-week research assignment, culminating with an oral presentation, and would have a major impact on her grade. Monica liked her social studies teacher and decided to talk with him about her worries. She explained that because she was adopted, she had very little information about her birth family. What she did know was upsetting to her and was not information that she wanted to share. She asked if she could have a different assignment and be excused from attending the oral presentations. She explained that it was painful to hear about everyone else's past and their happy little childhoods.

Her teacher responded by telling her to either make up something about her birth family or tell about her adoptive family, adding that no one would know the difference. Monica was crushed. She had been nervous about exposing her fears regarding the assignment, but now she felt dismissed, as if the teacher thought she was silly. She had trusted him, and he had not even listened to her.

It was necessary for her parents to intervene, and they were eventually able to give the teacher a clear understanding of their daughter's situation. As an alternate assignment, he directed her to write about Ellis Island and its role in immigration. This compromise tied in with the other children's stories about their ancestors, while providing a comfort level for Monica.

SPECIAL EDUCATION

Many parents panic when they hear that their child is being considered for special education services. They worry about the label and the subsequent impact on their child's life. Sometimes they refuse to allow testing to occur.

In reality, school personnel are not trying to get more students into special education. Before they even decide to request testing for a student, they have probably tried many educational interventions that were unsuccessful. Testing is just the beginning of the information gathering process, and your child may not even qualify for special resources.

When you are first contacted about testing, be careful what you say in front of your child. Try to keep an open mind, and if you experience fear or resistance from your child, be clear in your talks with him. Remind him that you and his teacher work as a team to help him do his best and that you are seeking more information about ways to help. Point out that your family likes to learn new things and that this is an opportunity. Assure him that you will not be making decisions until after you investigate the entire situation. Discuss the fact that you always have options and you can get help from other people. Help your child to feel safe and secure with the adults in his life by modeling the behavior of flexibility and confidence.

Sometimes parents would like to have an assessment done by the school. If that's the case, you can initiate the process by contacting the counselor, teacher, or psychologist. You may find out that your child exhibits a different set of behaviors at school and seems to be managing well. In addition, the school will need to know that you are spending every night and weekend reviewing and studying with the child just to keep him afloat. If you strongly believe that your child might qualify for special education, ask for testing or a conference with the psychologist. You may have to put the request in writing. What's more, a follow-up letter is helpful after a phone call. Be sure to document all communication in case you need a record of it in the future.

Some students who have a disability that does not qualify for special education can receive help with a 504 plan. For example, a student with a reading problem may have been on an Individual Education Plan (IEP) in the elementary grades. After intensive instruction, his skills might have improved so much that there was no longer any discrepancy between ability and achievement scores. The student would then be signed out of special education.

In high school, when the reading requirements intensify, he might struggle and need some adjustments with assignments. A 504 plan informs the teacher that some modifications and adjustments to the curriculum or teaching style will be necessary for this student's success. Other students who have never been on an IEP may also qualify for a 504 plan if they have a disability—such as HIV, ADD, or addiction problems—that does not fall under the special education guidelines.

After the testing is completed, you will be invited to discuss the results of the assessments and the options for your child. If special education services are warranted, you will become a member of a team that works to help your child improve. The team will prepare an IEP that will set annual goals and objectives for your child.

Many young children who receive services in the elementary grades get the boost they need and do not require help as they reach the upper grades. Early identification can prevent additional problems and may help your child enjoy school. Besides assisting the student, special education services can be positive in the life of a parent. You will have a supportive team helping you with the academic, behavioral, and social difficulties your child encounters. In essence, you will have an ally in the school.

Judy and Ted adopted two siblings who were three years apart. From the very beginning, Pedro, the older child, adapted readily, while Manuel cried and was fidgety. When he entered elementary school, he continued to exhibit behavior problems and was placed in an Emotionally Disturbed program. Judy and Ted appreciated the support and help from the teachers throughout Manuel's elementary years.

When he was a freshman in high school, he began testing the rules at home. Because Pedro was now a senior, he and his dad had scheduled a few college campus visitations, which left Judy at home alone with Manuel. On one occasion, Manuel refused to accept the limits that his mother was trying to impose. The two of them argued for a while with an increasing intensity. Judy worked hard to maintain her composure, but when Manuel threatened to throw a chair through the picture window, she called the police.

Manuel retreated to his bedroom and locked the door. By this time, Judy was frantic. She was livid about her son's actions and, at the same time, fearful about what he was doing in the locked room. While she pounded on his door, screaming with tears streaming down her face, she heard the doorbell. As she tried to compose herself, Manuel sped past her to answer the door. He had put on a pair of pale-blue flannel pajamas and looked angelic and scrubbed as he calmly answered the door. She heard him say in a sincere, sweet voice, "Oh thank you for coming, officer. My mom gets like this when my dad's out of town. Dad says she's going through menopause and we have to be understanding, but I'm a little scared tonight."

Watching this scenario caused Judy to fly into a major rage, and as she tried to scream out the facts through her tears, she knew that she looked like the one with the problem. The more the officers tried to calm her, the angrier she became. When they finally took down the facts for their report and made Manuel promise to stay in his room for the rest of the evening, Judy knew Manuel was the one who looked believable to the officers.

After a sleepless night, Judy was waiting at the door of her son's special education room at 7:00 A.M. She knew this was a place where she would be understood and supported. After processing the event with the special education teacher, Judy commented that she had always known that she had an ally in the school, but that she never thought she would be using that support for herself. She knew that the teacher was the one other person besides her husband who could help her unravel the complexities of the previous night. (Manuel went back to counseling, had a medication change, and became manageable again.)

If you are worried about labels or your child's self-esteem, there are two things to keep in mind. First, today's special education students are fully included in classes and social activities with the rest of the population, so they will not be spending the day in an isolated classroom. Second, if your child is having any problems in school, it is likely that the students already know it. If you want to check this out, just ask your child for the names of the smart students or the bad ones. They will tell you. You may also find out that your child already considers himself as different or dumb.

If your child is older and is being identified for special education services for the first time, a request for testing may come as a relief for you. Even if the child is new to your home, you will know if he has had a long history of school difficulties. The adolescent will probably view an academic assessment negatively and feel that this testing just proves that he is right when he tells people he is dumb. He may argue that he is not crazy and does not want to see a school psychologist.

Try to listen objectively to his complaints, because you may gain insight into his fears. If you have established good communication and developed an understanding of how your family approaches learning, you can wait a few days and then talk about the diagnostic information that the testing can provide. Another option is to call the school and ask a trusted teacher or guidance counselor to do the explaining. Sometimes a peer who is currently receiving special education, or one who has been helped previously, can discuss the positives. If you do not know of such a student, the guidance counselor may be able to suggest a candidate. Remain firm in your stance that you are gathering helpful information. No decisions can be made until your family has the data.

There are a number of advantages to a special education placement, even as late as high school. If a student has struggled because of a learning disability or a behavior problem, the academic help and support he receives can offer hope for a turnaround. Many high school students learn to advocate for themselves and to seek the accommodations that the IEP prescribes. Students have a better chance of passing state-mandated tests when they are able to have the special services their disability affords them.

For example, a reading-disabled student who is competent in math may have previously failed math tests because of the reading required for some of the problems. Once the teenager has a reader for the test, he is able to earn a much higher score. Students can also request accommodations when they take driver's tests and college entrance exams. Many families are surprised to hear that the benefits continue even when the student enters college.

PATRICE, A HIGH SCHOOL GRADUATE WHO WAS IN AN EMOTIONALLY Disturbed program, was enrolled at a university. She was aware that students with learning disabilities were using tape recorders, receiving extended time for projects, and taking tests in a separate location. However, she hesitated to visit the special services department at the school because her IEP accommodations were quite different from the learning-disabled students.

She needed to be excused from classes on days when she was too psychologically distraught to attend, and she worried that the professors would perceive this as a strange request. She was greatly relieved when the coordinator read over her accommodations and in a matter-of-fact tone explained the customary procedure for dealing with situations such as hers. When Patrice asked if the instructors would think she was weird, the coordinator commented, "Of course not. None of them even batted an eye when I told them about a student who was unable to function if there was too much of the color orange in a room. One professor even had to cover up an old orange bulletin board."

Tips About the IEP

If your adopted child has an IEP and this process is new to you, ask the school for information about your rights. There are booklets and printed materials that will explain everything you need to know. You will learn that you can request an IEP meeting any time you think a goal needs to be added or changed. It is not necessary to wait for the annual review. You will also learn that you do not have to sign the IEP form, and you can reject parts of the plan. Your family can seek help from a parent advocate, whose role is to attend meetings with you and help you decide the best path for your child.

HOMEWORK

Homework can create havoc in the lives of parents, teachers, and students. There are so many different viewpoints about its value that there is no firm place to stand. Many hurt children use homework to control and manipulate, causing a twenty-minute assignment to last for three hours.

Some teachers have strong beliefs that homework should be given daily, while others see little or no value in assigning it.

Some school systems demand that teachers give homework, and many parents insist upon it. Strong emotions arise when homework is discussed, and research supports every position. As a parent, you may or may not have a definite viewpoint, but if you have a hurt child, his school career is not the time to become a homework activist.

Bᴇᴛʜᴀɴʏ ᴋɴᴇᴡ ᴛʜᴀᴛ ʜᴇʀ ᴘᴀʀᴇɴᴛꜱ ᴛʜᴏᴜɢʜᴛ ᴛʜᴇ ᴡᴏʀᴋꜱʜᴇᴇᴛꜱ ꜱʜᴇ ʜᴀᴅ ᴛᴏ do each night were a waste of time. She didn't like them either, because she was not good at math and hated to practice. Each night, she would cry during the assignment. Her tears would cause her parents to launch a discussion about the value of doing twenty-five subtraction problems instead of five. She knew her parents thought the teacher was making a mistake, and she loved to listen to their dialogue about the flaws of the educational system. As a result, she felt supported at home and very seldom did her math homework.

■

You want to make life smooth for your family, so the best approach is to cooperate with the philosophy of the current teacher. Because your child will change teachers each year and there will be different policies, you will have a good opportunity to model flexibility, talk about individual differences, and reinforce the idea that change is a part of life. Your family can adjust and grow.

Elementary and middle school: In kindergarten and first grade, children do not usually have much assigned homework. If your child talks about what he did in school, express sincere interest and keep this discussion as a routine in your family life. School is the child's job, and it's as important as the adult's career.

By second and third grade, the child may have weekly spelling words or worksheets. For some children, the words are so easy that they do not need to practice at home. If your child has trouble with spelling, take time from your busy schedule to help him. Show him the importance of a little practice each day, rather than waiting until the last minute. The time you spend now to help your child develop good habits about homework is an investment for the future. Giving him the opportunity to develop discipline and responsibility is much easier when he is little.

If your child is hyperactive, find a way to help him settle down and create a routine. A distracted child will need more help from you. Try to make the sessions short, and even if you would like to avoid the task and rationalize that he already knows his spelling words, discipline yourself to establish the routine. Give him the practice of settling down and showing you how much he already knows. You are encouraging habits now in order to avoid conflicts later.

Be vigilant if you have a bright child who does not need time to study and can finish worksheets in a minute. While other children are learning that they must study to be successful, the quick child is learning that he does not have to do anything to excel. Parents of these bright children often observe that the children have school under control and feel fortunate that they do not have to take time to develop study skills.

By middle school years, the less-able student has really "learned how to learn," and he understands that a little hard work pays off in the classroom. He may have even figured out that staying on task in class helps him do better. Meanwhile, the quick child is learning that even though middle school assignments are not quite as easy to complete on the fly, he still can get by without too much effort. He has also probably figured out that paying attention to the teacher helps, and he may be able to do that and still fool around. The less-able child is working to potential, while the quick child is learning how to be an underachiever. Although these two examples are extreme, they do happen. Think about how you want your child to learn and then take steps toward that goal while he is young.

Upper grades and high school: If your adolescent has developed a pattern of being responsible and completing homework, you are fortunate. Many teenagers do not do homework. Sometimes it doesn't affect them; other times it causes them to fail classes. If your teen is failing, talk with him about the connection between homework and grades. Explain that because of the instability in his earlier years, he did not learn how to do assignments at home.

Take some time to help get him started by sitting down with him and offering hands-on support. If he is open to your assistance, you have a good beginning. Once he develops the homework habit, you will be able to encourage him to work alone.

If he resents having you help him and you end up with a "homework battle" on your hands, you may want to hire a tutor. Many families find that an outside person can teach their children the skills they need to raise grades—and they can accomplish this in a very short time. If you cannot afford a tutor, call the guidance department and ask about volunteers. Some schools have both adults and students available. Another possibility is to ask your child's teacher if there is a student in the class who might be willing to be a homework buddy.

Unfortunately, there is no quick fix to solve the homework problem. You must determine what the best situation is for your family. Some adolescents are so traumatized by past failures that they do not want parents to see how they struggle. They may be in such denial that they refuse to believe that anyone could help them, so they choose to continue the path of failure.

Anything that can be done to break this cycle is worth the effort. When a child realizes that he can be in charge of his learning by being consistent about completing assignments, it is a powerful lesson. He has learned that effort and hard work pay off. When his grades improve, he sees an additional benefit.

There are no shortcuts to gain the self-esteem that comes from self-determination. The student who gets by with minimal effort and barely passes, or the student who copies homework from someone else, is not learning to take charge of his own life.

Homework Tips

Following are some suggestions that have proven successful for parents whose children are struggling with homework issues:

- Set aside one night a week when the child teaches the family what he has learned in school.
- Go to school weekly to collect the child's assignments. (This has been done even for high school students.)
- Keep up with the child's assignments so you can casually include relevant questions and comments in daily conversation.
- Invite the child to teach you a daily lesson.
- Listen to biography or math-fact tapes when riding in the car with your child.

- Read aloud to your child from textbooks and find ways to make the content understandable and enjoyable. For example, read a paragraph from a science book and make up a story using the facts you've just cited.
- Get together with two or more families to form a homework club. Let the children take turns working at each other's homes.
- If you love math, offer to help two or three children other than your own on a given night. If another parent loves English or some other subject, let them take the children another night.
- Trade children with other parents for an evening and spend study time with someone else's kids. Children will often be more cooperative with adults other than their own mother and father.
- Accept the fact that some students can actually do homework while listening to music.
- If your homework-challenged child does well with choices, ask him something like, "Where would you like to do your homework—in the kitchen or in the dining room?"

The important element that leads to success with homework is to make the time as enjoyable as possible. If you find yourself resorting to threats and anger, reassess the situation and look for help.

YOUR CHILD AND SOCIAL INTERACTIONS

Forming friendships is an important part of development and school. Children with problems have a difficult time making friends, because they lack the necessary social skills. Fortunately, these skills can be taught, and teachers often incorporate them into daily lessons. Hurt children may need additional help, and there are many things parents can do at home.

Elementary grades: If your child is extremely immature, you may have to accept the fact that he is going to play better with younger children. Talk with his teacher to find out how he compares with others and ask for suggestions about what you should do.

It may be helpful to invite one or more of your child's classmates to your home. Discuss the visit with your child before the guests arrive. If your child has come from an orphanage or foster home, it's possible that entertaining a guest is not in his frame of reference. He will require much more coaching than a child who has been raised in a family.

Plan activities and snacks in advance. While the children play, stay within listening distance so you can become aware of the areas where your child needs help. Get involved only if someone might get hurt. Let the children work things out while you listen. If you must intervene, use diversion rather than reprimands. Remember that your child does not know how to act. He wants to do the right thing but is not capable yet.

Do not get discouraged when you hear him saying and doing all the wrong things. Focus on loving him and teaching him in small steps. When the guests are gone, you can talk about what was good about the visit and offer one thing that could be done to improve the fun in the future. Plan another visit to practice a new behavior. Role-play the situations that cause problems and practice saying the appropriate sentences. A child without friends usually knows that he is not well liked. You can talk about ways that help people be liked by others.

Seek assistance from other parents. Explain that your child needs additional practice in learning social skills and that you are trying to improve his interactions. Parents with socially adjusted children may be willing to help you and may reciprocate by inviting your child to their home for an activity. Your child can provide an opportunity for other children to practice their tolerance and acceptance of individual differences.

Upper grades and high school: When a child enters the adolescent years, parents may wish they could return to the days when their child had no friends. Although teenagers insist that peers do not influence them, friends often have the ability to impact one another dramatically.

Your child may be desperately trying to maintain the core values that you have instilled and may need more help from you in managing his social life. Of course, he is not going to ask for help or even know that he needs it, so you must observe and listen carefully. When children start to change friends or lose friends, it is helpful to investigate to find out the reason.

Some teenagers are making good choices when they drop old friends.

KRISTEN AND AMY MET WHEN THEY WERE IN THE THIRD GRADE. ALTHOUGH they had always been best friends, they began to drift apart in the seventh grade—the year that Amy decided to turn her attention toward the opposite sex. One of the ninth-grade boys had begun to phone Amy every night. Her parents finally put a stop to the calls, telling her she was too young for a boyfriend. Amy confided in Kristen that her parents were "out of it," and that she was still seeing the freshman boy. She warned Kristen not to say anything to her mother, because both families were friends.

Kristin's mom, who was unaware of the changes in Amy, was concerned that her own daughter was losing a good friend and becoming asocial. When Amy called to beg Kristen to go to a party, Kristin's mom insisted that she attend. Because she was so worried about Kristin's social life, it never occurred to her that her own daughter was making a good choice when she declined Amy's invitation. The only reason Amy begged Kristen to attend the party was because her boyfriend would be there, and she would need Kristen as a cover when she left with him.

■

Even though you may know a teen's parents and are confident that their child has values in common with your family, adolescence brings a new set of behaviors. Your child may be afraid to tell you that his old friends are experimenting with controlled substances or sex, especially if the parents are friends. When you constantly question him about old friends, you may force him back to a group that he is trying to avoid. By the same token, he may be leaving old friends so he can do the experimenting with a new peer group. If you can find other parents who share your values, support each other. Keep your network of communication open and make a pact to keep each other aware of pertinent information.

Parents often worry when their adolescent is not part of the "in" group or has only one friend. But if you have a good relationship with your teen and he spends a lot of time with you instead of with friends, it is far better than having him receive all of his advice about life from his peers. If you are confused or concerned about your teen's choice of friends or lack of friends, contact a trusted teacher or counselor. School personnel see your child for a good part of the day, and they can help sort out your concerns.

Use all the resources the school has available. Do not wait until it is too late for help. If you have a bad feeling about something in your child's life, trust your instincts.

ROADBLOCKS AT SCHOOL

Maintaining positive communication with school personnel enables you to resolve minor conflicts with the teacher or counselor directly. But if your child has a teacher who does not respond to your attempts at dialogue or your requests for understanding the unique needs of your hurt child, there are a number of things you can do.

Ask for a conference with the teacher and request that a counselor or principal attend to help with your efforts at communication. If you feel uncomfortable asking the principal, ask a friend or parent mentor to help you during the meeting. You can also ask your therapist or physician to provide input. If you fear that the teacher will retaliate and take out his anger on your child, put your concerns aside. The teacher will know that you are vigilant, and he will be very careful about what he says and will try to fulfill your requests. If you feel that the teacher and principal are closing ranks and are not willing to work with you, go to the next level for help.

Talk to members of the school board or the superintendent. Be sure to keep records of all your attempts at communication. It is unlikely that you will need to take such extreme steps, but in the event that you do, make sure your records are accurate. If you know that you are right about what your child needs, but you are being hampered by school personnel who do not have the expertise or the willingness to learn about your unique situation, you must find the way to change their erroneous perception. Arm yourself with facts and documentation from experts who do understand. Do not be intimidated when a teacher says he has twenty-three other students to worry about. You are only discussing one child—your child—who cannot succeed unless he is understood.

Many parents have had to fight to get services for their physically handicapped or learning-disabled child. But hurt children deserve help and adjustments, too. A teacher may have to get out of his comfort zone and recognize that he has something new to learn about the needs of one of his students. If his discipline methods do not work with your child, he may have to learn new ones. If his expectations about social interactions are beyond your child's capacity, he may have to find ways to bridge the gap. Although it is always better to work problems out in an amicable way, you have every right to fight for your child if his needs are not being met.

Bᴇɴ's ᴘᴀʀᴇɴᴛs ᴡᴇʀᴇ ᴋɪʟʟᴇᴅ ɪɴ ᴀɴ ᴀᴜᴛᴏᴍᴏʙɪʟᴇ ᴀᴄᴄɪᴅᴇɴᴛ ᴡʜᴇɴ ʜᴇ ᴡᴀs only six months old. As a result of the accident, he sustained severe injuries and was not expected to survive. Although he proved all the physicians wrong, his life was marked by severe disabilities.

A couple with careers in the fields of neurology and advocacy for the disabled decided to adopt Ben. They were fascinated by the recovery and tenacity of this child who managed to beat the odds. They knew he would require complex services all his life and were convinced that with their professional skills, they could pave the way for him.

They experienced their first roadblock when family members told them they were nuts to adopt such a difficult child and that there were "places for people like Ben." Because they did not have family support, they were extra-diligent in finding every resource available for their child. He had early-stimulation therapists, speech therapists, and occupational and recreational therapists. He was ready for school when the time came, and his devoted parents expected him to be included fully in the regular education curriculum.

They were surprised to find that at the initial kindergarten screening, school personnel suggested a restrictive placement for Ben. The parents held their ground, attended numerous meetings, and used every bit of their professional expertise to get the school placement they demanded. They had set realistic goals for Ben, and they wanted him to graduate from high school and seek additional education or training. Even though he might require supportive services, they wanted him to be able to fend for himself and become a productive member of society.

They had to fight the battle many times with teachers who believed that Ben would never learn to read. They endured teachers who paid them lip service while rolling their eyes when they heard the parental expectations. They listened to counselors, teachers, and principals tell them that they had too many other students to be able to fulfill the unique requests for Ben. But still his parents persisted. Once in a while, they would meet a teacher who would share their vision, and that would be a year when Ben and his test scores would soar.

Today Ben is in a community college studying for a technical degree. He advocates for himself and has surpassed his parents' expectations and dreams. The teachers, the guidance counselors, and the psychologists were wrong about Ben.

■

Most parents do not have the professional expertise that Ben's parents have, but passion for your child's success can be a powerful substitute.

You might be surprised to know that, in some schools, an adopted child is not permitted to use his new surname until the legal papers have been processed. If this bureaucratic rule is hampering your child's attachment and your claiming, perhaps it is worth your intervention. School systems profess that the needs of the child are their primary focus. If that is indeed the case, they might be willing to change some of their regulations if school personnel became aware of the negative effects on the child.

Likewise, school systems provide staff development for their employees, and the entire staff may need to learn about the life of an adopted or foster child. Parents have power that they do not always use. A few words to a member of the administration or to a school board can go a long way to help an individual child or all adopted children. Think of the positive results that could occur if schools would embrace National Adoption Month every November, allowing students and staff to learn about adoption and celebrate this important aspect of life.

HOME SCHOOLING

Some families explore home schooling for a myriad of reasons. Those who choose to do it usually do it well. Those who could never rise to the challenge generally send their children to school out of the home. The issue of home schooling is frequently the subject of heated debate, and we are never quite sure why it merits so much scrutiny. If a family chooses to home school, and they are doing it within the confines of their respective state's education laws and guidelines, why should professionals who are supposed to help and support families get so upset about where children learn to read and do math? There are children who do not learn well anywhere, and there are children who would learn quite well sitting in the middle of a field. This should be a family decision that is made with the child's educational and social needs in mind.

WHAT IS REALLY IMPORTANT?

School is important because it consumes most of the waking hours of our formative years and impacts so much of the future. The social interactions that occur daily are complex and can make or break a child's spirit. The best thing you can do for your child at any age is to arm him with the techniques he can use academically and socially. Teach him that he can solve problems, because he always has choices and can always seek help from you. If he makes a bad choice, help him to recover and view the mistake as a learning opportunity. Help him to know that he can count on himself and on you and that he is resilient. Teach him to be curious about everything and to try new things. These approaches will serve your child well throughout life. Use them yourself as you advocate for your child throughout his school career.

CHAPTER 7

ROUGH WATERS:
Surviving When It Feels Like Nothing Works

Many parents have tried everything they can think of. They employ every technique recommended by their therapists . . . and still their children do not change. This doesn't mean that the parents are incapable. It doesn't mean that the intervention is inappropriate. It simply means that some children have neither the capacity nor the desire to change—and that is a sad and difficult fact to acknowledge.

In the past twenty years, the idea that therapy can solve all problems seems to have seeped into our collective way of thinking. Even on a professional level, many mental health practitioners claim that they can treat anything. That is probably true—if "treat" means "to *attempt* to make better." However, if the definition is "to *make* the condition better," it is an untrue and irresponsible claim. Professionals and parents alike need to remember that individual differences in the population of hurt children guarantee nothing but individual results.

In nearly all other fields that help people, there exists a widely accepted understanding that not everyone will have the same outcome. Even in the best schools, some students don't make it through third grade. Even in the finest hospitals, some patients don't survive their diseases. While these students and patients may have been treated the same way as their counterparts, their outcomes were very different.

Parents and professionals must be allowed the same kind of latitude that exists in other areas. Parenting very difficult children and adolescents is precisely that—very difficult. Techniques that have a significant impact on one child will be like water off a duck's back to another.

In this chapter, we will help you address particularly challenging issues and develop strategies for bringing about some change. Keep in mind that your job as a parent is to do the best you can. *You cannot make your child change.* What you can do is construct situations and responses that will maximize the chances for change. You can hope for change. You can pray for change. You can even pretend that you see change (a ruse that may prove very helpful now and then). But you absolutely, positively, unconditionally cannot force a change that your child does not want to make. In fact, giving up this belief can help make it more likely that you will have influence on your child. In other words, relinquishing some control may give you more control.

SELF INVENTORY

Many people get stuck in relationship struggles when their own issues intersect with those of another. If your child's issues are a threat to your own state of equilibrium, it follows that there will be intensified emotional responses from you.

Jenny was sexualized in her birth family by her father, grandfather, and numerous uncles. As expected, she became extremely seductive in her relationships with other children and adult men. Whenever she had the chance, she would jump right into the lap of an unsuspecting man—even in church! Her adoptive parents were horrified and embarrassed each time this happened. As a result of Jenny's behavior, her adoptive mom was brought face-to-face with her own childhood sexual abuse. She was flooded with feelings that she thought she had dealt with years before.

This kind of situation creates great difficulty. Jenny's mother was challenged not only with controlling her daughter's inappropriate behavior, but also with managing and containing her own hurtful memories. Her pain would not allow her to disengage from her earlier experiences, and simultaneously, her efforts to help Jenny became more complex and riddled with emotional overtones.

When you are thinking of your child's most bothersome issues, it may help to do a self-inventory and ask yourself some of the following questions:

■ What about this is so painful for me?
■ Does it relate to some of my own concerns—either historically or currently?
■ Is my child actually betraying me or am I responding to another betrayal in my life?
■ How much of this is about me? How much of it is about my child?
■ Where do our issues intersect? What happens to me at this intersection?
■ What allows me to feel so disempowered by my child?
■ How do I keep falling into these traps from which I feel there is no escape?
■ Who else lied to me? Who else gave me their baggage? Who else "caused" me to feel this powerless?
■ Is this how my child feels almost all of the time?
■ What do I do to try to manage these uncomfortable feelings?

If you can successfully go through a process of understanding what triggers what, you can more effectively manage both the child and your own emotional responses.

Sometimes parents of extremely difficult children report to us that others tell them not to "take things so personally." Our response is, "How can you help but take things personally? They're being aimed at you!" Even though your child's disturbance has roots elsewhere, it is difficult to feel emotionally removed when you open your dresser drawer to discover that he has defecated all over your clothes.

Let's look at a parallel. It is probably safe to say that most criminals are not robbing or raping someone because of who the victim is. Yet we wouldn't dream of advising that victim not to take the assault personally. Similarly, when you feel hurt by something your child has done to you, telling you not to take it personally is a nonproductive suggestion. It is much wiser for you to take a personal inventory in the hope that you'll feel differently the next time around. You may even be able to come up with a response that allows you to feel more in control and less violated.

Another benefit of taking a look inside is the possibility of recognizing what you *can* change about you so you don't feel so vulnerable. Living with hurt children automatically brings hurt into the family, and people who are not accustomed to dealing with it on a day-to-day basis have difficulty adjusting. Conversely, children who are accustomed to hurt don't mind it anymore— whether it's their own pain or the hurt they "share" with others.

When faced with your child's pain and the hurt he's inflicting on others, you may feel the need to respond in a clinical manner. Certainly, many professionals encourage parents to act somewhat detached and thoughtful. That may be realistic in some cases, but it probably isn't possible in truly shocking situations. To help parents feel validated and empowered, professionals must judge them less and judge the children more. Parents who feel strong do not need to flex their muscles; they can rely on their true strength and ability to come up with good ways to respond to their challenging children.

When you have defined what kind of parenting you do, what kind of parenting you *can* do, and what kind of parenting will help your child, you will have the opportunity to develop and create more effective strategies that are uniquely yours. Your style is who you are. Odds are it has worked for you for years, and with some new additions and fine-tuning, it may just be able to help you and your child.

BEHAVIORS THAT ARE RESISTANT TO CHANGE

The behaviors that are most likely to persist are those that have become reflexive habits. These are often integrated into the child's fragmented personality, and he has come to believe that they are necessary for his survival. Let's take a look at one of them—lying.

Anyone familiar with attachment issues knows that one of the most frequently mentioned problems is lying—crazy, obvious, primary process lying. This specific kind of lying is first seen in early childhood when children begin to tell "stories," lies, and so on—before the child has any awareness that others can evaluate what he says. In other words, when young children lie, they assume that their parents will believe them. A four-year-old does not know that other people have brains that will both hear and judge what they say.

Children who have had early trauma that interrupts their development often continue this primitive form of lying long past its developmental appropriateness. It is reflective of developmental delay, and it frequently becomes habitual and automatic. That is why we encourage parents to avoid responding to a child's lie with a question like, "Do you think I'm that stupid?" The answer to that—from the child's perspective—is a resounding "Yes!"

Everyone has automatic, habitual behaviors. Think about casual conversation. One person says, "Hi, how are you?" The other, without thinking, responds, "Fine, thanks, and you?" Rarely does the exchange vary, and most people are comfortable with these predictable replies. In fact, when someone takes a detour and starts to expound upon how he *really* feels, many folks feel inconvenienced and think, "Why did I even ask him? Now he'll go on forever telling me about his woes."

Along these same lines, the child who is a habitual liar simply goes on automatic pilot. His brain begins to compose a lie even before a question is completed. He is preparing for something bad to happen, but because he cannot predict what the questioner may ask, he comes up with a premature and inaccurate answer.

PARENT: "Denzel, did you . . . "
CHILD: "No!"

The child has responded reflexively without regard for the question. Once the response is out of his mouth, he is committed to defending his answer. The upshot? The lie gets bigger and more complicated. The angry parent then launches an investigatory pursuit, which allows the child to hang onto his belief that the parent must have some doubts. After all, if there were no doubt, why would there be further inquiry? An interactive process soon develops, as each player is committed to proving his respective point.

When dealing with an automatic liar, it is important to interrupt the process immediately in order to end it. The dialogue might go something like this:

PARENT: "Denzel, did you . . . "
CHILD: "No!"
PARENT: ". . . breathe today?"
CHILD: "What?"
PARENT: "I was just wondering if you breathed today."
Or something like:
PARENT: "Denzel, did you . . . "
CHILD: "No!"
PARENT: "Oh." (Then walk away from the interaction.)
CHILD: "Did I *what?*"
PARENT: "Oh, never mind."
CHILD: "What?!"
PARENT: "Oh, I was just going to say, 'Did you want to go to the mall and get those new shoes today?' But since you don't, I think I'll finish cleaning the garage."

By generating unpredictability, the parent may finally cause the child's process to be sufficiently interrupted to reduce the automatic nature of the response. Once the child begins to get the point that he cannot predict what is going to be asked, he may be "forced" to wait for the completed question.

A few pointers may help you fine-tune your lying-reduction program. First, if you know your child is a chronic liar, why even ask him if he did anything? You already know both answers—his is no and yours is yes—so there's no point in asking. If a lying person isn't asked too much, he obviously lies less. It is far more productive and infinitely less infuriating—for you—to tell him what you would like or what you already know. Here are two examples:

PARENT: "Did you have a . . . "
CHILD: "No, I didn't have a snack!"
PARENT: "How did you know what I was going to ask you since I didn't even finish the question?"
CHILD: "You always ask me stupid things like that!"
PARENT: "Randolph, we *do not* talk like that in this

house!" (Don't look now, Mom, but Randolph just *did* talk like that in your house.)

CHILD: "Like what?"

PARENT: "With a bad attitude. Anyway, I know you ate fourteen cookies because that's how many were left in the package before you went to school. I saw a big pile of crumbs on the counter, so I *know* you ate the cookies."

CHILD: "Sarah ate some cookies yesterday, and I did not eat fourteen cookies. I did not eat *any* cookies!"

PARENT: "Then how did all of those crumbs get there today?" (This is the kind of comment that gives the child the impression that you may have some doubt. It also "forces" him to respond with an explanation.)

CHILD: "Sarah must have dropped them yesterday."

PARENT: "Randolph Harrison, I will not have this lying going on in this house!" (Look again, Mom.) "I know that I cleaned the kitchen after breakfast this morning, and there were no crumbs."

CHILD: "Well, you must have missed some because, *for real,* I didn't have any cookies. I'm telling the truth!"

PARENT: "I know you're lying! In fact, every time your lips move, you tell a lie!" (If this is true, by now the child must be thinking, *If you know so darn much, why do you keep asking such stupid questions?!*)

CHILD: "I'm telling the truth!"

PARENT: "Well, I don't believe you, and just for that, you are not going to have any dessert tonight!" (Big deal. He's already eaten fourteen cookies.)

CHILD: "That's stupid."

PARENT: "Just for that, you're not going to have any dessert for a whole week!"

CHILD: "That's not fair!"

PARENT: "Haven't I told you a thousand times that life's *not* fair?" (If you have, in fact, made that statement a thousand times, do you really think saying it one more time will have any effect?)

This scenario could go on and on without accomplishing anything. Let's take a look at some other ways to approach the problem.

PARENT: "Randolph, could you come here, please?"

CHILD: "In a minute. Can I come at the commercial?"

PARENT: "Yes, at the *next* commercial will be fine."

(He comes into the kitchen.)

CHILD: "What?"

PARENT: "I'd like you to clean up those cookie crumbs while I peel the potatoes."

CHILD: "I didn't put them there!"

PARENT: "I didn't say you did. I just want your help in cleaning them up so I can get dinner ready faster."

CHILD: "Can I do it later?"

PARENT: "You could, but the commercial is just about over, and you'll miss the next part of the show if you wait much longer. Here's the dishrag. Just wipe up the counter and toss the crumbs in the sink."

CHILD: "This sucks. It isn't fair. I didn't make those crumbs."

PARENT: "Well, I don't know who did, and I really don't even care. I just know you always do a good job helping me get ready for dinner." (He shrugs and cleans the counter.)

CHILD: "Okay. Is that good?"

PARENT: "Great. Thanks."

Or at dinner . . .

CHILD: "What's for dessert?"

PARENT: "Oh, the cookies in the cupboard."

CHILD: "Can I get them?"

PARENT: "Sure, Randolph, that would be nice."

CHILD: "The package is empty!"

PARENT: "Oh, I can't imagine that. There were plenty left this morning. Oh, well, I guess we'll have dessert tomorrow."

Although there is still interaction in the latter scenario, it is less chaotic. The parent doesn't get into a pointless battle, and the child has fewer opportunities to engage in the automatic activity he has mastered—lying and defending himself.

When he defends his lie, he is doing it for himself, as well. That is why a parent might observe that the child seems to truly believe his own lies. If this is the case, it most likely is the result of having defended himself too often. Reducing the *volleying* about lying should also reduce the lying. Think about children bickering with one another: "Did not!" "Did so!" "Did not!" "Did so!" When you engage in a battle like this, not much good will result.

We hesitate to tell people what to say and how to say it because prescriptions don't exist. Different situations call for different interventions and responses. It is therefore important for parents to develop an understanding of what drives the child's misbehavior, what will interrupt that behavior, and how they can take charge of a situation in a way that will make it work for both parent and child. There is no single way to do this. A diversity of effective solutions stems from the knowledge, frustrations, and experiences that individual parents derive from their children and adolescents.

Timothy was a demanding sixteen-year-old. He had experienced profound neglect in his early years, which resulted in a long-standing impact on his overall development. He had made significant changes in many of his difficult behaviors, but an offensive one remained. He continued to soil himself during his waking hours—at school, at church, and at home. He never seemed particularly bothered by it. The odor was probably familiar from his early life, and he was just "too busy" to do something "boring" like going to the bathroom.

After much frustration and embarrassment, Timothy's mother stumbled upon a great curative idea. Tired of the briefs he'd been wearing for years, Timothy wanted boxers. For a while his mother resisted, claiming that she wasn't going to spend money on boxers when he kept ruining the underwear he already had. She then had a revelation that hadn't dawned on Timothy—what would happen when he soiled himself while wearing boxers? Gravity, that's what.

So she bought Timothy some colorful new boxers, and he excitedly put them on for school. Predictably, he did what he always did—soiled himself. Now, it doesn't take a rocket scientist to figure out what happened. Boxers + gravity + baggy pants = a huge mess on the floor, not in his pants. Talk about natural consequences! Timothy's classmates teased him for what seemed like forever. And gravity taught him a lesson that no person had been able to get across. And that was his last day of soiling.

When dealing with profoundly difficult children, it is helpful to explore parenting resources, to talk with other parents, or to look inward. A combination of these three strategies is better still. As we have often repeated, the *Parenting with Love and Logic* materials provide an invaluable framework for helping your child get rid of his old ways. However, you need to remember that *you* are what makes any strategy work. The strategy alone will not do it; logic alone will not do it; love alone will not do it. The merging of all of these components—and the way in which you deliver them—may give your child a reason and an opportunity to change.

REPARENTING . . . OR GETTING YOUR CHILD UNSTUCK

The initial task faced by parents of hurt children is helping their child "get unstuck." When thinking of getting a car out of the mud or snow, most people know that you simply cannot move forward without digging deeper into the mess and getting more stuck. Instead, it is necessary to back up a bit to gather the momentum that will help propel the car forward. This exercise may have to be repeated numerous times before there is any noticeable movement.

So it is with children of trauma. In most cases, they need to go backward before they can gain any real forward momentum. In short, they need what they need, even if it seems inappropriate for their age. And, of course, it is the parents' job to determine what they need and to provide it.

Children and adolescents who are *very* stuck will need more repetition, more normalizing experiences, and perhaps, more consequences. While it is reasonable to expect your child to respond to you, it is also reasonable to make yourself "respondable." In other words, he needs to know that you are present and central in his life. You cannot assume that he knows what every other child his age knows.

Marty had just moved in with his new family in late April—his first real home after a series of foster placements and group homes. He had been removed from his birth family when he was four, but as a result of legal entanglements, he was never previously placed in an adoptive family. He seemed to be getting along well with his new mom and dad, and he looked just like most other fourteen-year-olds. He had fashionable clothes, rather good social skills—at least superficially—and everyone considered him the average adolescent.

As mid-May approached, he heard and saw Mother's Day advertisements, but didn't pay much attention to them. After all, he had never before had a mother for whom he needed to buy something. When he awoke on Mother's Day, he was surprised to find that both of his parents were upset because he had forgotten to buy a gift or a card, or to acknowledge the day at all.

Obviously, his parents had assumed that he would respond like other boys his age. His father could have prevented this awkward situation by explaining how Mother's Day was celebrated in their family and by having told Marty that he would help him think of something special for his mom. Most fathers of younger children would have done this automatically. Had Marty's father done so, the boy could have had a new learning experience, and his mother could have felt appreciated and recognized.

Marty's dad was wrong to think that because Marty presented so well, he knew what to do in situations like this. In an attempt to give his new son as much leeway as possible, he didn't want to intrude upon his adolescent autonomy. So, for very admirable reasons, a father missed doing what would have helped both his son and his wife experience a better Mother's Day.

■

Parents should not assume that limits necessarily interfere with the child's or adolescent's development. Limits help heal the "breaks" that a child has experienced, just as a cast holds broken bones in place long enough to let them heal.

Keeping the child close to the family—and involving him in family activities, chores, and day-to-day life—helps to promote growth, attachment, and both external and internal regulation. While some adolescents may attempt to compare themselves to others their age, parents should not be lulled into thinking that they should give in to the adolescent's protestations of, "But everyone else is doing it!" Their child may actually be testing them in an effort to see just how much they will limit, regulate, and control them — in essence, how much they will care and love them.

MICHAEL, AGE SEVENTEEN, WAS VERY COMFORTABLE BEING WITH HIS FAMILY. He had lived with them for three years and spent a lot of time in the company of his parents. In fact, there were many occasions when he would choose to stay home rather than participate in an out-of-home activity.

When he was invited to a party with both boys and girls his age, he asked for permission to attend. His parents said they would think about it, and they assumed that Michael wanted to go. Because they knew the family hosting the get-together, they said they thought the party would be fun. As soon as Michael heard this, he became irritable and uncooperative. His parents had not seen this kind of behavior for a long time, and they wondered whether or not the party was influencing his acting out.

They decided to tell Michael that he could go to the party, and they would spend the evening at their favorite restaurant, which was adjacent to an arcade. Michael replied, "Aw, that's not fair — I love that place!" His parents saved him by replying, "Well, you can go with us instead if you like." The next day, Michael came home from school and reported that he told his friends he couldn't go to the party because he "had" to go out with his parents. He had resorted to using the single most acceptable excuse to peers. He was comforted by his "out" and was able to back out of something he obviously didn't want to do.

■

Older children, including adolescents, need nurturing and containment. Those who missed out on what "should" have happened in early childhood need even more. Parents can often take clues from what their children say about other kids and their parents.

Whenever the family discussed freedom and curfews, or suggested calling other parents for information on a teen activity, Tom, fifteen, would casually mention, "Oh, you don't need to call Bert's parents. They never care about what he does. He can do whatever he wants."

What Tom is saying, however indirectly, is that letting someone do whatever he wants is equivalent to not caring about him.

And that, quite simply, is scary to most kids. It is better to err on the side of restriction than freedom. Odds are, these hurt children were once very unrestricted, unregulated, and unnurtured. For someone to hold them, limit them, and demonstrate obvious concern sends a most important message: "You are loved, protected, and safe."

Will most children make this connection? We think the answer is yes, but that does not mean that you should expect a thank-you immediately upon making a decision that may not be perceived as nurturing. Watch for changes in the child's mood. After the initial flurry of protests, evaluate what you see, not what you hear. Observe the child. Is he more cooperative? Is he relaxed? Is he hanging around you? How long has he stayed angry? Behavior will tell you much more than his words. And, remember, the most severely disturbed children will probably not get the point, but as we have stated before, they may not get the point regardless of what you or any professional does.

CHILDREN FOR WHOM NOTHING WORKS

If your child or adolescent exhibits the behaviors or combinations of behaviors listed below, you will, with utmost certainty, need to undertake focused, intensive treatment. You probably do not need to wait very long before making the decision to access professional help. These problems are rooted in very early damage, and if they continue, they will often escalate. If many of these behaviors are present, assume that you need to get help—sooner rather than later.

Post-placement adjustment does not take a long time, and even if your child is from another country, you can expect that he will begin to fit into your family rather quickly—if he is going to fit in at all. Do not wait for years of troublesome behavior to pass, assuming that he is "getting used to" your family and culture. A honeymoon phase should not extend into years. If it does, you may be in a terminal phase, which means that what is happening will be going on for a protracted length of time, or perhaps forever.

Some of the most serious symptoms that hurt children may exhibit are:

- Injuring, mutilating, or killing animals on multiple occasions
- Seriously injuring—not just hitting or arguing with—other children on multiple occasions
- Repetitive attempts at setting fires
- Repetitive, intentional self-injury
- Repetitive sexualization of others—children, adults, animals
- Smearing feces, drinking from the toilet

Many children have some or all of these behaviors. They may also exhibit other symptoms mentioned in chapter 1. Early intervention and treatment may lead to remediation or elimination of such serious problems. However, it is imperative to consult with someone who has the necessary expertise to address issues of this magnitude. Traditional psychotherapy, child-centered psychotherapy, play therapy, traditional family therapy, and behavior modification plans will not begin to help these severe situations.

The next chapter, "Life Preservers," may give you the direction you need to help children who require more intervention.

CHAPTER 8

LIFE PRESERVERS:
Discovering Help from a Variety of Resources

There is no book, therapist, agency, or Web site that can meet all of your needs. Geography, finances, parental involvement, severity of the child's needs, culture, developmental age, and sibling issues are a few of the pieces that make all family mosaics different. Each situation calls for involvement on different levels, and it is for each family to decide. Following are a few of the common issues faced when parenting a hurt child, and some ideas of when, where, and how to ask for help.

SUPPORT

Support is a great way to end isolation, normalize your experiences, and find useful resources. Learning that other families share your bewilderment, pain, and issues helps invigorate and validate parents.

Many parents want everyone—teachers, family, boss, and the grocery clerk—to understand attachment issues and respond accordingly. This desire wears out the parents and makes them seem like crazed zealots. If people are really interested in learning, lend them some books. Otherwise, take their comments with a grain of salt: "If you'd stop being so harsh, your son would be fine." "Aren't you lucky to have such a great child!" "You are a saint!" "What did you expect?" "Give him back."

Just remember, before you knew your child, you wouldn't have believed it either.

A FAMILY CAME FOR TREATMENT WITH THEIR DAUGHTER. "THE AGENCY MADE us read *Adopting the Hurt Child* before we went to Russia to get her," they said. "We thought, 'How silly . . . no child is like that, and even if she were, we can fix her.' Now here we are, looking for help."

■

If you need support, call local adoption agencies (look in the telephone book) and ask for parent support groups. We have one at our office, and it has been great to see the parents begin to joke, share ideas, offer respite, and support each other. There is nothing like being able to tell the truth about your situation without judgment. Several of our families—from Ohio, Michigan, and Illinois—met on the Internet in an online chat group and discovered that they all used the services of our office. They began to book appointments at the same time so they could go out to dinner just to laugh and share.

All you really need for a support group is a few families, and agencies can often help you find those. Ask to be put on as many mailing lists as possible to receive notice of statewide adoption conferences, trainings, and other events. Attend a matching picnic— where prospective adoptive parents and waiting children meet to get to know one another—even if you don't want to adopt again. They always need volunteers, and other parents will be there to chat with and to learn from. Even if you adopted internationally, you can sign up with the local public agency to learn what is available.

There are many support groups on the Web, and several of them are geared to a specific situation.

■ Go to www.attach.org, click on "Links and Resources," and you're on your way! There are numerous listings for parenting techniques and support groups.

- Families who would like a Christian support group might try www.adoptionjewels.org.
- Families who adopted from China could go to www.members.aol.com/RADChina/index.html.
- Families who adopted from Eastern Europe might like www.eeadopt.org.
- Additional resources are listed in the back of this book.

FINANCIAL ISSUES

Paying for professional services is difficult for many parents. There are several avenues to explore.

- If you adopted domestically, you may have, or should have, a subsidy package. To learn what your state offers, go to www.nacac.org and click on "Subsidy," then on your state. If you don't have Internet access, call North American Council on Adoptable Children (NACAC) at (651)644-3036, and leave your question. If you didn't know at the time you adopted that you would need all these services, most often your subsidy can be reviewed and adjusted.
- If you didn't get a subsidy and think you should have, read *Accessing Federal Adoption Subsidies after Legalization* by Tim O'Hanlon. It is available by calling Tapestry Books at (800) 765-2367, or online at www.tapestrybooks.com.
- Some states have money for post-placement or post-legalization services. Many states receive federal money because they increased placement numbers, and they are spending it on these services. Check with your local Department of Human Services, Children's Services, or your state's Department of Human Services (usually in your state capital). Ohio has a program called Post-Adoption Special Service Subsidy (PASSS), which offers families financial assistance for post-legal services if they adopt domestically or internationally. If you are politically minded, get such a program organized in your state.

- Victims of Crimes money (if your child is an abused child, he might qualify) is usually administered through the state's Attorney General's office.
- Family Preservation services are available usually through Children's Services.
- Think out of the adoption box. There may be services available elsewhere in the community. For example, if your child is developmentally behind, check out Early Childhood Intervention Services. If he has an identified medical problem (such as cerebral palsy), go to the agency that helps families with that disability (United Cerebral Palsy Association).
- Check your insurance. If your doctor orders occupational therapy, it might be covered for your child. If you use the service on your own, it may not be covered.
- Keep current because rules and regulations can change. Sometimes agencies get federal grants to offer services—that's why it's good to be on their mailing lists—and are looking for families to help.
- There is some tax relief in some states and in the federal government for parents who have adopted a child. Check with a tax expert each year to be sure to get your deduction, which will give you more money to spend on services. Call the Casey National Center for Resource Family Support at (202) 467-4441. This organization created a federal tax benefits booklet that highlights adoption, foster, and kinship families. You can also visit their Web site at www.casey.org/cnc.
- Those of you who like to help change things might want to join Voice For Adoption, P.O. Box 77496, Washington DC 20013, (202) 543-7372. This group will keep you current on legislation and will tell you how to help create funds for post-placement services.

EDUCATION

Most states now require education classes before adopting from the foster care system. These classes help some parents, but many feel it is another roadblock that they simply do not need.

If you're among the latter, and wish you had paid better attention during the classes, you can usually go back to the sessions you need. If you heard about attachment three years before a placement, you may need to refresh yourself. If you are planning to or have already adopted internationally, many agencies require no education, but you might want to attend these classes anyway. There is no such thing as too much knowledge.

Many agencies offer ongoing training for foster parents. Even if you aren't a foster parent, you might be allowed to attend a class. Call the agency and ask for the training department.

The North American Council on Adoptable Children (NACAC) has a huge annual conference. It moves around the country and has many workshops on a variety of subjects. The resource room is wonderful! Many speakers allow their sessions to be recorded, so if you can't attend, you can buy the tapes from NACAC. You can write to NACAC at 970 Raymond Ave., Suite 106, St. Paul, MN 55114-1149; call (651) 644-3036; or visit www.nacac.org.

Another organization that offers a yearly conference is the Association for Treatment and Training in the Attachment of Children (ATTACh). You can reach ATTACh at P.O. Box 11347, Columbia, SC, 29211, by phone at (866) 453-8224, or on the Web at www.attach.org. Many of the association's sessions are also available on tape.

There are many books available for children, teens, parents, and professionals. A good resource to begin with is the *Adoption Book Catalog*, available from Tapestry Books. There are about sixty pages of books available on attachment, adoption, infertility, birth parents, and international adoptions, and it is fully annotated. Tapestry will send you one if you call (800) 765-2367, or request one on the Web at www.tapestrybooks.com.

Adoptive Family Magazine is another good resource that features many articles for families regarding all types of adoption. Contact the publication at *Adoptive Families* magazine, 2472 Broadway, Suite 377, New York, NY, 10025, or call (800) 372-3300, or visit the Web site at www.adoptivefamiliesmagazine.com.

The National Adoption Information Clearinghouse offers a great deal of information, and much of it is free. You can write to 330 C Street SW, Washington, DC, 20447, call (703) 352-3488, or visit www.calib.com/naic.

SOCIAL SECURITY

If you adopted domestically, chances are your child has a social security number. You will need to change his name once the adoption is final, so when he retires, the money is in the right account. If you have reason to fear the birth parents, you might want to get a new number, because the social security number makes the child traceable on the Internet. Check with the agency because a new social security number might change your subsidy payment number.

If your child is adopted internationally, he becomes an American citizen when the adoption is legal. Get him a social security number immediately because you'll need it when filing your tax return.

THERAPY

If your parenting alone is not changing your child's behaviors, he may need therapy. Make sure the counseling meets the child's needs. Simply picking someone close to your home from a list of providers is not helpful. Ask people from the support group or the adoption agencies—people who understand attachment—for a referral. Try the organizations, too. Ask the therapist how many children he has treated with your child's particular issues. He might work wonders with many children's problems but know nothing about attachment issues and their treatment. Contact groups such as ATTACh, Heal The Heart, the Attachment Disorder Support Group site, and others listed in Resources for information on therapists trained in this field.

Another resource is Theraplay®, which is *not* the same as play therapy. These therapists offer an interactive way to increase attachment through structure, nurture, challenge, and engagement. (See the listing in Resources.)

WHEN NINE-YEAR-OLD DON CAME TO OUR OFFICE, WE WERE THE THIR-teenth professional group to be involved. No one else suggested attachment as an issue, but we soon discovered it was at the heart of his problems. The in-home therapist asked if she could continue to visit the family home weekly just "to learn about the process." Don's mother said, "You can come if I don't have to pay you, but why should I spend money to train you?" The therapist never came back.

■

If a program is helpful—if a therapist is making strides with your child—stay put. Otherwise, look elsewhere. It is not your job to make therapists happy. Your role as a parent is to find the best services for your child. See chapter 9, "Finding Useful Help," for more guidance on this topic.

Want to know what is normal? Read some developmental books. Give the child time for an adjustment period, which will vary with each individual. Factors that affect the length of this period include age, life-history, and number of moves. For every three months in an institution, you might subtract a month developmentally. For example, if the child was fifteen months old when adopted from an orphanage, he could be ten months old developmentally. These are only general guidelines and are meant to help you figure out when to ask for help.

We often get calls that run the gamut of extremes: "We got off the plane a week ago. Is he attached to us?" Probably not, because he just met you. "We have had him for twelve years, and we knew at ten months that things weren't right." So, what took you so long to get help?

SPEECH

It is fairly clear to most people that when a child has a lisp or can't say his Rs he needs speech therapy. Less obvious are children with receptive language problems. People assume these children understand everything they hear, but they often do not. The problem can have several sources: poor early speech development due to neglect; early, untreated ear infections causing muffled sounds; a problem with processing (Mom speaks at thirty miles an hour, and the child hears at ten miles an hour); English as a second language; or lack of vocabulary.

CINDY WAS REMOVED FROM A NEGLECTFUL HOME AT THIRTEEN MONTHS. AT age six she was told she was going to be adopted by her foster mom, and she immediately burst into tears. "But I want to be a ballerina!" she wailed. The social worker and the mother exchanged confused glances—they had been so sure Cindy would be happy about the news. Their statement to the child meant, "You're going to be adopted, and you'll get to stay with the foster mom you love forever." But Cindy didn't hear "be adopted." Instead, she heard "be a doctor," because her foster mom had once told her that she could be a doctor when she grew up. "I don't want to give shots— I want to dance!" Cindy cried. Clearly, what was said and what the child heard were very different things.

OCCUPATIONAL THERAPY

Many children who were neglected or abused, were moved around, or spent their early years in an institution need occupational therapy (OT). They seem on track when they are walking or climbing, but perhaps they never learned to chew and swallow correctly. The result is that eating and mealtime are a problem. Some children lick the skin below their lips until it is chapped. Others have difficulty using utensils, pens, or pencils.

An indication that an OT evaluation is needed might be a child's inability to climb the stairs without alternating his feet long after he is developmentally supposed to be able to do so. Or his crawl might be off, even if he is older. A child should be able to crawl with alternate feet and hands—left hand with right leg, right hand with left leg.

Aʟᴀɴ ᴡᴀs sɪx ᴡʜᴇɴ ʜᴇ ᴡᴀs ᴀᴅᴏᴘᴛᴇᴅ ғʀᴏᴍ ғᴏsᴛᴇʀ ᴄᴀʀᴇ. Hᴇ ʜᴀᴅ ʙᴇᴇɴ neglected as a child and lived in two foster homes, one of which was abusive. Meals in his adoptive home were a nightmare! Alan spilled every liquid, threw tantrums when the foods on his plate touched each other, and was awkward with a fork. We suggested going backward until he could be evaluated by an occupational therapist. His mom bought a divided plate so foods didn't touch. A raised lip around the rim helped push food onto his fork. A toddler "sippy cup" ended spills, and toddler silverware bade farewell to the utensil war. While these solutions were developmentally incongruous for a six-year old, they were just right for Alan. The family meals settled down, and everyone was happier.

Many children also have sensory integration problems—colors, sounds, touch, smells, and textures seem very different to them. They may require less-cluttered rooms, deeper touch, or other adaptations.

SIBLINGS

Living with a hurt child is not easy—particularly for the sibling of one. Sometimes things at home are so weird that the healthy child doesn't want to invite friends to witness the tantrums or the swearing or whatever the hurt child is doing. Sometimes parents involved in therapy, OT, or support groups forget to spend time with their other children.

Be sure your other children know exactly what is going on. If there is danger—such as sexual acting out by the hurt child— be sure the others know what to do when he approaches them. If the child is violent, his siblings may be afraid that they can't protect their parents or themselves. Develop a code word and teach it to the siblings. If Mom or Dad says the word, the children are to call 911 for help immediately.

Many hurt children have a need to know that their birth siblings, foster siblings, and/or orphanage mates are all right. It is a kind of survivor's guilt—I'm okay, but what about everyone else? Sometimes they are preoccupied with thinking about others.

MARK, THIRTEEN, WAS PLACED WITH HIS THREE SIBLINGS, BUT COULDN'T safely stay in the family. Another family adopted him and invited his siblings and their parents to his legalization. His sixteen-year-old sister was very happy that he was secure and settled at last. However, when the judge announced that Mark was legally adopted, she recalls, "It was like a knife went into my heart. He would for sure never come back, his new parents could keep me out of his life, and he would never be my brother in the same way. He had new parents and grandparents. I lost my brother all over again." Even though she knew Mark was safe and happy, her worrying about him seemed to take on a life of its own.

MARRIAGE

We have a joke at the office that none of our families get divorced because no one wants custody of the child! Be sure that you take care of your marriage while rising to the difficult challenge of parenting a hurt child. Writing notes, supporting each other in front of the child (who is often an expert at polarizing parents), and spending time together are all necessary.

THE JONESES ADOPTED A SIBLING GROUP OF FOUR, AND THE AGENCY PROvided the services of a sitter if they wanted to attend a support group. They accepted the offer, bought dinner at the drive-through of a fast-food restaurant, fell asleep in the car, and returned home four hours later. It was great! They got the support they needed—even if it wasn't quite what the agency had in mind.

You may need a tropical cruise, but perhaps the best you can do is get up fifteen minutes earlier to have coffee together or stay up fifteen minutes later to cuddle. However you do it, make time for each other.

TAKING CARE OF YOURSELF

It is impossible to tell people how to take care of themselves. Some require quiet time to read a book; others need time to get their nails done, others need a day at the art museum or the ball park, and some just want to take a nap. Each individual needs to find a way to keep refreshed, optimistic, and alive. In a survey available at www.eeadopt.org, 65 percent of the parents who had adopted responded that they were suffering from post-adoption depression.

INFERTILITY

Not everyone adopts because of infertility, but if you did, your feelings of loss and anger may rekindle as you help your child deal with those same issues. Why do people who abuse children have five . . . and you have none? You did everything to have a child. You did everything the agency said to get a child, but the child didn't fix your infertility. You are no longer childless, but you still cry when you get your period. If this is still an issue for you, you may need some support. Visit an infertility clinic, do some reading on the subject, try counseling, or do some research at www.resolve.org. If you adopted simply because everyone said you would get pregnant if you did so, that is simply a myth. Most people who have infertility problems do not get pregnant just because they adopt.

DISRUPTION

Some parents want the hurt child out of their house and are surprised that this is not an easy task. If your child was placed domestically, there is a time between placement and legalization when you can request removal. This is called disruption. In international adoptions, when legalization occurs in the home country, and after the legalization of domestic adoptions, the child is yours—as if born to you. If you want the child removed, it is called dissolution and is usually very difficult.

Adoptive parents are sometimes shocked when an agency replies to their request for removal with, "We will help with services, but he is yours now." Some private agencies will replace children through a private adoption—if they have a family and the relinquishing family will pay the fees. If you choose this course of action, you *must* be sure it's legal in your state. In some states, for an agency to take custody of a child after legalization, the parents must be charged with neglect, abandonment, or dependency. If the child needs residential treatment, the plan will be for him to return home after treatment, and you will be asked to complete a case plan. Residential treatment centers are very expensive, and it is unlikely that a parent or agency can afford to keep a child in one for many years.

CULTURAL ISSUES

It is nice if you can help your child appreciate his birth culture through dance, books, dolls, language, and food. But keep in mind that these things can also trigger memories for your child.

DANIELLA WAS SIX WHEN SHE CAME TO AMERICA FROM RUSSIA. AT EIGHT, her parents took her to a Russian deli in the city. She instantly went into a fetal position, overwhelmed by the smells, food, people, and language in the store—so reminiscent of her home. The clerks looked and sounded like the staff of the orphanage where she spent her early years, and the memories made her feel sad. As soon as her adoptive parents comforted her and she processed her feelings, she was able to enjoy the experience.

■

Different children can process the same event differently.

THE ROBERTS FAMILY ADOPTED TWO KOREAN CHILDREN AS INFANTS. WHEN the boy was eight and the girl was seven, the parents took them to a Korean festival with dance, food, and lots of activities. Their son loved it, but it made their daughter very sad. She crawled into her adopted mom's lap, and said, "So many Korean moms keep their children. Why didn't my mom keep me?" The same event, the same adoptive parents, completely different reactions.

■

The cultural issues that cause problems in families are things like:

- Johnny comes from a culture where money is used for drugs, and food is obtained by stealing. He arrives in an adoptive home . . . and steals food.
- Shana comes from a culture where children are raised in orphanages. To her, children are the family and she doesn't know what parents are for.
- Derek comes from a culture where any kind of problem results in a move to another foster home. As soon as he begins to love his foster parents, he will act in a way to ensure that he gets moved. It hurts less if he moves *before* he develops feelings for the family he loves. And he *knows* he will move—he always does.
- Sally comes from a culture where people enter her room at night and sexually abuse her. She wakes up at night screaming.
- Douglas comes from a culture where you eat by the clock. He doesn't understand his body's cues that indi-

cate hunger. Whenever he sees food, he thinks he should eat it. And he doesn't stop until the food is gone.
- Lynn comes from a culture where babies share beds. Every time you get her up from sleep, she sadly peers down looking for her "sister." She misses her crib mate.
- Janet loved her birth mom, who beat her regularly. Now Janet hits people she loves, because she learned that's the way love is expressed.
- Anna came from an orphanage where food was often stolen if you didn't eat fast and guard your food. Now she can't understand why everyone tells her to "slow down!" when she's eating.

HOMELAND TOURS

In recent years, there have been increasing numbers of homeland tours for children adopted from other countries. We believe that the decision about the feasibility of this concept needs to be child-centered. Are you being driven by the trend, by the child's genuine interest in his country of origin, or by your own need to expose your child to his birth culture? Any homeland visit should be in response to the child's need for such a visit. Perhaps it should be delayed until late adolescence or adulthood, when the adoptee is able to put things together in some sort of conceptual framework.

You must remember that culture is the way you grow up, not the place where you were born. Quite simply, children adopted from other countries grow up American. Even families who arrive together from another country are often unsuccessful when they try to get their children to retain their language and culture of origin. Kids adapt quickly, and they want to be like other kids. So if Filipino parents living in the United States have difficulty getting their Filipino children to embrace their culture, what are the chances of a white American family succeeding at bridging cultural gaps?

This is not to suggest that exposure to birth country issues shouldn't be undertaken, but parents must follow their child's lead in this arena. If Russian-born Darius doesn't want to take Russian classes, then he probably shouldn't. Conversely, if he expresses a desire to do so, his parents should explore the options.

Every child is going to have his own viewpoint on this issue, but parents need to remember that whatever they do, they should do it because it will somehow benefit the child.

MARCO, A CHILD FROM LATIN AMERICA, WENT ON A HOMELAND TOUR. HIS parents spent a lot of money and effort to make sure everything was well planned. They went to museums and restaurants and visited places of interest for most tourists. Marco's responses included, "It was boring to go to those museums. The food was gross—a Wendy's® burger would have been better. And I'm glad I don't live in those little dirty houses with chickens running around!"

Angeline, another Latin American child who went on the same trip, commented, "I had a great time. It was interesting to try the food and to see how the people live there. I felt better about my adoption knowing what my life would have been like if I'd stayed with my birth family. I now understand what 'poor' means, and it's no wonder my birth mom couldn't keep me."

Two different children . . . same trip . . . two different experiences. One size doesn't fit all, and it's important to take time to think about what fits *your* child.

We can guarantee one thing: if your child is emotionally disturbed, a homeland trip will *not* make him better. He will simply be disturbed and disturbing in Russia, Korea, Costa Rica, China, or wherever.

The entire arena of birth family and birth country issues is huge and should not be taken lightly. These issues need to be acknowledged; they need to be heard and understood. In the end, parents need to make the decision with the child's needs in mind.

HOLIDAY HORRORS

No, it's not your imagination. Holidays, birthdays, and Mother's Day can be triggers for a lot of children. And many of them hate surprises.

WILLIAM WAS RAISED FOR FIVE YEARS BY A MENTALLY ILL MOTHER. HE NEVER knew if he would be smothered in kisses . . . or knocked across the room. He spent the next five years in foster care and residential treatment. As a result of his early life with an unpredictable mother, he hated surprises and made everyone miserable at Christmas and birthdays. His new mom finally gave up her fantasy of a happy boy sitting beneath the Christmas tree. He went shopping with her, saw the presents in advance, and they simply appeared on Christmas morning. His mom wrapped surprises—just a few small treats—for his stocking. It was not what she wanted, but it made for a Merry Christmas.

■

Other children just don't understand what is expected.

MIKAIL CAME FROM RUSSIA IN AUGUST. HE WAS SIX. THE FOLLOWING MAY, his teacher helped the class make cards and gifts for Mother's Day. His new mom was thrilled as he squirreled away his treasures. When the day came, his dad went up to Mikail's room to help retrieve the gifts and handed them to his wife. Mikail burst into tears. Why was this mom stealing the gifts he so carefully made for his Russian mom? He thought Mother's Day meant your birth mom came to visit.

■

Be prepared to dump some of the holiday confusion and get rid of those Norman Rockwell/Martha Stewart fantasies. You may have to be low-key.

BIRTH FAMILY CONTACT

Most of the children adopted from the child welfare system have had much contact with their birth families. Some of them may continue to have contact with their birth relatives, and many think about contact in the future.

The current trend toward openness may lead you to think this option is for everyone, but that is *not* the case. You must remember that many birth parents have seriously hurt their children, and some have been convicted of crimes against them. In instances such as these, openness may not be safe for either the child or your family. As a responsible parent, you would not expose your child to any other dangerous people . . . or even to situations that might cause him to worry. It is the same with his birth parents.

As the adult in charge, you must carefully evaluate all suggestions about contact with birth relatives. Here are some questions that may help you consider whether or not to pursue or respond to inquiries about contact:

- Will contact with birth relatives be helpful to the child or adolescent?
- How will it be helpful?
- Will contact be safe?
- If this person were not biologically related to the child, is he or she the kind of person you would trust to be in the child's life?
- Is the contact for the child, or is it to satisfy some ideologically driven professional?

The answers to these questions—as well as your own perspectives—will guide you to your decision. Openness is not for everyone. Having an open adoption with a birth parent who carefully planned for her child's adoption is completely different from taking a trip to prison to visit an abusive birth parent.

On the subject of visits with siblings—sometimes they're helpful and sometimes they're crazy-making. When they are productive, your child's behavior won't deteriorate for weeks before and after the visits. If chaos reigns, you must rethink the purpose of the contact.

No one has all the answers. There is no magic pill that works for everyone. Not all children are alike. Neither are all families. The more you know and understand about loss, your child's history, and the resources available to you, the easier the path to a happy family.

CHAPTER 9

FINDING USEFUL HELP:
Connecting with the Right Therapist

Once people have reached the point where they recognize the need for professional help, they should be able to access it relatively painlessly. Unfortunately, this isn't always the case. This chapter may provide you with some guidance and insights regarding what kind of help you should seek.

Help that is not useful is probably worse than no help at all. So be proactive, and get precisely what you and your child need.

Adoptive families often find that they need the assistance of professionals to help them address difficulties. In fact, nearly all of the adoptions in the United States today—including those that begin in other countries—involve children with a diversity of special needs. Many times, families can handle the problems themselves, but it is more common for them to solicit services from mental health, health, or educational professionals.

We continually hear horror stories from desperate families who have been judged, misjudged, and poorly handled by mental health professionals. One would think such practitioners would be beyond some of the comments shared with us:

173

"Why would you adopt such kids?"
"What did you expect when you decided to take in three kids like these?"
"You shouldn't take their behavior personally."

Each of these comments reflects a complete lack of understanding of adoption, the adoptive process, the adopted child, and the adoptive family. Professionals are sought out for their help, not for their criticisms and second-guesses about the family's motivation. The last thing that a family in distress needs is to be blamed by a therapist.

Another frequently heard complaint is from families who have been told, "Why don't you just take the child back?" Back where? Do these same therapists suggest that solution to married couples who are having difficulties? What do they say to families who have problems with their birth children?

The first thing that families should do when looking for a therapist is to check with other adoptive families. The Internet is filled with adoption-related chat rooms and information sites. Families are clearly the best source of information, and our experience leads us to believe that most adoptive families have done their homework. They know about their problems—and potential solutions—and other resources.

While interviewing a prospective therapist may be a bit uncomfortable, it can be done. We would suggest asking about his experiences with adoption, severe behavior problems, loss and grief, and anger. If you think your child has severe attachment difficulties or Reactive Attachment Disorder, ask about his experience with these diagnoses. What is his treatment approach?

Following is a list of components that we believe are critical to adoption-related therapy:

- Parents should be intimately involved in the therapeutic process. Individual, child-centered treatment is most often not helpful for serious problems.
- Parents should be seen as a part of the treatment team. After all, they are the *only* ones who can actually help heal the hurt child.
- The child and therapist should not have confidentiality that excludes the parents. The adults in the

family should know everything that the therapist knows.

- Therapists should not enter into bargaining with the parents on the child's behalf. For example, "If Jamie has been nice, can she stay up a bit later?" Such bargaining undermines the family's balance of power and gives the child an ally—the therapist—in his attempts to manipulate the family. Such triangulation of the parents and therapist is not helpful.
- The family's value system must be respected. The therapist should support the parents in their efforts to instill their value system, irrespective of the therapist's beliefs.

Families must do their homework before embarking on a course of therapy. Too many people have had bad experiences that cloud later attempts at therapy . . . or even preclude the family's interest in trying again.

Once you have chosen a therapist and have become confident in him, it is then necessary to follow through with his directions. Most adoptive parents are *not* responsible for creating the difficulties their children have, but they *are* responsible for helping to correct them.

This chapter was first printed in *Jewel Among Jewels* newsletter, Spring 2001. www.adoptionjewels.org.

CHAPTER 10

ASK AN EXPERT:
Questions and Answers About Hurt Children

These questions and answers were originally published in Dr. Keck's column, "Ask An Expert," which appears in *The Connection,* the newsletter of the Wayne County Children Services Board in Wooster, Ohio. A diversity of issues is addressed here, and we think it would be helpful to share the information with our readers.

Dear Dr. Keck:

We have a fifteen-year-old adopted son who has ongoing difficulty with anger. He has had an inner rage since he was a little child. He has also been hyperactive since he was three. At that same time, our second child was adopted. We are not sure if there is a correlation between our older son's behavior and the addition of a second child to the family.

We have closely monitored his diet in the past and believe it has helped control his anger outbursts. We are frustrated, though, because our son does not deal with his anger. He just walks away without addressing the issues or his emotions.

Do you have any suggestions on how to deal with our

son's anger? Also, what types of consequences work best for teens?

Concerned Parents

Dear Concerned Parents:

Anger is a problem that many parents see with children who have had early loss, trauma, and/or separation. Anger that begins in early childhood is certainly different from that experienced by many adolescents whose anger is more related to issues of separation, individuation, and autonomy. Early anger that continues to increase in intensity is most often related to some sort of early trauma. In the case of the adopted child, one would need to know something about birth family history—particularly as it relates to personality issues—his history within the adoptive family, and any events that may have precipitated the onset of the anger.

In all probability, the hyperactivity you mention is not related to the addition of a second child. If the child is truly hyperactive—that is, diagnosed with Attention Deficit Hyperactivity Disorder (ADHD)—it should be assumed that this particular disorder is of biogenic origin and was present from birth. The addition of children to a family can always change the dynamics, but I do not feel that it would result in issues related to mood and hyperactivity.

Regarding your son's diet, the research with which I am familiar has not indicated any significant relationship between diet and behavioral difficulties.

I am not certain at this point if you will be able to do anything about such long-standing anger without professional intervention. If parenting techniques and parenting interventions were going to be of help to remediate this child's anger, I suspect it would have already occurred. For the professional to be of assistance, he would first need to understand the origins of the anger. He could then begin to help your son understand how these original issues are currently being triggered.

Any discussion of consequences related to outbursts of anger would need to be rather extensive. I would simply refer readers to *Parenting Teens with Love and Logic* for parenting strategies and consequences that help remediate a wide range of behaviors.

Dear Dr. Keck:

Four months ago, my husband and I adopted our second special-needs child through our local Protective Services agency. We are excited about the prospect of increasing our family by at least two more children. We have received some suggestions from our adoption worker to wait a while before bringing in another child, but we feel we are ready to have another child placed with us. What would be your suggestion regarding the length of time to wait after finalization? Thank you for your help.

Adoptive Parent

Dear Adoptive Parent:

My immediate answer is: *it depends*. I think all questions regarding adoption should be answered this way. After all, we know very little about what makes a good placement and what causes a disruption. Adoption practice has run a course of many trends, and I think we should be wary of most of them.

The bottom line is: kids need to move into permanent placements as quickly as possible. While we sit around waiting for the right amount of time to pass before a child or a family is "ready," the child's developmental clock continues to run. This clock does not wait for our professional thinking, adoption practice, current trends, or anything else.

"Temporary" for children is very short—and should be very short. Just think of how long it seemed from Christmas Eve to Christmas Day when you were a child. How long does a school year last for a child? A long time! An adult's idea of time is extremely different from that of a child.

Keeping this general thinking in mind, there are some things that you should think about when making placements close together:

- How is the family doing with the child already placed?
- How is the child doing in the placement?
- What would another child mean to the first child?
- Is the next placement going to happen eventually? If so, why keep the new child waiting any longer?

There are so many children waiting that I think we should move to permanency as soon as possible. If you are feeling that you want another child and there is no concrete reason *not* to begin the process again, it should probably begin. Obviously, I don't know any of the details of the situation, so there may be circumstances that caused the adoption worker to counsel against this specific placement. However, I think all of us working in adoption need to challenge our own long-standing beliefs about what *we think we know*. Adoption professionals must constantly reevaluate their beliefs in an effort to facilitate and expedite getting kids into what we all talk about—families.

■

Dear Dr. Keck:

My question is in regard to my eleven-year-old adopted son. He has a disturbing behavior of urinating in various places around his bedroom—places like out his window, in a hole in his closet, and on the carpet. One time that we are aware of, he even defecated in his closet. We have tried various techniques to help him stop, like keeping a bucket in his room to go in if he has an emergency. Nothing seems to work. He doesn't consistently do this behavior. Sometimes he will go a whole month without doing it, but then he starts again.

I want to know why he does this, and do you have any suggestions on how to stop the behavior?

Frustrated Mother

Dear Frustrated Mother,

The problems associated with elimination are frequently seen in our office. Most of the children who have had severe trauma and have developed attachment difficulties have elimination problems.

Children who have been hurt early in their lives seem to be continually trying to eliminate things from their lives—closeness, love, pain, and control by others. Their elimination difficulties are most often intentional and focused on sending a message to their parents. Without being too explicit in a publication such as this, let me say that your son is *doing* what many people say when they are angry—he is showing you *"Urinate on it!"* He is giving you *defecation*! I think you get the point. This behavior is offensive, and that is exactly why it is so popular with angry children. He knows that you have absolutely no control over this part of his body, nor his life. His point is to offend, and I would guess that he is being successful.

Another component of this activity is that it may re-create the sensory memories of the birth home. Many children are left alone for hours or days without being changed. When they create those old smells, they may get some sense of comfort from the familiarity.

While you cannot *control* this behavior, there are some things that I have found to be helpful. I often say to the children and adolescents with whom we work, "You know, Colin, you seem to be the kind of kid who likes gross things in your room like pee and poop. I have an idea. I'm going to ask your parents to allow you to be in charge of all of those things in the house. You can clean the toilets to give your mom a break, you can clean up after the dog—and let's throw in the litter box as a bonus. I think all kids should get to do what they like to do, so let's try this for a while and see how it works!" Most often, these kinds of chores will eliminate the problem behavior.

I have had great success with these problems, and I encourage you to be creative as you think of ways to create logical consequences for your son's offensive behavior.

■

Dear Dr. Keck:

I believe that all children need, and should have, a safe, permanent, loving family. Should adoption be the goal for all teens who are in foster care? Should it be the goal for teens in long-term foster care where reunification with the biological family is no longer a court order or considered? How should a public children services agency best explore the issue of adoption with a teen who expresses doubts and fears regarding the possibility of an adoption?

Concerned Adoption Assessor

Dear Assessor:

This question is one that often comes up in adoption circles, as well as among the public. I think that we begin to find the answer to this question by asking another: "What is the alternative?"

After all, most of us have more years of involvement with our families after age eighteen than we did before. Most people experience support from their families throughout their lives. Just because the public children services agencies do not maintain involvement after the legal age of majority does not mean that the lives of those children becoming adults can go on smoothly without a family.

We have attempted to address this dilemma by developing independent living programs. With all due respect to these intentions and efforts, I must say that I believe it is the rare individual who is truly able to be self-sufficient at age eighteen. This is even more difficult when you consider the fact that the children within the system are even less prepared for independence as a result of all of their early trauma and broken foundations. I think we could agree that most adolescents need a family if they are going to develop into productive, functioning adults. We can try to alleviate our collective guilt and discomfort by developing sophisticated plans, but we cannot change human development.

This being said, I believe we need to attempt to place children and adolescents in adoptive homes. Long-term foster care denotes something temporary; adoption implies permanence.

Most adolescents will have some fears and reservations about adoption. However, it is our job to help them work through those. I think they have the same fears when presented with the alternatives: no family connections, no support, no safety net, and ultimate responsibility for managing life's many issues. If an adolescent absolutely refuses to discuss adoption and continues to indicate that he does not want to be adopted, I feel that we have to pay attention to his claims. His two choices should not be adoption or long-term foster care; they should be adoption or foster care until he is left to his own devices to survive. This presentation is not only truthful, but also one that may help him make a more well-informed decision.

The individuals with whom I have worked who were adopted during adolescence have valued their families, for the most part. They are happy to *finally* have what their peers have—a parent. While it may take them some time to begin calling their parents "Mom" and "Dad" directly, they very quickly seem to take pride in referring to "my mom" or "my dad" while talking to others. When people say (or think), "He's too old to be adopted," they are really saying, "He is too old for a family." How many of us would ever say that about ourselves?

■

Dear Dr. Keck:

A child's life book often offers therapeutic value when children are placed in adoptive homes. Do you recommend that the adoptive parents review the life book with the child, or should a therapist do this? What if the child wishes daily to review the life book with a parent, and then becomes sad as a result? Should the parent put the life book away for a while? How would you recommend the parents handle this situation?

Interested Adoption Assessor

Dear Assessor:

Life books seem to have great importance for many children. We need to remember that only those children whose lives have been seriously interrupted are the ones who end up developing a life book. We hope that such a book will pull together the fragments of their broken lives into one document that they can review. Children often like to look through their life books because this activity helps them reflect on where they have been. The linkage may also be valuable in helping them get a clear understanding of why they are, where they are, and how the past relates to the present.

I certainly think the family can review the life book with the child if the child wants to do so. The focus of work with the life book in the therapeutic situation is different from the family's review of it. However, I believe the life book should be available to, and accessible for, the child when he wants it. Depending on the age of the child, the parents may want to have the life book in a place where he cannot get it directly but knows where it is and needs the parents' assistance to retrieve it. Many children have been known to destroy different parts of their life book, and it is for this reason that the parents should be involved when the child wants to see it. If the child is destructive, it is a good idea to make color photocopies, particularly of the photographs that are not available elsewhere.

It seems that if the child wants to review the life book on a daily basis, this may be an issue that should be addressed thera-peutically. That amount of involvement seems a bit excessive to me, and unless it is for short periods of time, it would be neces-sary to understand the child's wishes more clearly. If, on the other hand, he wants to see the life book a great deal during cer-tain periods of time—such as holidays, his birthday, and so on—I do not think that is inappropriate. If he is clearly agitated and has negative behavioral responses to involvement with the life book, I would suggest that the family talk with a therapist about this process. An outside party may be able to develop a clear understanding as to what triggers the problems generated by the child's review of the life book.

I would suggest that the parents put the life book away only in rare situations. If a child is destructive, I think it is appropri-ate for the parent to maintain control of it. Things that are destroyed will be hard to replicate later on, when the child may, in fact, be interested in the material. If the life book continues to be a source of extreme discomfort, as I said before, I would sug-gest that the parents get some professional help.

In closing, I would like to encourage people to write life books in an honest manner that reflects the actual traumatic events in the child's life. In our practice, we have seen many well-developed, beautifully done life books with a content that leaves one confused as to why the child was ultimately removed from his birth family. The purpose of a life book is to provide the child with a realistic view of his life. This view will almost always include very painful and uncomfortable situations. If the worker's discomfort interferes with producing a completely honest docu-ment, the child's confusion about his removal will be com-pounded. This confusion will make the child's attachment and adaptation to the adoptive family more difficult. One needs to remember that the life book should reflect in a very accurate way all the details of the child's life. One should resist the temptation to gloss over or make things sound nicer than they, in fact, were.

■

Dear Dr. Keck:

We adopted a relative's child who was initially placed with us after being severely abused physically before the age of one year.

This child is now twelve years old and directs a considerable amount of anger toward me, but not my husband. He is also disrespectful and defiant toward other females, such as teachers and a swim coach, but does not act this way to men in the same roles. Why does he do this to women when it was his birth father who beat him? What would you suggest we do to handle this? Also, we are considering therapy. Should we look for a male or female therapist? Will there be any difference?

Mother in Need of Support

Dear Mother:

This question often comes up as frustrated families from around the world are confronted by the very same scenario you describe. The most simple and direct way to answer this is to say that all early attachment interruptions involved the child's loss of trust in the mother's capacity to both *love* and *protect*. Even though you describe a situation where the abuser was his birth father, on some level, perhaps even unconsciously, he holds the mother figure responsible because she did not keep him safe. Because you, his current mother, are in that role, you are unlucky enough to be the target of his wrath.

I recently saw a five-year-old boy who exhibits a huge amount of anger toward his adoptive mother. The family reported that he never talks about his birth mother. The very first part of our conversation went as follows:

> DR. KECK: "So you're a little guy with a lot of mad, huh?"
> CHILD: "Yeah."
> DR. KECK: "Where did you get all of this mad?"
> CHILD: "From Heather." (His birth mother)
> DR. KECK: "How did she give this mad to you?"
> CHILD: "She didn't take care of me. She left me alone.
> She locked me in the closet."

You can see that even a disturbed five-year-old was quite clear about what was going on. This was my very first contact with him, but he continued throughout the session to talk about how he gave all of this "mad" to his adoptive mom now.

It is also common for children to generalize this anger to all women. They see women as weak, unable to protect, incompetent, clueless. Conversely, they see men as strong and competent. That is how they often split the family and the couple.

Obviously, you have attempted to deal with this for many years; and because it has not been resolved, I think it makes sense for you to enter therapy. Your son will need to resolve this problem if he is to function in the world. After all, his first boss may well be a woman. I don't think you should worry about the therapist's gender, but rather his competence. Whomever you choose should be strong, directive, and have a clear understanding of adoption, loss, grief, attachment, and trauma. You should avoid any therapy that is child-centered and nondirective. You and your husband should be involved in the therapeutic process and not left out of any part of it. Your child needs to "get repaired" *within* the context of the family and *not* outside of it. As parents, you are a critical component of the treatment team.

■

Dear Dr. Keck:

We are the parents of a seven-year-old boy whom we adopted from an overseas orphanage. At the time of the adoption, we were made aware that he had a younger brother who was also in the orphanage. We were told that this child was not free for adoption at that time, but we would be notified when he was. We were also told that we were the first choice for his placement because we had adopted his sibling.

Three years have passed, and we have never been contacted by the organization regarding this child. We have not shared with our son the fact that he has a sibling, and it is our understanding that he was not aware of his brother because they were separated due to their age difference. We now question whether we should share this information with him. Someday we hope to take him back to his country of origin—and possibly visit the orphanage—but we want to make sure he will be emotionally able to handle that trip before we go.

It does not appear that his brother will ever become a part of our family, so we do not know if sharing this information would create more of a feeling of loss for our son. He has expressed that he would like a brother, and we are afraid that telling him would make him question why his sibling cannot live here with us.

Do you have any suggestions on how to handle this type of birth family information? Are we cheating our son out of this knowledge by not telling him, or are we protecting him?

Family-Focused Parent

Dear Parent:

Thanks for asking a question that is a frequent concern of adoptive parents. Let me start out by saying I strongly believe that *all* information that is known to the parents, social workers, or anyone in the adoptive child's life should be shared with the child. This information is about the *child* and therefore should be within his knowledge base.

So many adoptive children feel like they are missing parts of their own lives, and the truth is—they are. Parents and professionals can help "patch up" these holes by providing details about the child's life. For people who have grown up in the families into which they were born, such details often seem unimportant. That is because they *know* about their lives . . . they do not have gaps that no one can explain to them. Adoptees, on the other hand, have gaps—some of which will never be completely filled. So it becomes incumbent upon the parents to do what they can.

We also should share information early in the child's life. Some people want to wait until the child is "old enough to understand." That is too late. In fact, waiting to share information almost always backfires on the parents. The child then thinks, "I wonder what else they know about me that they do not think I am old enough to handle?" Waiting until later brings up issues of trust.

As parents, we are always talking to infants and children about things they do not understand or even know about. Just think of how people talk to babies. While the infant certainly does not understand, this talking helps development and prepares him for when he will eventually comprehend.

I would not make a big deal about sharing this information with your son. You do not need to have a "serious" talk. When *you* are comfortable and a convenient time comes up, you can introduce the information casually. But I would not wait much longer. In all probability, this is a much bigger issue for you than it is for your son.

An example of how to do this might be as follows: You are together when something comes up about siblings—anyone's brother or sister. You can say something like, "Do you remember that you had a little brother in the orphanage? Well, we were told that you did, and I am just wondering if you remember him." After this, you can follow your son's lead regarding whether or not to continue talking about it. Inevitably, it will come up again at a later point, and you will then have the opportunity to discuss it further.

One final point: many people are talking about doing homeland tours. I think it is best to follow the child's lead. This endeavor should be for the child and not to help parents feel like they are doing something they should be doing. Younger children often are not interested at all in such tours, but I think an older adolescent can benefit greatly—if he initiates the idea. I was on one of these tours, and I clearly remember that the kids were much more interested in eating at American fast-food joints than "experiencing" the foods of their birth culture. Remember, each child is an individual; one solution is not good for every child.

■

Dear Dr. Keck:

I am the adoptive parent of a thirteen-year-old boy. He is the birth son of a family relative whom we see very frequently. My son is not aware that this relative is his birth mother, though he does question who his birth parents are. I do not tell him about his history, because his birth mother does not want him to ever know her genetic relationship to him. She has made it very clear that I am not to share this information with my son.

I do plan on telling my son his genetic heritage when he reaches the age of twenty-one. I consistently tell him this when he asks questions about his birth mother. Part of me questions whether this is a good plan. I believe at age twenty-one he should be able to deal with the truth and any repercussions from his birth mother; she has threatened never to visit us or allow her other birth child to visit my son if their genetic linkage is told.

My other concern is how to handle the possibility of my son discovering the truth before he is twenty-one. There have been occasions where people comment on my son's resemblance to his birth mother and birth sibling. I worry for both of these children if their genetic connection is ever revealed. I am concerned that they will lose trust in adults. Do you have any suggestions on what to do if my son is told who his birth mother is?

Confused Parent

Dear Parent:

Your question is a rather complex one. However, it is one that, unfortunately, frequently comes up in kinship adoption situations. I want to offer some general responses that may help people. However, I believe the situation is much too complex to give you an answer and strategy for addressing this problem without having more knowledge of the case situation and without knowing you.

Truth in adoption has certainly become the goal of most adoption professionals. The very issue that you mention in terms of the child's losing trust in adults is ever-present when full disclosure has not occurred. We often think that individuals are more able to handle something at age eighteen, the current age of legal majority, or at age twenty-one. Neither of these ages has any particular magic connected to them, and one should be careful about assuming that highly charged information will be easier to handle at an older age than earlier on in one's life. While I know only what you have mentioned in the question, I certainly would suggest that your son will feel a certain amount of anger and betrayal given the fact that he has had an ongoing relationship with his birth mother but is not aware of who she really is. This sense of anger and betrayal will not necessarily be irresolvable but I suspect it will be rather complicated, and you will need much professional guidance in handling this situation.

From your question, it is clear that you have thought about all of the most critical issues, and I certainly concur with your many concerns about them. I encourage you to meet as soon as possible with a professional who is experienced in adoption-related issues for more specific guidance and direction in this very complex situation. I commend you for addressing this question at this point in time, because it suggests to me that when you feel it is comfortable to handle this with your son, you will do so having considered many of the important pieces that are sure to emerge.

■

Dear Dr. Keck:

I am concerned about my adopted son going away to school-sponsored overnight camp next year. He was sexually abused prior to his adoption and has since acted out sexually. We have put safeguards in place in our home environment. My concern is for him when, or if, he goes away to this overnight camp next year. He would be put in a position of sleeping with other boys in a cottage supervised by high school counselors.

What recommendations would you have for this type of situation? We are struggling with whether we should send him to the camp, because we do not want to place him in a situation he is not prepared to handle. In addition, we are concerned for the other children. We are also considering sending him for the day and having him return home at night.

Your input on this topic would be greatly appreciated.

Worried Parent

Dear Parent:

Because I don't know just how sexually reactive your child is, it is difficult to give you precise guidance. However, I think you have been wise to build in safeguards at home. These kinds of boundaries protect not only others but also may provide enough external regulation for your son to keep him "in line." Children and adolescents who have impulse control impairments, or who simply make very poor choices, often benefit from being externally guided. The hope would be that after enough external regulation, the individual will develop internal regulation. That is what happens, after all, in normal development. Parents control, guide, and direct until the child can do some of these things himself.

If this is the first time he will be unsupervised by family, I, too, would be uncomfortable with the overnight situation. I assume that the school program is attended primarily by children without severe difficulties. If so, they may not be prepared for the possibility of what could occur with a child who has sexual arousal and impulse problems. To prepare them with complete information may not be wise, nor will it necessarily prevent any kind of acting-out attempts.

Some things I would want to think about are:

- How sexual is he?
- Has he been sexual with age mates?
- Has he been sexual with younger children? Same sex? Opposite sex?
- Is he apt to be a victim of another such child or older supervising adolescent?
- How long ago did he attempt anything sexual?

Even after thinking about and reviewing these issues, I believe I would choose the safe side and opt for one of the following: plan an alternative family activity with him for the time he would be camping or, as you suggested, allow him to go for the daytime activities and get him immediately at bedtime and return him before breakfast. Of course, I imagine that you will need some sort of reason for others as to why this is your plan, but I'm sure you can come up with something creative!

While there is always a tendency or desire to "normalize" things for children with problems, it does not help them to put them in situations that may be exactly what they don't need. Even your son, depending on his age and level of adjustment, may feel that he might not make the best choices in certain situations. There will always be another opportunity to do a camp activity if this one doesn't work out.

Parents should trust their knowledge about their children, and I think it makes sense for them to allow their knowledge and their feelings to lead them to the best decision.

■

Dear Dr. Keck:

I am the parent of a seven-year-old adopted child who was placed with us at the age of four after living in an overseas orphanage. The behavioral and emotional problems he had at the time of placement have improved considerably. He continues to demonstrate a strong need for control, though, and his behavior and attitude in this area frustrate his father and me.

Our son wants to be in control at all times. He acts like a know-it-all, even with adults. He wants to control things that he does not even understand, such as which direction to go in the car. He will try to control what is on the car radio. Also, he will try to control what I do when he isn't even in the house. For example, he tells me that I shouldn't leave home while he is away, and then he acts annoyed if he realizes that I did, in fact, go somewhere while he was gone. His other forms of control are demonstrated by his deliberately not following rules or adult direction. Do you have any recommendations on how to handle this type of attitude?

Adoptive Parent

Dear Parent:

You describe one of the most common personality characteristics in children who have had early deprivation and/or trauma. In treating children with attachment difficulties, this behavior is one that we see very frequently.

During your son's first year of life, he was supposed to learn about trusting others to meet his needs. Dr. Foster Cline estimates that an infant learns 50 percent of what he will ever learn about trust in the year following his birth. That is quite a lot! Had your son experienced positive nurturing, appropriate external regulation by loving parents or caregivers, and sufficient physical and psychological stimulation, he would in all probability not have the control issues you describe.

So, what can correct this? You will probably have to take a few steps back in order to be able to go forward. In other words, you may need to do some things with him that seem too "childish," given his age. He needs to learn that you *can* and *will* control him directly. When he gets the message, he will begin to develop trust. When he develops trust, he will need to control less, because he knows that you are capable of both controlling him and keeping him safe.

Too many parents make the mistake of giving the child who is a "control freak" wide boundaries, thinking he will respond positively. Actually, this scares children who have had shaky beginnings. They think something like, *If my parents can't control me, they also can't protect me.* We too often forget that control equals love for the infant, child, and even some adolescents.

One adolescent with whom I was working said to me, "My dad won't control me at all. He acts like I really want to do everything I say I do, so he always says yes to things. I think that if I asked to kill myself, he would say yes." This is quite telling . . . and insightful. Only through safe, nurturing external regulation can children develop the internal regulation they will need later in their lives.

For strategies in dealing with control issues, you might read *Parenting with Love and Logic* by Foster Cline, M.D., and Jim Fay, as well as *Adopting the Hurt Child*, which Regina Kupecky and I wrote. If control is the major issue and there are not a lot of other problematic behaviors, I think you could get some benefit from short-term therapy, which should focus on repairing the early damage your son experienced.

■

Dear Dr. Keck:

Respite is something that this agency attempts to offer the adoptive families with whom we work. Often we find that families are uncomfortable about using respite. They seem to either feel guilty about taking a break from their adopted child or do not want to impose on family or other types of respite providers. Would you please give us your opinion on the concept of respite? For example, how should it be used? How often should it be used for a particular child or family, and is there additional information that this agency and adoptive parents should consider when arranging respite?

Post-Adoption Social Worker

Dear Social Worker:

These questions regarding respite certainly are timely. I have recently been talking with a number of families who find themselves in critical need of having a break from a very difficult-to-live-with child, and at the same time, feeling very uncomfortable about having the child spend time away from the family.

Respite actually needs to be seen as one avenue for a change in routine and for a break for both the child and the family. It should not be punitive, and it is perfectly acceptable if the child enjoys his respite stay and the family enjoys the time that the child is with the respite provider. Sometimes families who are extremely frustrated and angry about the many difficulties they experience on a day-to-day basis do not feel that the child should enjoy the respite experience. Respite does not need to be a negative experience for any of the parties involved, and it is perfectly acceptable if everyone enjoys the process.

Many families find that regular respite gives everyone the expectation that a break is scheduled. Sometimes this alone is enough to enable a family to manage difficult times preceding and following respite. Clearly, the ultimate goal of most families, I suspect, would be to eventually avoid having to use respite. However, determining when respite is needed must be made primarily by the family, in consultation with the social worker and/or therapist.

Sometimes families are frustrated by the respite program. The respite providers report that "he was just fine, and we didn't have any problems." This should be expected, because most children do not exhibit their most serious difficulties and/or behaviors while they are in the respite situation. There are some exceptions to this, but most children do quite well in respite.

One reason for a change in the child's behavior in respite is that the demands and expectations for intimacy are fairly minimal. The child knows he is there for a brief period of time, and the respite provider knows that she is fulfilling a functional role. Most respite providers certainly are not in competition with the parents; and because issues around intimacy and permanency are not present in respite situations, the child's insecurities, angers, and fears will probably not emerge.

Regarding the questions about how often respite should be used for a particular child or family, I feel there is no answer to this. Each situation must be evaluated independently, and the answer should develop out of a good understanding of the child and his relationship with the family. The family's needs should guide professionals in making a decision about the frequency of respite. Some families may benefit from monthly respite, while others might benefit biweekly. Still others may need respite only a few times per year. An attempt to give a more specific answer would diminish the critical nature of a case-by-case evaluation.

In closing, I think it is important for agencies to advocate for families and support their interest in, and need for, respite. Any attempts to suggest that they are not fulfilling their parental responsibility by utilizing respite is counterproductive to our overall commitment to empowering parents to raise their children in an effective manner.

■

Dear Dr. Keck:

My fifteen-year-old adopted daughter exhibits self-mutilation behaviors. She will do things like cutting and scratching her arm with a safety pin to the point of bruising. She has also cut herself with glass. These wounds have been described as "superficial" at times by mental health professionals, but as a parent, I am very concerned. I would like to know why someone would do this to herself. I cannot understand what she gets out of this, other than the obvious attention, which would not be worth the pain to me. My daughter has also had a recent suicide attempt, where she overdosed on medication. Is this related to the self-mutilation behavior?

Can you help us to understand these behaviors, and tell us what we should do to help our daughter?

Troubled Parent

Dear Parent:

The subject of self-mutilation and injury often comes up when people are involved with troubled children and adolescents. This particular kind of difficulty is of much concern to parents and professionals.

Unfortunately, the pattern of self-abuse is often an ongoing one that frustrates those around the child. Most people who cut, burn, scratch, or otherwise injure themselves report that they do not experience pain while they are doing the act. Some say that they feel the hurt afterward.

There is probably not just one reason that certain people engage in self-destructive activities. Adolescence is a tricky period of time, and one needs to diagnose very carefully. It would be easy to assume that your daughter has borderline personality features, but many borderline features are seen in normal adolescent development. If her pattern has been continuous and has repeated itself, then I believe there is reason for serious concern.

It is the unusual individual who would cut herself simply to get attention. It is more likely that the attention is the secondary gain, while self-stimulation and arousal is the primary object of her action. Some people who do this kind of behavior have had early sensory deprivation; in other words, their brains may not process their sensory experiences properly. Some adolescents with whom I have worked have said, "When I cut myself, I feel like the living and not like the dead."

The suicide attempt may be an extension of the hurtful behavior you describe. Suicide attempts always need to be assessed quickly for lethality, and you should seek to interrupt the pattern of increasing self-mutilation and/or repeated suicide attempts or gestures.

I believe that the kind of problem you see with your daughter can be effectively treated. One seventeen-year-old with whom we have worked had an extensive pattern of self-abuse—severe cutting and burning. Since treatment began, he has not repeated any of these kinds of behavior. This is not to suggest that treatment is always so effective, but rather to say that you should know there are optimistic outcomes for a problem that is often seen as being resistant to therapeutic intervention.

■

Dear Dr. Keck:

I am the adoptive parent of a ten-year-old boy who was placed with me when he was six. He has an extensive history of emotional disturbances and mental health problems. He is currently in outpatient counseling—something he has been involved in since he was first placed with me.

My son has many problems, but lately his stealing has escalated. It is this behavior that concerns me the most at this time. My son steals anything. For example, he takes things from people at home, at school, and at relatives' homes. He steals money, food, and personal belongings. He can verbalize right from wrong regarding stealing, but he continues to steal. When asked why he steals, he answers, "I don't know."

What are your recommendations on how to handle this behavior?

Apprehensive Parent

Dear Parent:

In reading your question, a number of issues come to mind. I believe that it would be important to know about the experiences of your son's early infancy and childhood. One would also need to understand the history of emotional disturbances and mental health problems. Other questions to be asked are: Is the current course of therapy productive? If so, in what way? What issues have been helped? What issues, other than stealing, remain unaddressed?

I am not certain that I have enough information from your letter to give you any sort of in-depth answer that would be helpful to you. It sounds as if your son's problems are well entrenched, and I would imagine that the only way to interrupt his manner of thinking and behaving is through a focused-treatment approach. Generally, the kinds of problems you present are associated with one of the following diagnoses: Reactive Attachment Disorder, Conduct Disorder, or Oppositional Defiant Disorder. Because I do not have enough information to suggest any sort of diagnostic impression, I believe that a thorough assessment would be helpful. A diagnosis should lead you to a plan for intervention.

The kind of stealing you describe is very common among children who have been diagnosed with Reactive Attachment Disorder. They tend to steal from family, friends, and relatives much more frequently than they do from strangers, stores, or other places of business. Their stealing is frequently done in a rather overt and obvious way, and often they do not make any successful attempts to hide what they steal. In fact, they often appear to be almost proud of what they have stolen and behave in a way that ensures getting caught by their parents.

At this point, I would suggest that you have an assessment specifically to look at attachment issues because there certainly are strong indications of this disorder in what you write. After that, I believe that someone would be more able to help you develop effective strategies for managing your child's behavior.

■

Dear Dr. Keck:

I would like to know if you have any suggestions on how to best prepare an older child for adoption. This particular child has lived with the same foster family for three years. For a variety of reasons, he cannot be adopted by that family, but there is an adoption plan for him with a family in another city. I am very concerned about how to best prepare this young man for the move from the foster home to the adoptive home.

He is dealing with so many issues, including coping with the loss of his birth family, the foster family, and his therapist. There is also an older birth brother who will not be making this move with him at this time for a variety of complicated reasons. There is hope that he can eventually be placed with his brother. Another issue I have to work with is how to have the foster parents best assist with this transition. At this point they are feeling their own sense of loss and are trying to cope with that. Any suggestions you may have would be very appreciated.

Caring Adoption Worker

Dear Adoption Worker:

We always need to remember that most decisions about child welfare involve pain and hurt—even those that are intended to be of assistance. Therefore, there is probably no way to alleviate the pain and loss associated with this move. It will be yet another complication in the child's life, but one that may ultimately be mitigated by a successful adoptive placement.

We often take too long to act on the decisions that we make, and we do so in an effort to minimize the painful processes we face. However, I think that once a decision is made and it is acceptable to all of the parties involved, we should act right away. Sometimes people want a child to complete the school year. But transferring into a new school near the end of the year may afford the child the opportunity to see where he will be going in the fall. That may eliminate a summer filled with anxiety and uncertainty about the future. It may also give the child an opportunity to make some friends before the summer break.

There is rarely one *right* way to do anything in adoption practice. Honesty and fast movement toward permanency—coupled with involvement of the child, foster parents, and adoptive parents—should facilitate the transition.

The foster parents will need to decide how they want to be involved. Is this comfortable for the child and the adoptive parents? The adoptive parents should be given a maximum amount of input regarding all of the decisions made, because that is how they will truly begin to be the child's parents.

As I said in the beginning, there is not an easy way to deal with hard situations. But reasonable, common-sense approaches seem to be more helpful than the most carefully planned clinically/professionally correct decisions. We often delay acting in our efforts to help and end up extending the child's uncertainty as a result.

■

Dear Dr. Keck:

How would you suggest that fathers become more involved in the direct parenting of their adoptive children? I am used to a more "traditional" family model, where the wife/mother takes the more active role in parenting while the husband/father is more focused on job and house maintenance. With our special-needs child, my wife appears to require more assistance. What suggestions do you have for fathers to become more active in parenting while still managing the other duties in life? Thank you for your assistance.

Willing Father

Dear Father:

It's good that you have realized that you cannot expect your wife to do most of the child rearing, because parenting requires high levels of involvement by both parents. A frequent complaint from the adolescents I see in therapy is that they want to spend more time with their fathers. Most of these teenagers are very high-functioning, yet they continue to want and *need* parental involvement.

The child with special needs will require even more parental involvement. Children who have experienced early difficulties in their lives most often blame their mothers for whatever happened to them. Therefore, they often target their new mothers with great anger and venom. Simultaneously, they often *seem* to have higher regard for their new fathers. This process, alone, begins to split the couple. The mother becomes the target of anger and the father becomes the good guy . . . playmate . . . mediator. All of these roles assigned to the father by the child serve to undermine the mother's parental role and authority.

Fathers can be immensely important in the child's journey to healthy attachment and adjustment. First of all, it is incumbent upon the father to *support* and *believe* his wife. He needs to fulfill the husband role, and the child must come to see the parents as a *single unit* that is not subject to division. Even though a father may not see and experience the child's most intense feelings and behaviors, he must believe his wife's subjective experiences. Without spousal support, the wife will have more difficulty mothering the child.

The child must come to know the father, as well. For many children in adoptive families, having a father is a new experience. Many of them have had numerous men in their lives if their mothers had multiple boyfriends, but very few have had a real *father*. That is another reason they don't target fathers so much—they don't know quite what to do with them because they never had one.

The father's role is very important for both boys and girls. He can be a powerful role model for them as they attempt to figure out life and its many complications. I believe that the parental role for the father is much more critical than the many external, concrete duties often associated with fathers—job, breadwinner, house maintenance, and so on. As the child grows older, he will remember much more about time spent with his dad than he will about the quality of his dad's "handyman" status.

Time, lots of it, can be rather easily managed in many cases. If you are running errands, take the kids along. If you are fixing something around the house, have the kids help. Most kids can do something, even if it would be easier to get through the job without them. I think that we often think *quality* time can substitute for *quantity* time, but I don't believe this is accurate.

■

Dear Dr. Keck:

My question has to do with our ten-year-old foster child, who has come to us as a result of a disrupted adoption. The child can be very frustrating to deal with at times, because when confronted about something she has done, she does not wear down. I will know she is lying about something because it is quite obvious she is the only person who could have done it, and she will continue to proclaim her innocence. I am just trying to get her to tell the truth about the action, but she is very stubborn. Actually, I don't know if you would call it stubbornness or defiance. Anyway, she will continue to deny having done something or accepting any responsibility for the wrong deed. Basically, she simply lies about what she did. I will give her consequences for the lying, such as extra chores or exercise, but these do not seem to have any effect. Do you have any suggestions on how to handle this behavior?

Frustrated Parent

Dear Parent:

Lying is one of the most bothersome things that can go on in a family. It undermines trust at all levels, and without trust, most people feel extremely frustrated.

The kind of lying that children with attachment difficulties do is called primary process lying, and it clearly points to developmental delay. It is a specific form of lying that is first seen in early childhood when children begin to tell "stories." A normally developing ten-year-old would have conceived a different type of lie. She would engage in lies in a self-protective manner to *avoid* trouble, not to *cause* it.

After telling a child not to lie over and over, parents need to adopt new strategies. People who lie want others to believe them. Sometimes saying something as simple as the following will interrupt the child's lying pattern: "You know, Sarah, I know you're a kid who likes to lie most of the time, and in a way, I'm kind of glad I figured this out. Now that I know this, I won't have to waste any time at all wondering if what you are saying is true. That will give us more time together having fun. I'll just know for sure that most of what you tell me is not true — that way, I won't have to bother you or myself with trying to figure things out or being a policeman. If I find out that you have told the truth sometime, I'll be really surprised." This kind of response takes the child's energy out of lying. You, the parent, are no longer running around trying to *prove* the child wrong. When parents do that, the child gets the idea that just maybe the parent believes her — even a little bit. After all, if you are so sure that what you are being told is untrue, why would you investigate?

Some children lie automatically. By this I mean that they begin to construct the answer even before the question has been completed. Therefore, they are bound to come up with the wrong answer or a lie. For a child like this, it is helpful to attempt to make statements instead of asking questions. If you know that each time she answers something she's lying, reduce the number of times she has the option to do that. Frequently, in therapy, when I know a child is about to lie, I'll say, "Please tell me a lie, *not* the truth." This confounds him so much that he seems almost driven to tell me the truth!

The bottom line is this:

1) Eliminate, or minimize, the angry response because it seems to liven things up for the child.
2) Assume that a child who always lies is lying, and let her know that.
3) When she tells the truth, fake a heart attack, grabbing your chest with a surprised look and saying, "Oh, no! Please don't tell me the truth, it's too much for me to handle!"—or some other very surprised action. This works much better than a tutorial, boring comment such as, "Well, finally you say something true. Aren't you proud of yourself?" That will drive her back into finding a lie as fast as she can go.

■

Dear Dr. Keck:

My husband and I have adopted a biracial child whose birth mother committed suicide. We are wondering how to address these sensitive issues with him. We believe we should be honest with him about his mother and birth history, but we want to be sure he is at age readiness for this information. Can you give us any suggestions?

Unsettled Parent

Dear Parent:

It is certainly good to see that you are interested in discussing birth-family issues with your child. It is rather difficult to give specific ages at which things need to be addressed. It is probably best to use your child's questions about his life as a guide for what you need to address. Most children, whether birth or adopted, generally begin to ask questions about how it is that they were born or came into the family. You can use this opportunity to begin discussing adoption and other issues that may arise afterward. Racial issues will also begin to emerge, and when they do, you will be able to discuss them. Many parents are overanxious to address everything all at once and to talk about adoption long before the child is able to have any conceptual understanding of where babies come from.

As with many other issues, suicide is a conceptual issue about which children have very little understanding. I believe it needs to be shared, but it should be done in the context of some related issue. It is also one that your child, at this point in time, would be unable to comprehend. Again I would encourage you to let the child's interest and questions guide you in how and when you explore the issues you mentioned. While secrecy causes the development of many other difficulties, flooding the child with details that he does not and cannot understand is of no value. Feel free to take your time, because you will have many opportunities to discuss relevant concerns with your child.

■

Dear Dr. Keck:

My husband and I are preparing to finalize the adoption of a six-year-old boy who has been in our home more than six months. My question is, How should we handle his attention-getting behaviors? One behavior he displays is laughing at inappropriate times. I feel this laughter stems from defiance, because it happens when he is given an order. His other attention-getting behaviors include making weird noises, silly babbling talk, and rolling around on the ground. He has been diagnosed as ADHD, but I believe he has control over these behaviors. We are currently attempting to ignore them to decrease their frequency. Do you have any suggestions for how to best handle them?

Embarrassed Parent

Dear Parent:

One of the first things I would want to know is what leads you to believe your son's behaviors are attempts at getting attention. Certainly, if they are, a more critical question is whether or not they are intentional. Intentional behaviors require a very different response from behaviors that result from a lack of attention—that is, those that occur out of the child's ADHD. Behaviors that occur as a result of ADHD are most often not intentional in a child who is six years of age, and given the appropriate psychotherapy and perhaps medication, a child with ADHD can be effectively treated.

If the child's negative behaviors are intentionally directed at inviting your involvement with him, the picture begins to change a bit. I would recommend reading the book *Parenting with Love and Logic,* which will provide you with very effective ways to manage a wide range of childhood difficulties. I believe you will find these strategies helpful to your child and to you, as well.

Regarding the issue of irritating noises, I would suggest that you have a mental health professional rule out the possibility of Tourette's syndrome. Once it is ruled out, I believe that you can then begin to develop a strategy for allowing natural and/or logical consequences to provide your child with a life-learning experience. In most cases, ignoring a behavior will result in two things. First, the behavior will increase in frequency and intensity. Second, after a period of time, if ignoring the behavior is helpful, the behavior will begin to diminish and finally cease. However, I do not believe this strategy should take an extended period of time, because behaviors that are intentionally directed will most often not respond to simply ignoring them. If you have tried for an extended period of time without success, it is time to make some changes. Again, I probably would suggest you read the book I mentioned, and I am sure you will find some relief in a much more relaxed, fun style of parenting.

CHAPTER 11

PARENTS AND CHILDREN TALK BACK:
Stories from Those Who've Been There

Parents and their hurt children have an abundance of wisdom and insight. We thank them for sharing part of their lives with our readers so that others may heal. And we thank them for caring for and about their children. We thank the adoptees for sharing their hurts and their stories of their healing.

The families who have opened their hearts to us comprise couples and single parents . . . children adopted from foster care or through international channels . . . toddlers, children, or teenagers. Their stories differ in many ways, but these families all are on the same journey to healing and love. May these glimpses into their lives help your hurt children join your family in a healthy way.

A SINGLE MOTHER'S STORY

It is human nature to want to blame someone or something for mistakes and/or failures. Often we blame ourselves. More often we try to shift the blame to others. When we adopt a hurt child, we want to blame someone for his behavior, or lack of feeling,

or any of the many shortcomings that are commonly attributed to these "tainted children."

I recently acquired my second child who has Reactive Attachment Disorder. I now have three adopted children, and every day is a new experience and a new set of adjustments. I learn something new about all three of them—and about me— every day.

The most important thing I have learned since adopting my children is that, although I must hold the children responsible for their actions, I must *not* hold them responsible for what they have become. Despite their shortcomings, I have to constantly concentrate on breaking down the walls that keep them from receiving my love—the walls that can prevent me from loving them. These walls cannot be destroyed unless I am willing to fully realize that children do not become troubled by choice. I must constantly be watchful of what their words and actions really imply.

It is easy to become cynical—to come up with one-liners in order to maintain control. But there is danger in this practice. The cynicism can take over or cloud our feelings. It can lead us to treat our children as if they are the enemy. Taking control of the situation is one thing. Letting the situation get in the way of loving the children is another.

More often than not, I have been quick to judge every out-of-the-ordinary action, outburst, or expression of anger. "She is just being a brat." "They must have spoiled her." "He just never learns anything." But now that I have my newest "acquisition" (I hope she will be my daughter one day), I have taken a fresh approach to dealing with these children. The reasons for this new approach are to maintain a modicum of sanity, keep an open mind and, most of all, to keep an open heart.

Now, for example, when someone throws a tantrum, I handle the situation on several levels. Of course, I deal with the behavior. But before that, I ponder whether my child is really throwing a tantrum as a result of an immediate situation or reprimand, or because some past memory has been triggered. Then I allow the tantrum. I don't interrupt it. But, while the tantrum is in progress, I hold the child in a secure way. I don't show my anger. The outburst seems to be coming from a much younger child. She is not really aware of what is going on. She is screaming and crying real tears, but she is not really there with me. But I hold her securely all the same.

I encourage her to release all the anger she has at the time. When she "returns" to me, I hold her in my arms. I speak to her gently and work through the situation. I let her know that I love her and that she is mine forever. I have found that this approach has caused her to more readily trust me and to bond with me. It has made it easier for me to love her. I hate tantrums as much as the next mother, but I love the baby I am holding after the tantrum subsides.

I have made it a practice to pause before I judge my children's actions or displays of emotion. When in doubt (which is most of the time), I hold them. I make them feel safe. I show them I am there for them. I let them really know I love them — I make them feel I love them.

They are children! They are children! They are children! Find it in your heart to treat them as if they are the fragile and impressionable babies they really are — not the enemy. It makes it easier for you to love them. It makes it easier for them to receive your love, and to love you in return.

Mary Kaye
A single parent of three children adopted internationally

A STORY OF APPRECIATION: THE PUZZLE

Imagine being handed a jigsaw puzzle and being told to put it together. When you look at the pieces, there are no colors. Everything is gray, and some of the pieces are kind of rough around the edges. There is no picture and no directions. You and your family are all on your own. You work and study this jigsaw puzzle. Try this piece and that one. Over time you are finally able to put a couple of pieces together, but for every couple of pieces that you are able to fit together, you have tried and discarded many more.

Some days you can't even stand to look at the pieces or walk by the puzzle. Some days you work and work to find just one piece to fit here or there. You study everything and nothing helps, and out of frustration you take your hand and sweep everything off the table onto the floor.

This job is made even more difficult by other people coming in and telling you, "Those pieces don't fit. You are doing this all wrong." And still other people asking you, "Why—why are you wasting your time? It probably won't be a very pretty picture even after you get it put together."

Then one day a very special person comes into your life with the gift of hope. This very special person, your Reactive Attachment therapist, is able to add color to your pieces. He brings you framework, patterns, and best of all, a guiding hand. After many sessions and years of hard work, your puzzle is almost completed. Yes, there are still a few pieces missing, and some pieces of the puzzle are ragged and tear-stained. But even with these flaws, it's the prettiest picture ever—for it is the picture of your family—a family that has color and framework— a family that has struggled and worked, laughed and cried together.

Joyce
An adoptive mom who, with her husband, adopted their son at age six following his placement at age two.

AN INTERNATIONAL ADOPTION

I knew while I was in China that my daughter had not had a great start and had experienced neglect. No matter how loving or clean or well cared for she seemed, she spent the first part of her life in an orphanage, and that could not have been a wonderful experience for her. Just the fact that she did not have one-on-one care was enough to have an impact on her. Wouldn't that have an impact on anyone?

I was certain when I brought her home that I had somehow, benignly, added to her stress. I became another change in her environment and, although I hoped I was the best and the last change she would experience as a baby, she didn't know that and responded accordingly. Sure, she loved the steady supply of food and the toys and books and her beautiful nursery. But still she seemed uncomfortable in my arms, she did not like to look too long at me, and she did not always just "take" to all the changes the way I thought she might.

Sometimes she "took" a little too easily. It was hard at first to figure out why my daughter seemed so confused and upset. Or why at other times she seemed just the opposite—so clearly happy and content and cheerful and friendly and loving. Was she just "being a baby" as so many assured me? Or was something wrong like my heart told me?

What was I thinking? Was I expecting her to call me "Mommy" in China or on the plane ride home? Was I expecting her to prefer a quiet house and her own room when all she had really known was a noisy, children-filled orphanage? Was I expecting her to respond to me with a special bond and pure love and rapt attention when it was in her best interest and necessary for her survival to respond to whoever fed her in China?

I had spent a great deal of time considering how my life would change as a parent, but what I failed to consider adequately was how changed my daughter's life would be. In addition, I am a little embarrassed to say that I spent more time online with my adoption support groups—discussing the merits of a certain stroller or baby carrier—than I did preparing myself for the eventualities of adopting a child who had experienced trauma and change.

And change, even good change, is stressful for some people. That includes babies. I sometimes get irked when my little routine is upset, or when something I expect to happen doesn't. And I can negotiate that irritation in my mind and overcome it, or deal with it, or be irritated by it. My daughter could feel the irritation but could not articulate it. What frustration she must have felt in those early days! What joy to finally be with a loving mother! What a roller coaster of emotions!

Most adoptions are stories of crises. Children are surrendered by birth parents for critical reasons, not sport or whim, and it is amazing that adoptive families so often do not get that. They tuck it away and whitewash the story (or make it worse than it is) and do not acknowledge the hard and painful fact of adoption— that it is because of some other family's crisis that they are parents at all. It is certainly hard to think about—a tiny baby in a state of crisis—but we must at least acknowledge it if we are to address the needs of the children we have chosen to adopt. We have to see the whole story, so that when our children feel the confusing and uncomfortable parts of their pasts, we are prepared as parents ought to be—to be the adults in the situation.

In an effort to provide for our children's every material need and creature comfort, we have failed to recognize that they are emotionally numb with pain, grief, anger, rage, and confusion.

Just because they lack the language to express it to us, these babies are a far, far cry from the blank slates we think they are. We must then redouble our efforts to not only recognize but to seek out signs that they are uncomfortable in their own souls.

After all, they have lost *both* birth parents, at least one if not several caretakers, their homeland, their friends, and everything that was familiar to them. Has that ever happened to you? How can we suggest that it is not remembered through a body memory or a primal memory?

It is disconcerting to go to an adoption agency event or a Chinese reunion and be the only parents to admit that your child has attachment issues and to have everyone look at you with pity. The disconcerting part is that, in the group, most of the children have the same symptoms your child has, and you know very well that they are in the same boat as your child. But the parent doesn't see it. That's the worrisome part. It is also frustrating to hear about the children from China who miraculously do not have the same problems as the "other" internationally adopted children or domestically adopted children.

Instead of investigating the worries I had about my daughter's physical and emotional well-being, the professionals from whom I sought help—pediatricians, social workers, other (supposedly more experienced) parents—joined a "confederacy of denial," repeatedly assuring me that it was just a "getting adjusted" stage. It wasn't. A mother's intuition—and, yes, adoptive mothers have it, too—is usually on the mark.

Your baby needs quantity time in a secure, stable, warm, and loving environment with you, the parent, at the epicenter. Your child does not need a schedule filled with activities, play groups, lessons of every kind, and other external stimuli, including other children and adults. Nor does she need loud noises, conspicuous consumption, and more toys than she knows what to do with.

You, as the parent, need to see that your baby is responding "normally" to an "abnormal" situation and learn how you can make it work. What I did not expect is that it would hurt my own feelings to be rejected by a baby who could not yet identify me as her mother. But I had to understand that it was nothing personal and that there were techniques and professionals who could help us. What I also had not counted on was how hard it would be to access that very help. Without a more open acknowledgment of the challenges we may encounter as adoptive parents, the professionals and agencies who can provide saving help are difficult to identify.

Sarah
A mother who adopted a nine-month-old girl from China

ON DISCIPLINE

My husband and I feel as if we were very well prepared by our social worker for the behaviors our children may exhibit. Catching on to the "Love and Logic" principle of parenting is a whole different story! It takes a lot more time, thought, and imagination than traditional forms of discipline and punishment, such as grounding. Although it is more time-consuming, it works! We have learned that it is important to have fun and to stick together as a united front. No matter what!

Kellie
*An adoptive mother of two children adopted domestically,
one from an adoption disruption*

THE POEMS OF A WAITING CHILD

The Girl Inside the Box

The girl inside of the invisible box
She Bangs.
She Screams.
She Knocks.
No one pays Attention
To the Voice inside of Me.

She Waits

She Waits At The Door For Her Father
She Waits For Her Mother
She Stops Waiting.
She Knows That They Will Not Come.
But, She Still Loves Them.

The Dungeon

Once there was a girl,
Who felt that she lived her whole life in a dungeon.
She had no way out.
Why people treated her the way they did
She does not know.
She did a lot for her siblings,
Yes, she might have made some mistakes
in her life.
But not to get treated like she did.
She feels like people care about what she did wrong
Not what she did right.
The reason she feels like she lives in a dungeon
is because she has no freedom.
No one believes her when she says anything
They assume it is wrong.
At times she would sit in her room
And cry and pray
That someday she would get away from all of that.

Pity

Days of sunshine have gone away
Pity for you—pity for me.
Now my future days are gray
As I sit below this saddened tree.
The grass has died.
The flowers have crumbled.
For I feared that you had lied.
Words of sadness I have mumbled.
Although I know the sky won't fall,
Not being heard—not being seen,
I feel as if I am one inch tall.
People can be so cruel, so mean.
So my hurt spills into this paper.

Stacey
*A domestic adoptee who entered foster care at the
age of nine and was adopted at fourteen. These poems were
written when she was eleven and waiting for a family.*

AN ADOPTIVE MOTHER'S ADVICE

- Swallow pride. Ask for help. Ask for help. Ask for help. Keep asking till you know that you've found the kind of help that you need.
- Read! Read! Read! For example, *Adopting The Hurt Child*, *Parenting with Love and Logic*, and other "Love and Logic" materials, such as audio books.
- Pray! Build a support system. A pastor, share groups, Bible study groups, and parenting groups are some ideas.
- Accept that a healthy mind and body are far more important, in the long haul, than academics. Your home should be a security blanket for every member of the family, not a battleground for topics like school work.
- Sit down to supper in your home at least four or five days a week. If that doesn't seem possible, reevaluate your family schedule. Sitting down, as a family, meets an important emotional need.

Mrs. H.
An adoptive mother of a domestically
adopted child just shy of eight years old

WORDS FROM A TEENAGER

I was nine when I was adopted. I really didn't know what a family was or what it meant to really be part of a family. So when my foster mom at the time told me I was going to be adopted, I didn't really know what it meant. I thought that it was going to be just another one of the many foster homes that I had been in. I didn't think it would be permanent.

When I first met my to-be parents, we went out to eat and I called them "Mom" and "Dad." To me, a mother and father were just people who were there and who you stayed with. I didn't know that a mother and father were people who loved you and helped you, not someone who left you with strange men and did mean and hurtful things to you.

At the time, I didn't know what the word "love" meant either. Now I know what love is, and I know what real parents are. I love my adoptive family *very* much, and they are the most important people to me.

I started going to Dr. Keck's counseling center when I was a freshman. Before I went to Dr. Keck, I still thought highly of my birth mom, if that's what you could really call her. I didn't know my birth father. I thought my birth mother was going to come back and get me, and everything would go back to the way it was before I went to foster care.

When I started seeing Regina at Dr. Keck's office, I began to realize how wrong my birth mother was and how much she had really messed up my life. I also began to realize how much I had put my adoptive parents through and how much they loved me no matter what I did.

I don't hate my birth mother. I just hate the things she did to me and the things she didn't do. Now I have a *wonderful* mother to look up to and love, to be there for the things that my birth mother was never there for when I was growing up, and who loves me just as much as I love her.

My parents have done so many things for me that I don't know where to start. I ran away several times before I started going to Dr. Keck, and my parents still loved me. There is one situation that I remember very clearly. One night when I was about ten, my family went to Bible study and I hurt my ankle while I was there. Well, I told my mom it was broken and I needed to go to the doctor. She had been a nurse and looked at it, told me it wasn't broken, and we went home. I cried the whole time, and said how bad it hurt and kept telling her it was broken. When we got home, she gave me an ice pack and had me elevate it.

The next morning, I got up and I was limping on it. We were supposed to meet my grandma at the store, and my mom said she wasn't going to take me if I was limping. I argued and cried and argued some more. When my mom and my brother and sister were on the way out, I yelled at her and told her that I hated her. As soon as they left, I took a bag, packed some clothes, and got my bike and rode away. Needless to say, I stopped at a friend's house who knew my dad, and he took me back to the house. When my mom came home, boy, was she mad! Not only because I had yelled at her and told her that I hated her, but also because I ran away. We joke about it now, but that is just one of the many instances when my parents have shown their endless love.

To parents who may adopt or have adopted, I think the most important thing is not to give up on the child, and no matter what, don't stop loving them. What they need most, whether they realize it or not, is love. That is the best thing you can do for that child. If they push you away, show them more love. The worst thing that you can do for a kid is give up. Most kids have had people give up on them, so they are used to that. But if you show them that you aren't going to give up on them, that will be another of the many ways of showing how much you love them. I know this from personal experience.

Amanda
A domestic adoptee who was adopted at age nine
and wrote this at age seventeen

AMANDA'S PARENTS' PERSPECTIVE

I think we are doing well, with periods of anxiety mixed in. Amanda seems to be truly attached, but struggles with terrible judgments, poor social skills, and impulsiveness. So we still have ups and downs, but without the anger level she used to have. We feel blessed with the outcome. We have made some moves that made the difference.

I think the most important thing we did to turn Amanda toward us rather than away from us was to follow the instructions of the therapist! We had to deal with, and let go of, the hurts and anger with her behavior, which made us available to be attached to. We tackled the tough subjects with her, talked about her feelings, her past, and our love for her. We held her every single day those first six months. We still hold her two to three days a week, at seventeen years old. It is an excellent way to connect with her and for her to connect with us. Yes, she is still frustrating, irritating, and tests our limits, but she is able to come around and accept our direction and advice without that underlying anger that was always present before.

To other parents, I would suggest total compliance with the therapist. Do everything that you can to follow through with their advice. That may mean therapy for the parents, but if you truly want to connect to your child, you have to be available to be reached by them when they are ready. Keep their "illness" in perspective and keep looking at the big picture. Try not to get bogged down by the day-to-day hassles. It is very hard, but you have to let the little stuff go in order to get to the big stuff.

I think what convinced me that Amanda was truly "fixed" was the ease with which we could get her to come around when she would begin a downward spiral. Before therapy, nothing that we did had any effect. We have become masters at redirecting her, and all it takes is taking the time to connect, and then speaking to her about how much we care and why her choices are pushing us away. It always works.

I have learned how strong our marriage is and how important it is to present a solid stand to these kids. I learned I don't deal with stress well, and I am trying to correct that. But I have been left with daily headaches, and I feel that a "post-traumatic stress" reaction sometimes still occurs when Amanda does something unexpected. I think it is important to take care of yourself during these times. It can leave lasting impressions on your health and relationships. I also know having a support group of family, friends, and church has been very important.

I still worry about Amanda's future. But at least now I know she will have one! We tease her that when she is thirty-five years old and "gets weird," we will have to go to her house to hold her and straighten her out and teach her future husband to hold her, too! There is probably some reality to that! She wants to be normal and even asks if certain behaviors are "normal." Sometimes she will tell us, "I feel weird today." So we are proud of her for coming as far as she has and pray she continues in the same direction!

Peg and Dean
Amanda's parents

AN INTERNATIONAL STORY
FROM AN ADOPTIVE DAD

When adopting internationally, and the kids speak another language, don't expect the "International Language of Hugs and Kisses" to get you through the first six months! People will tell you that all the kids need is love. Don't fall into that trap. You are delusional if you lead yourself to believe that. The kids will need a lot more, probably more than you will expect. Get ready for the onslaught. It will take time, but with the right help, you can get through it—or at least on the right track.

If you think you are going crazy, it is because you are! Acknowledge your feelings and fears. Most important, be sure to know your wife is telling you the truth. The kids treat her differently, *a lot differently!* The worst thing you can do for your family and your marriage is not to support your wife (or vice versa). It is a prescription for disaster.

Be prepared for antisocial behavior. Your kids have probably experienced things that kids (and adults, for that matter) should never have experienced. Try to remain resilient and keep your sense of humor. It is not an easy thing to do. Remember that your kids were not raised with the same experiences, values, and so on, that you and your spouse were. You cannot parent the way that you were parented. It simply won't work.

We adopted older Caucasian kids who, when dressed up, look like they've lived with us in suburban USA all their lives. Don't be fooled. Our kids are not from here, and although they "look the part," they have a long way to go to fit in. Our kids were seven, five, and three when they came from Russia. They had never heard of a home run, a strike, John Wayne, GI Joe®, the Yankees, Apollo 11, or the Cleveland Browns. Their cultural contexts are limited. So often, they don't know what to do when interacting with other kids their age. They simply were not raised here, and while they fit in somewhat, they have rough edges. We have often said that it would have been easier to adopt from Asia, so at least people would know the children were from another part of the world.

The most important thing we have done to foster family attachment is to develop family traditions. We were childless, so we needed to build a family. We celebrate the adoption anniversary with "Gotcha Day" every October 1. We have cake, ice cream, and party hats, and the kids look forward to it. We have formalized Friday night video night as "Family Night." We eat dinner as a family, at the dinner table, and we work to reduce interruptions.

We limit sports for the kids to one sport per child per season. Overextending and over-scheduling are a bad mistake. These kids can only take so much stimulation. The same goes for family vacations and family events. Be careful of the stress, stay relaxed, and travel at the children's pace.

We stress proper English language. Watch the slang and accents, so the children can learn English correctly from the start. It is an awesome responsibility. The children don't know bad English from good English. You have to teach them.

Take a long-term perspective with your kids. Their hurt can destroy you and your marriage if you let it. Keep your expectations in line and don't expect them to go to college unless they are up to it. Maybe completing high school is a good and realistic goal. This was a big adjustment.

It took a long time for the oldest, who was seven when adopted, to accept that he is here for good. He may never fully accept the fact, due to his delusion that he was wrongly taken from his birth mother by the Russian authorities.

Bob and Margaret
Adoptive parents of three Russian children

THE VOICE OF A CHILD

Dear Dad,
    I love you because you are my dad.
Love, Marina

Marina
Bob and Margaret's daughter, age six

MOTHERING A CHILD OF SEVERE TRAUMA

Not too long ago, I was asked whether, knowing what I know now, I would still adopt our son. I didn't even have to think about the answer. I remember looking at my inquisitor strangely and saying, "Of course! Why would you even ask that?"

I guess in reality, though, anyone who has known us during the last six years might ask that same question. We've battled with counties, hospitals, teachers, school administrators, schools, schools, and more schools. We've had to restrain our son and watch as others restrained him. We've spent nights listening to him scream out in his sleep and toss and turn so violently in bed that we were sure the metal frame would break. We've spent countless hours in school meetings, therapy sessions, and court. Would I change any of that? Of course. But the thought of not having our son would be like asking someone if they'd mind cutting off their right arm.

Parenting a hurt child is the single most important thing we will ever do. We have been able to take a very frightened and extremely angry eleven-year-old and watch him develop into a very bright, caring seventeen-year-old. We have stood by as he shed the years of abuse at the hands of his mother and of the child-welfare system—including two horrendous years in a residential treatment center where he was gang raped, locked in seclusion for hours, and survived multiple attempts on his life by his roommate.

Parenting this child has been a roller-coaster ride. There have been times of chaos, times of extreme stress, and times of intense disappointment and explosive anger. But along the way has also been the most amazing development of a child who came to us with every set of initials tagged on to his "diagnosis"—ADHD, PTSD, ODD, and PDD, along with so many other disorders and syndromes. We have watched this child who came to us so drugged up on prescriptions that he was often like a robot, and now he is off all medication.

He was only eleven years old and was taking higher doses of medication than an adult twice his size would have been prescribed. We've watched with pride as this overmedicated child has struggled to get off all medications and learn what dealing with emotions is really like. At the age of seventeen, he's learning for the first time what anger and frustration are like and how to handle them successfully. We've cheered him on as his psychiatrist told us that he no longer needs to see him, that none of those initials and labels pertain to him anymore.

At the beginning, we told him that we would love him, take care of him, and provide him with the opportunities and tools he would need to realize his full potential, whatever that may be. We told him if his potential was Ds on his report card and he could look at us and say he had done his best, then we would celebrate those Ds. We could only give him the opportunities and tools, coupled with a secure and loving environment. He was the one who would have to do the work. He could become a victim of his past or a survivor of it. But whatever he becomes, it is *his* success, not ours.

Beverlee
An adoptive mom

HER SON'S STORY

I try not to remember being in residential treatment. It was supposed to be a short-term respite while my foster mom was recuperating, but it turned into a long-term nightmare. I was lucky because my foster parents were allowed to take me to their house for weekends and holidays. If it wasn't for them and for my adoptive family, I know I'd be in bad shape now.

At first I went along with being adopted, because it got me out of the residential center. As time went on, though, things changed, and I was glad to be adopted for lots of other reasons.

I still get to visit with my foster family, which I'm happy about. They're very important to me, like a favorite aunt and uncle. My parents have become good friends with them, too, and have always been willing to drive the three hours to let me visit them a couple times a year. And we talk on the phone sometimes.

Even though sometimes I get angry at my parents and I'll tell them they're not my real parents, I know that they are the best and most real parents I could want, and I know how lucky I am.

Fred
Beverlee's son, adopted from foster care at age eleven

COMMITTING TO A TROUBLED CHILD

When Stephen first came into our lives, he wasn't awake. He was eight years old, and we were his tenth family. He couldn't crawl correctly, and his run and walk were very awkward. He ran into things and people (even though he was looking right at them) and didn't seem to know where his body was in space. He gave artificial little hugs and patted our backs lightly with no emotions.

His communication skills were delayed, especially in intimate situations—like being in a family. He didn't appreciate things, especially beauty, art, and kindness. He said "thank you," but his eyes and his voice were sad and empty. Stephen could sit in a restaurant and order from the menu like a little adult and converse with the waiter, but he couldn't look us in the eye and hear the words "I love you" or admit or apologize for any kind of wrongdoing. He understood "the rules" very well, which is why it was good we didn't have too many. If he knew the rules, he could manipulate when he would get into trouble and to what degree, which meant he was in control.

He could (and still does) attempt to delay our leaving to go somewhere as a family and sabotage our going at all. He attempts to embarrass us in public. At school, he would lick his classmates, throw tantrums, scream at the top of his lungs, and jump up and down like a three-year-old. He threw three-hour rages at home, shook his bed, swore, broke the bed, and worked the door hinges until the door fell off. He bruised us in more ways than one.

The thing that had a huge impact on him was when the police took him from home one week before his legalization and placed him in a detention home for one night. We picked him up in the morning, and he thought we were nuts. People had given him back for less than that. A week later we adopted him. The most important thing you can do for a detached child is keep him.

Stephen was nine when we began intensive therapy. We were promised by the therapist that even if he didn't get better, we would. During the intensive, Stephen remembered things that had happened to him, and some of it was horrible. We were the parents he hardly knew, and we would sit on the other side of the wall watching his life unfold on a TV screen. There were times we wished we could jump through the screen and stop it—his pain and ours were so great.

We also knew that he wasn't alive like other kids. His eyes had no life in them. He didn't experience joy, disappointment, love, or sadness. He was angry and fake. Since then Stephen has gone up and down—mostly up. Some of the things we learned may be of help to others.

Be responsible. Be realistic about your expectations of the child. Set aside the techniques that have worked with other kids—you'll need to be creative with this one. Weird stuff works. Learn to step out of the chaos and be supportive rather than engage in fighting. Give up being embarrassed. Your child's behavior is shocking to people, so expect mixed reactions. Your child's life is more important than anyone's opinion of you or your child—or your methods of dealing with him. Have a strong relationship with your partner—you will need it. Nurture this relationship every chance you get. Try to remember that you have other children. This child will bring stress into your home that you never knew could exist. Keep a sense of humor. Learn to laugh at the situations you find yourselves in.

What we have learned is that we are stronger than we ever thought. We have a great capacity for unconditional love. We learned where our boundaries needed to be—don't overextend, don't take on the responsibility of other people's children, learn to say no, and don't take personal responsibility for the behaviors of the child. Don't suffer—let the child suffer, because he is the one who needs to learn the consequences of his actions. Don't feel that you have to take the advice of people who don't have a clue, but mean well—like the principal, the neighbor, your mother, the police, the teacher, and the former therapists. Trust yourself and the attachment therapist.

We did not always have the immediate answers. They sometimes came later, and we could always use them next time. This experience profoundly and continually opens us up and gives us a new understanding of all people, especially troubled ones. We learned that Stephen's pain is so very deep that we may never understand the level of harm he experienced.

Finally, we learned that these children are very worth it. (We are now adopting two siblings, both diagnosed with attachment disorder.) They have something buried inside them that is screaming to live again. What they lost may never be fully recovered again—but certainly much of it can be. Stephen's pain is powerful, but commitment and unconditional love are powerful medicine.

Lucy and Michael
Adoptive parents

ALWAYS ROOM FOR MORE

We always scoffed at agency policies requiring two years between placements. So, against agency advice, we adopted two separate children within nine months of each other. Hannah arrived in the fall at age three months. Her adjustment was fairly easy, but was intense in that she needed "a holding" about four times a day. The older two children adored her and she was doing well, so we thought "why not."

Sam was born in June. He was a dream baby, and slept through the night by six weeks. He spent his days cooing and looking intently into our faces. Hannah (now thirteen months old) spent her days plotting how to get rid of him.

I will never forget the day Sam came home from the hospital. Hannah was sitting on a king-size bed when we walked in with her new brother. She took one look at him, looked at us, and screamed and shook her head "No!" That was what the next six months were like. She threw toys at him, tried to pull him off our laps, refused to sleep at night, stopped eating table food (she wanted all bottles like her baby brother), and now needed to be "held" about six times a day. No one could have prepared us for how horrible it was.

Now, at five and almost four, they are the best of friends. Up until now, they have shared a bedroom. Due to a new addition on our home, they will soon each have their own room. Now we have two of them screaming and saying "No!" They want to stay together.

We believe all four of our kids are well attached to us. That process has been fun—and sometimes demanding. But even more fun has been to watch these four biologically unrelated children develop close sibling bonds. Because of the age differences, the two younger ones see the oldest as a "third parent." If Mom or Dad is not available, they go to him for assistance. The two oldest, although competitive in their relationship, share many common interests. Now, at fourteen and nine, they are both in baseball. That has served to strengthen their bond. The nine-year-old idolizes his older brother. The fourteen-year-old lovingly (most times) sees his younger brother as a pest.

As an adoption professional, I look at my children and wonder how we can ever separate siblings. Children's losses are so great already—how could we remove them from the last remaining connections? I cannot imagine my children not having each other some time in the future.

*** Candy and Jim***
Adoptive parents of four children,
three international and one domestic

A CHILD SPEAKS

When I first came to my family, I was five and a half, small, and very scared. I was shaky. After a while, I trusted my mom a little more, but I was still scared. I still had some fear inside of me. I was so shy I didn't talk too much. My orneriness made me hide, and I didn't want to come out and let anyone see me unless they came to me.

Now I am still shy and ornery, but I am not as fearful as I used to be, and I come out. I trust my mom a whole lot.

Robyn, age ten
A domestic adoptee who was adopted with
her brother at age five and a half

STRENGTH IN NUMBERS

I've had many children go through Dr. Keck's intensive treatment in Cleveland. I look to all of the caseworkers as angels, and Dr. Keck as the miracle man! I feel that many children could benefit from the therapy that is provided at the Attachment and Bonding Center of Ohio . . . and many parents, also. I look forward to every appointment—not only as an appointment for my children, but also as therapy for me. My kids sense when an appointment is approaching . . . maybe just so I'll have something to talk about. I just know that I ask for a lot of advice and am willing to try almost anything if it will help my children.

I find it most interesting, though, that many kids have attachment issues but there is not one cure-all for the disorder. It's a very individualistic disorder with an individualistic cure. One needs to try almost anything and everything! As a parent of children with attachment issues, it's vital to focus on the basic emotions: mad, sad, glad, and scared. It's very frustrating when mad is sometimes acted as sad, and sad and scared are often shown as mad. One just wishes that the true emotion would be exhibited.

It is a wonderful moment when the hurt child's emotions match what she is showing. I'll never forget the moment when Robyn actually cried and showed sadness in her eyes when she was sad! (This happened when her foster sister left.) It made me cry and, of course, I had to share the moment with someone (Regina!).

I now have six children—some are a real part of my family, and some are not. None are all of the time . . . yet. I hope this will happen someday, but if it doesn't, I know that I am not to blame. My goal for my children is to provide them with a sense of security and make them respectful, responsible adults.

Natalie, Robyn's mother
A single mother of six children
adopted from the foster care system

A VOTE FOR "MOTHER OF THE YEAR"

My mom should be mother of the year because she tries to help anybody she can. She has adopted six kids. Every day she gives me work, and it pays off. In third grade she helped me become one of the smartest kids. My mom works at South Middle School and she tries to work with other kids.

She is always giving things and always taking people into her house. When I got in trouble, she never gave up on me. She is always there when I'm hurt.

I would've been in foster care all my life if she didn't take me in. My mom is strict because she doesn't want me to grow up and be on the street. My mom also saved two cats that are still alive.

When she does something, she does it all the way. She goes to meetings to help solve the problems of the kids in her class. I've always wanted to take her somewhere to tell her I appreciate her kindness. She does not do things for gifts. She does them because she likes to. She deserves a really, really big and nice gift.

Dionntai, age eleven
Natalie's son, a domestic adoptee who was
adopted at age eight

A VOICE OF EXPERIENCE

Suggestions that I would give other parents:

- Research any and all emotional and health problems the child has.
- Let the child know, from the beginning, what is expected of him.
- Never feel guilty about a consequence.
- Call other adoptive parents to discuss the problems.
- Don't expect family and friends or neighbors to understand why you do what you do. They can never understand, because they have never lived in your house.
- No manipulations! Make sure you and your spouse discuss and clarify.
- Make natural consequences when you can.

- Never show any signs of embarrassment—no matter what your children do in public.
- Get your children involved in activities and keep them busy.
- Do a ton of family activities. The child has no idea what a "normal family" is.
- Always listen to the child.
- Always set a good example.

Marjorie
An adoptive parent

THE DAUGHTER AGREES

Teach them all kinds of stuff, do extracurricular activities like soccer, baseball, or cheerleading. Spend a whole day with the family. Talk to the kids—ask them about their problems and how their day was. Be active in all that your kids do.

Carla, age thirteen
Marjorie's daughter, adopted at age nine

A LIFETIME JOURNEY

What we have learned since beginning our journey to parent a hurt child:

- Attachment and trust are the same thing.
- Anyone alive is attached to something or someone. Infants who are completely "unattached" to anyone or anything die.
- The infertility that parents experience and the adoption that children experience create wounds of at least the same magnitude.
- Our daughter will have issues of safety, trust, and abandonment for the rest of her life.
- We have seen tremendous progress in our child and believe there is validity in the research and theories about the plasticity and resiliency of the brain. That information, however, does not change the reality of the situation. The devastating effects on the brain of severe neglect during infancy and early childhood will

generate lifelong issues for our daughter, regardless of the interventions we have used, and continue to use, to help her attach to us.

- The emotion our daughter experienced at the moment of her abandonment by her birth mother seems to be the emotion she presented most often before beginning her grief and loss process. This emotion of anger/rage served the purpose of keeping her close to her birth mother, and vice versa. Our attempts to help her "release" that anger could have sent the message to her that we expected her to give up, in favor of us, the only person she was truly attached to. We believe that raising our awareness of the conscious and unconscious messages we are sending to our daughter, as well as correcting the inappropriate messages in ourselves, is part of responsible parenting.

- No matter how much we thought we had to offer our daughter when she first came to us, it did not make up for the loss of her birth family. She just was not grateful to be with us.

- Our expectations for the kind of attachment we wanted our daughter to have to us caused just as many attachment problems for her as her previous abuse, neglect, and trauma. We either had to let go of our expectations or assume the responsibility for our part in contributing to her inability to attach to, or trust, anyone. So we let go.

- Our daughter reflected our own issues back to us as soon as she walked into the door. Her level of hyper-vigilance allowed her to have an unbelievable ability to attune to our own childhood wounds and unresolved issues on every level. Our responses to her behavior came out of our own need to survive this perceived threat to our emotional, psychological, and physical safety instead of her needs for survival. And we were the adults!

- The moments when we ignore or underestimate our child's "survival intelligence quotient" are our greatest mistakes. Honoring our daughter's survival skills—instead of seeing them as pathological—helps us to shift our responses to her.

- Progress in our daughter's ability to trust us comes during the moments we meet her where she is, instead of expecting her to meet us where we are. It is interesting that we ever think we are in a better place than our children. Owning that sense of arrogance is tough.
- We have had to accept our limitations in being able to help our daughter feel safe in the world. By doing so, she has seemed to be less anxious. Trying to prove to our daughter that she is safe with us is a waste of time. We end up losing precious chances for reciprocal enjoyment with her when we try to prove to her how wonderful we are.
- The therapists who have helped us the most are the ones who believe that the child's sense of emotional and psychological safety is improved when the parents also have a sense of emotional and psychological safety in the world. These therapists are the ones who are brave enough and skillful enough to address the parents' childhood wounds and unresolved issues. What's more, they actually believe that the parents are able and willing to do their own emotional and psychological work. The very best therapists are the ones who know that they have attachment issues themselves, like every other human being, and are willing to do their own emotional and psychological work, as well. There are no quick fixes or magic pills. It is a journey for every human that takes a lifetime.
- Our daughter began to learn in school, dropped her oppositional behavior and violence, and actually appeared happy for several months. We asked her what helped her the most to be the happy child she was becoming. Her response was, "I decided I didn't want to be mad anymore." Our daughter has taught us that no one can make anyone do anything. Free will is an incredibly powerful force. It is more powerful than the best parents or the most skillful therapist.

Becca and Kevin
*Adoptive parents who adopted their now ten-year-old
daughter at age four and a half from foster care*

A MOTHER'S VIEWPOINT

Prior to adopting Mindy six years ago, I attended every seminar, class, and training session offered. None of this prepared me for the reality of adopting a hurt child. We lived in turmoil and chaos, and both of us were upset all the time. When I read *Adopting The Hurt Child,* I recognized my daughter's problems. I had lost all confidence and little hope for success until we came to the Attachment and Bonding Center.

For the first time, Mindy talked about what had happened in her birth home and her multiple foster placements. During this time, she really became my daughter of the heart. I admired her strength and realized the pain from the adoptee's perspective. During this process Mindy began to trust me, and I believe she feels bonded with me today as we continue working on other issues.

We have both grown in this process—we continue to grow. We still have many obstacles to overcome, but I do know we will make this adoption a success together.

I thank you from the bottom of my heart for helping Mindy and me.

My advice to other parents—never, never give up, and be open to changing and learning from your child. Learn to be your child's greatest advocate, and you will be proud of what you can accomplish.

Kathy
Adoptive mom to Mindy

A DAUGHTER'S VIEWPOINT

Kathy writes, "When we discussed the new book, Mindy became very upset thinking of all the losses in her life and was unable to write her thoughts. We are writing this around a holiday, and holidays generally trigger sadness. With Mindy's permission, I share her thoughts":

I did not want to be adopted. I always hoped my birth mother would rescue me from foster care. When my mother was murdered, I gave up that dream and wanted to be adopted by my current foster family, but they would not, or could not, adopt me. I began preplacement visits with another family, but they changed their mind and did not want to adopt. I just wanted to be adopted so I did not have to move around so much.

I felt rejected by my birth family, my foster family, and the potential adoption that failed. I was so scared to be adopted and really did not understand it very well. I was afraid my new mom would "get rid of me," too. I still sometimes struggle with being scared that she will get rid of me.

Mindy, age fifteen
A domestic adoptee, placed at the age of nine

GONE, BUT NOT FORGOTTEN

When I chose to adopt, I decided on foreign adoption. The potential of losing the child once I had a placement was minimal. But after two very costly foreign adoptions and the desire to further increase my family, I decided to adopt a child through the public foster care system.

My new teenage daughter came with excess baggage. She had been in the system since she was eight months old. She had severe emotional problems. Because I already had one child with Reactive Attachment Disorder—and I'd had him for four years—I was up for the challenge. Yes, *I* was up for the challenge. But this was a decision made for my family, including my two children (both under eight). I knew this from the start, but I am a risk taker—so I took the risk with my eyes wide open.

I worked relentlessly with my daughter for several months. Although my personal challenge to parent her was manageable, I had to weigh the situation from the perspective of the whole family. Without spelling out the details, let it suffice to say that she became a threat to my two younger children. We worked through many difficult months. But gradually I began to realize that having this troubled teenager was becoming dangerous.

I am very stubborn. I don't give up easily. A lesson I repeatedly preach to my children is never to start something you don't plan to finish. When faced with the choice of my new daughter versus the remainder of the family, I had to violate my own rule. I could not finish what I started! But, in this case, the decision was easy. It was fast and it was confident. And it was painful!

Actually, having her out of our home at first was a relief. The prior several months had been action-packed. And the action had gotten more intense by the minute. Although I had been able to connect emotionally with my daughter, her actions toward the rest of the family began eroding the relationship we had established. Then she did one hurtful thing too many, and I was forced to choose between my family's safety and my quest to mother her. The choice was obvious. I disrupted the adoption.

My feelings during this transition period were mixed. I was happy to see the boys relax. But it was difficult to think that this was probably my daughter's last chance at having a family. I was angry. I was sad. I was betrayed. I was in mourning.

The healing process was long and difficult. My friends were very supportive. My extended family was happy. I felt that the county representatives were cold and/or ambivalent to my feelings, which was hurtful. At times I felt that I had failed. I was sad that my daughter was incapable of receiving my love. Most of the time, I feel proud that I made the right choice for my family.

The disruption was more than two years ago. Recently, my ex-daughter telephoned me. She called to tell me she was sorry. She had grown enough to know she had lost something very special.

I was surprised at my own reaction to the call. I learned something about myself. I liken it to what a Catholic priest who left the order after twenty-five years once told me: "Once a priest, always a priest." Whenever he hears a siren, he feels compelled to stop and see if there is someone in need of spiritual help.

My ex-daughter called me. She needed to talk to me. She wanted to know if she could call me from time to time. I cried. I said yes. Once a mom, always a mom.

Vicki
Adoptive mom

RISING TO ENORMOUS CHALLENGES

About thirteen years ago, my husband and I began the life-changing journey of adopting a total of nine special-needs children. They came to us one at a time, beginning with a sixteen-year-old boy and following with a tiny five-year-old girl with spina bifida. A year later, we begged our social worker to let us try to adopt Jon, a handsome eight-year-old boy who was being treated at a children's mental hospital. After he had been with us for about a year, social services reluctantly allowed us to adopt his nine-year-old birth sister. Next came Kristin, who joined us as a two-day-old infant—my first baby, but our fifth child. When Kristin was three, eleven-year-old Brad came to us from a disrupted adoption. Most recently, we have adopted a sibling group of three brothers, ages one, two, and three.

My kids are wonderful, and while the journey has been long, it has also been the most rewarding challenge we have ever undertaken. It has required every ounce of creativity we could muster, humor we didn't know we had, dogged determination, and the flexibility of a yoga master. We have learned to appreciate little things, take nothing for granted, stick together like super glue, and when all else fails, laugh. We now know the value of a hug, the awe of being trusted, the terror of abuse, and the immeasurable worth of a child.

The road between the anticipation and the reality of becoming parents has been filled with many challenges. How long can you hold a spitting, kicking nine-year-old in the jewelry department of a retail store? Can you be arrested for disrupting the Sunday morning peace when your eight-year-old colorfully curses out the elderly ladies breakfasting at a fast-food restaurant before church? Does it matter that you are now considered mentally unstable by family and friends, and you sometimes question your own sanity? In addition to the "normal" hazards of parenting, we have become experts at dodging flying objects, speed-dialing poison control, patching holes in sheetrock, and explaining why one would be suspended from school for threatening to kill the principal.

Suddenly, after we became students in the "school of parenting kids with special needs," we learned a different way of measuring success. I actually found myself rewarding my son for a raging fit that lasted only ten minutes. (The usual amount of time for such expressions of rage was an hour or more.) As we shared a root beer float, I told him just how proud I was that he was able to control himself so quickly. And he hadn't spit on me during the whole fit! He was able to see that he has the ability to stop his out-of-control behavior. We felt like a team. This was success!

When my daughter began inventing stories where she made good choices and saw herself as the heroine instead of the victim, a friend asked, "Don't her wild stories bother you?" No, this was success! My four-year-old pushed away his broccoli and said, "I don't want it." Time for a nutrition lesson? Nope! This child had never felt full before and had even eaten until he threw up. This was success!

My job became considerably easier when I learned to view each situation from my child's perspective. My ten-year-old's refusal to have her picture taken or to appear in family videos was completely understandable when I realized she had been the victim of child pornography. My nine-year-old's obsession with how much gas was in the car could be tolerated when I learned that he and his younger sister had been forced to sneak into gas stations and steal gas when their car had run out of fuel. When my husband and I became willing to look beyond our frustration and seek to understand what motivated our children, we could help eliminate the behaviors that resulted from the early trauma.

Adopting older, special-needs children meant changing my preconceived ideas about what my family would be like. I had always expected two or three little "clones" of myself and my husband. These ideal kids would think pretty much like us and, of course, share most of our values. But the kids we adopted are unique little survivors who have blossomed in spite of everything life has thrown at them. While I realize that even though I have helped shape their values, their characters are built, in part, by experiences that I will never be able to fathom. They have learned to trust in spite of a cruel world. They have learned to see themselves as valuable, partly because of how precious they know they are to me. They believe the cycle of abuse can be stopped—because they are living proof that it can.

There is no way to express the joy I feel today when I look at my family. We have taken "the road less traveled by. And that has made all the difference."

Lisa
An adoptive mom of nine special-needs children, including Keri and Brad, whose stories follow

A RESISTANT ADOPTEE ACCEPTS LOVE

I am nineteen years old, and I have lived through nightmares most people wouldn't even know how to dream. I was betrayed by my birth mother, who felt that satisfying her boyfriend was more important than protecting her daughter. I was molested by hitch-hikers and sold for child pornography—all before the age of seven. When I was seven, the department of human services "saved" me.

They removed me from school one day via police car and deposited me in a strange shelter for children. My clothes were taken, and I was given a new set. I was treated for lice and housed in a room with a four-year-old who cried inconsolably for her mother.

Where were my mother and my brothers? I cried myself to sleep. In about six weeks, a foster family came to take me "home." I was to be a playmate for their daughter, but I guess I scared them when I began to talk about things "nice girls don't talk about." I was sent away. I wasn't a good playmate after all. My possessions were packed in garbage bags, and I was sent to a therapeutic foster home. That meant I was really bad. My therapeutic foster mom was pretty sharp. I didn't scare her—even when I told her the worst stuff.

She always meant what she said, and she always told me exactly what she expected of me. I wanted my mom. I hated this intruder. I let her know I hated her. I threw terrible fits, kicked her, cursed, and caused embarrassing scenes. She held me. I began to like feeling safe. But when she got a boyfriend, I was sent away.

No one would ever trick me into loving them again. I was taken in by the therapeutic foster family who had my older brother. I didn't know it at the time, but they wanted to adopt me. I liked being with my brother again, and I wanted to stay. These people might work out. After all, they hadn't sent Jon away, and he had even threatened to kill them. But the department said this family had too many kids, and I was taken away. Oh well.

My next foster family lived right next door. The man shook me. I could make him lose his cool really easily. He and his wife liked to dress me up and show me off like a doll. I felt like a pet. I could work them pretty well. They couldn't take it, and apparently no other foster family wanted to try, so I was sent back to the family that had my brother. They actually asked to have me back, but I was sure it would last only until they really knew me. Well, this time *I* would decide when I would leave.

The family didn't have many rules, but the rules never changed. I remember having to be room-bound one day, and my foster mom brought her supper into my room and ate with me because she was sad that I had to eat alone. I remember being held while I screamed that I hated them, and then when the anger was all gone, she would rock me to sleep. I remember having family pictures made and wishing I was part of this family. No! I was determined not to let them make me love them. It was time to leave.

I made up some really awful stuff about their home and told the neighbors. The neighbors reported them and my family was investigated, but they didn't send me away. I did all the bad things I could think of, but I couldn't make them even threaten to send me away.

We did fun stuff. Vacations, birthday parties, swimming, camping, and shopping trips. I was always treated the same as the other kids. My dad made up nicknames for me and wrote songs just for my sisters and me. Slowly, I let my guard down. I felt safe. They let me be me. They didn't tell me what I could or should feel. They just loved me for who I am.

They believed I am brave and smart. They noticed when I felt proud of myself, and they were proud, too. We had parties for improvements, not perfection. A C instead of a D meant party time. They never told me I had to love my birth mother in spite of what she did. But they understood my love for her. They never told me how awful she was, but they understood when I hated her. They believed in me, so I began to believe in myself. I had fun, and I began to see that life was more than surviving. They gave me the power I needed to make my life what I want it to be. I am a product of their love as surely as if I were conceived by them.

Keri
Lisa's adopted daughter

HOME AT LAST

I begin college in about three weeks. I am eighteen years old. When I was two, my birth mother left. I was taken care of by my birth father's parents until he remarried a year or so later. Then I went back to live with my dad, stepmother, and her four children.

There were five kids and one on the way. My dad runs away from problems, so his job would keep him gone for months sometimes.

I wet the bed, I had hemophilia, and I wasn't liked by my older stepsiblings. I was trouble. My stepmom would tell my dad when he got home from work, and he would shake me. One time I had a cerebral hemorrhage and almost died. I was four. I would try to eat, but I was so nervous that I would throw up. They put me in a mental hospital. I was five. I said I wanted to die.

My father and stepmother decided I could live with my birth mom. They sent me on a plane to Georgia with my older birth brother. My birth mom had boyfriends and worked a lot. We lived in motels. My brother taught me how to steal food to eat. Mom locked us out when she was with her boyfriend. My hemophilia went untreated, and sometimes I cried because my knee hurt. Then my mom said she was going on a trip with her boyfriend and she couldn't take care of me. She left me at a shelter for kids. I waited for my dad to come get me.

The people at the shelter didn't know how to treat my hemophilia, so I was hospitalized. I waited for my dad to come get me. I was sent back to the shelter. I waited for my dad to come get me. DHS found a foster home for me. I waited for my dad to come get me.

The foster family was very strict. I never did anything right. I couldn't even figure out what they wanted. I got paddled. I didn't do my chores right, so I didn't get to eat. I lost lots of weight. I wet the bed, so I got paddled and had to take a cold bath. Every day, I waited for my dad to come get me.

The social worker said this family was going to adopt me, and they filed the papers. I told them my dad was going to take me home. They let me call my dad, and I asked him to come get me. He said he had too many kids. The family said if they didn't adopt me no one else would, because I had hemophilia and I was too old. I would be a foster kid forever, moving from home to home. I was ten.

I became very depressed. They paddled me more. One day, I showed my bruises to my friend Jon. He told his parents, and they told my caseworker. Jon's parents asked to keep me. The caseworker said that his family had too many kids, but I could stay until they found another adoptive home for me. They never found one, so I got to stay.

My mom and dad were very patient, and I knew exactly what they expected. They didn't yell, and they respected my opinions and my feelings. I always had choices—and the choices had consequences—but they let me make my own decisions. Their rules made sense. They didn't give up on me, even when I gave them trouble or embarrassed them. I felt like they liked me. We did fun things together, like camping and whitewater rafting. At first I was just with them because my dad wouldn't take me back, but slowly I grew to love them. They are my family now, and even though I have seen my birth dad again, I no longer want to live with him. I am home.

Brad
Lisa's adopted son

STILL FEELING THE PAIN OF NOT BEING ADOPTED

People need to feel loved at all stages of their lives. As a twenty-eight-year-old woman, I still feel that being adopted would be the single most important thing in my life. Most people would see this as maybe an insecurity and not understand this need.

I was signed off for adoption at age thirteen and spent most of my life in the foster care system. Moreover, I feel that I had missed out on something by never being adopted. This has left a large void in my life, and I don't feel as though it will ever be filled. Although I did have good points in my childhood, I feel like I missed out on having a normal home life. Even though I was not legally adopted, I did emotionally adopt my cottage parents at the Florida Sheriffs Youth Ranch, and I feel like they are my family.

Locating my biological parents helped to fill some of the void. But it did not give the fulfillment I need. I am still, to this day, trying to fill the emptiness that lingers. However, I do have a good relationship with both my biological parents.

Being unable to conceive a child as yet, my husband and I are seeking to adopt a child through the HRS system, because we both feel that we could teach him love and family values.

Don't get me wrong—I have a full and happily fulfilled life. I am a great wife, a good friend, and a wonderful aunt. I have a great family, but I will always feel like I missed out on having an adopted family.

So when you are thinking about the choice of what age child you would like to adopt, please remember that every child needs a family.

CM
A young woman who grew up in the foster system

A CHILD'S GRATITUDE

Thank You
    for riding through the rough waters
    of changing with me.
Thank you for holding my hand.
And thank you for waiting.
Thank You
    for believing in me
    when I pushed you away.
Thank you for taking the time to help me find my way.
Thank you for standing beside me.
Thank you for each day
    you were there for me . . .
Thank you for being there for me
    when I needed you most.
Thank you for making all my dreams come true.
In 1996 there was no one I could turn to or talk to,
Then in 1998 there was you who brought all my dreams to life
And gave me the best family ever.
    Love,
    Your son

A sixteen-year-old adopted at thirteen.

CHAPTER 12

AUTHORS' SMORGASBORD:
Reprinted Articles About
Hurt Children

Over the past few years, we both have written short articles or commentaries for organizational newsletters and decided to include some of them in this book. They include a smattering of information—some of which has been addressed in other chapters—and are not in any particular order of importance. Glance at them as you wish. We hope they will help to punctuate the lessons and wisdom we have tried to impart in *Parenting the Hurt Child*.

"THE PINOCCHIO PRINCIPLE"

While training in England, Regina encountered a man who proclaimed, "I don't believe in anything that doesn't exist in fairy tales or mythology. Attachment issues don't. Therefore, they can't exist!" Although his statement made little sense to her, Regina quickly replied, "Pinocchio!" When she returned home to the United States, she rewatched the Disney film, and there were all the behaviors, containment, and eventual healing. As a result, she wrote "The Pinocchio Principle." Enjoy!

"When children who were naughty become good, it gives a new smiling appearance to the whole family."[1] That quote from *Pinocchio* is what I wish for all families parenting hurt children. And because every cause needs a mascot, after rereading the tale of Pinocchio and watching Disney's version, I wholeheartedly nominate Pinocchio. Although most of us remember his nose growing as he lies, it was not until I reviewed the movie that the striking similarities between the tale and parenting a child with attachment disorder jumped out at me.

First there is Geppetto, a kindly, lonely, single father whose only wish is to have Pinocchio be a "real boy," to fill his life with joy. The fairy (social worker) brings Pinocchio to him and says, "To make Geppetto's wish come true will be entirely up to you. . . . Prove yourself brave, truthful, and unselfish, and you will be a real boy." It's not exactly the respectful, responsible, and fun-to-be-with principle quoted in attachment therapy, but it's close.

Does Pinocchio listen? No. Pinocchio, although not a real boy, becomes mobile, and in his first dance (that honeymoon ended quickly) kicks Figaro, the cat (cruelty to animals), sets a fire, burns his finger (self-injurious), and pollutes the fish's bowl (destructive to property). As they try to sleep, Pinocchio asks questions about sleep and school, why this and why that (persistent nonsense questions).

Undaunted, poor Geppetto continues to work hard, hope for the best, and parent Pinocchio. Poor Geppetto. He needs to form a support group fast. Pinocchio, having no conscience, is given one by the fairy, in the person of Jiminy Cricket. He is a great guide, but unfortunately he is not integrated by Pinocchio, who continues to plague Geppetto with truancy, running away, and poor peer relations.

He lies to the fairy, and his nose grows and grows with each obvious untruth. The social worker (oh, I mean the fairy) bails him out once again, but the young puppet doesn't learn from past mistakes. He continues to choose bad peers, indulge in abnormal eating patterns at Pleasure Island, and adds fighting and destruction of property to his crimes.

---

1. Carlo Collodi, *The Adventures of Pinocchio* (New York: Knopf, 1988), p. 1.

Even his conscience, Jiminy Cricket, bemoans in a moment of despair, "After all I've done for him!"

His father, even facing death, continues to feel guilty and laments in the whale's belly about poor Pinocchio, who was such a good boy. Well, as we all know, the story has a happy ending. After Pinocchio receives the help he needs (containment in the belly of a whale), his fairy does turn him into a real boy. A very happy ending for all.

Pinocchio is a delightful way for parents and children to discuss some attachment issues in a fun, nonthreatening way. Rent it, buy it, enjoy it, and put some laughter in your life. I give it two thumbs up!

This article originally appeared in the February 1998 issue of Connections, a newsletter of ATTACh, the Association for Treatment and Training in the Attachment of Children.

"IT'S THE SAME, ONLY DIFFERENT"

It seems that everyone involved in adoption has a strong and somewhat fixed belief about what is right. The right way to match parents and children . . . the right way to arrange for visitations . . . the right time of year to make a placement. The truth is, there are probably as many different "rights" in the adoption world as there are adoption agencies and professionals. We do not know the perfect way in which to facilitate this complex blending of families, and no one can claim that their methodology will ensure a successful outcome. What professionals must do is cooperate and focus on the macro picture: adoption is, in essence, the act of providing a permanent home for a child who has not had one. To highlight this and other pertinent facts, Regina and Jacqueline H. Smigel, LSW, a therapist from the Attachment and Bonding Center of Ohio, wrote "It's the Same, Only Different."

In the late 1800s, when the Orphan Train rode into town with scores of children in need of families, little or no information was available to the families who took them in. Today, with ready access to the Internet, public libraries in every town, bookstores on every corner, and multiple "special interest" groups continually sponsoring workshops and conferences, adoption information is readily available to anyone who wants it. The amount of information can be overwhelming, leaving many adoptive parents lost.

In a well-meaning effort to help those searching for information, the field has become so specialized that at times we can't see the forest for the trees. For example, there are multiple Internet sites for Reactive Attachment Disorder, all of which focus on different sets of children—American, Eastern European, Russian, and Chinese—as if the causes, symptoms, behaviors, and treatment differ depending on the child's nationality. If we all give up a little of our uniqueness and join hands together, what a powerful force we could be to change the lives of the children we love.

The term "special needs" is one that sends chills down the spine of a potential adoptive parent, because it suggests that the child has a severe intellectual or physical impairment. In truth, the adoption world defines "special needs" as any child who is not an infant, is part of a sibling group, had prenatal exposure to drugs and alcohol, has had multiple caregivers, or who has been the victim of neglect or abuse. In essence, nearly all adopted children, regardless of their place of birth, fit the definition. (However, only American children are eligible for subsidies to help parents with these special needs.)

Among the many assumptions that prospective adoptive parents have are:

- Children adopted internationally do not have special needs. (Based on the definition above, they often do have special needs.)
- Birth parents are a threat to the permanency of adoption. (In our combined forty years of experience, not one of our placements has been disrupted by a birth parent.)
- Knowing difficult information about birth-parent family history—such as alcohol abuse, drugs, or violence—is damaging to the child. (*Knowing* the history is not what hurts the child—the fact that it

happened at all is what caused the damage. Sharing the information can, in fact, be healing.)

■ There are no Caucasian children waiting for adoption in America. (In truth, approximately 46 percent of America's waiting children are Caucasian.)

As you can see, these assumptions are not valid, and parents should not make a lifetime commitment based on them. Instead, they should use resources to get good, current information on all types of adoption before making choices for building their family.

One issue that all adoptees face, regardless of their origin, is that of profound loss. Whether the adoption occurred because of a well-thought-out plan made by birth parents, a governmental policy, poverty, death, neglect, or abuse, the child has lost an integral part of himself—his birth parents! The loss of birth parents is the universal loss that all adoptees face.

They also experience a myriad of other losses, which can include loss of siblings (birth, foster, orphanage-mates), caretakers (foster parents, orphanage staff, group home/treatment center staff), familiar foods, smells, drinks, toys, clothing, noises, and language. In whatever combination, these losses can be overwhelming for children. Joining forces with other adoptive parents—regardless of the nature of the adoption—gives parents the tools, knowledge, and power to play an active role in helping their children fully grieve their losses and eventually move beyond them.

Protecting ourselves by denying the true issues that the child faces keeps the issues alive and prevents healing. By mere definition of neglect, it is undeniable that children placed in orphanages at birth or at a young age are, in fact, victims of neglect. This is not because the orphanage staff doesn't care for and love the children. Instead, it is because a child's individual needs cannot be met in a group situation.

Out of necessity, children living in orphanages are forced into a routine, without the freedom to respond to physical and emotional cues relating to hunger, discomfort, bathrooming, pain, thirst, or a desire to be nurtured. The result is a pseudo-independence that mirrors the self-parenting label attached to neglected children in America.

A three-year-old adopted from the American foster care system who is overly independent, refuses help, or won't ask parents for anything is easily and quickly identified as having a problem. The same behaviors in an internationally adopted child are often lauded as signs of intelligence and self-sufficiency. Part of the solution is that parents must care for the child in a way that helps her begin to heal from past neglect and learn to trust her new parents.

This is done most effectively by using activities such as rocking, bottle-feeding, singing, playing with baby toys, eye contact, and massage. This is vital to overcome the consequences of chronic neglect—no matter where it happened. There is sometimes resistance to regression and "babying" children who are not chronologically babies, but rest assured that college applications do not ask students when they gave up the bottle, stopped singing lullabies, or quit sleeping with a teddy bear. After all, when stressed, most of us long to be nurtured and taken care of, and adoption creates stress for both child and parent.

Like the issues of loss, attachment, and neglect that were previously discussed, other adoption issues—such as identity, control, loyalty, rejection, fear of abandonment, feeling different, self-esteem, and trust—are the same for adoptees regardless of the circumstances surrounding their adoption. Some children will negotiate these issues with ease, while others will need professional help to heal.

Viewing your child's needs and issues from a narrow focus of her country of birth or ethnic origin may rob the family of opportunities for growth and healing. We can all learn from one another and from the lessons of the past. Reinventing the wheel each time a new country opens up to adoption trivializes that which has been learned by adoptive families over the years.

The challenge for adoptive parents is to learn as much as possible from each other, and, in turn, to share their experiences and knowledge with others. For example, domestic special-needs agencies often require preplacement classes to prepare parents for adoption-related issues. This is not to slow down the process but is in response to feedback from previous adopting families about the importance of having this knowledge base before the child was placed in their home.

Those adopting children from other countries are not often required to attend such classes but could expand their readiness for special-needs children (as defined earlier) by doing so voluntarily. Knowledge is power, and arming yourself with the power to help your child develop into a healthy person can never be wasted. After all, adoptive parents of children from the United States, South America, China, Romania, Korea, Russia, Guatemala, or anywhere else are all in the same boat. Isn't it time we started rowing together?

An edited version of this article, entitled "We're All in This Together," originally appeared in the July/August 2001 issue of Adoptive Families, a magazine published by Susan Caughman.

" 'YOU AREN'T MY *REAL* PARENT'. . . AND OTHER JOYS OF PARENTING ADOPTED TEENAGERS"

Adolescents are often the topic of discussion when addressing parenting issues. Some people feel utter terror when they think of the teen years, and others wait to see their child bloom into a questioning, thinking, conceptualizing individual. The challenges of adolescence are compounded by the fact that this difficult period is not limited to the ages of thirteen to nineteen. The world is populated with eleven-year-olds who are quite pubescent, and twenty-year-olds who are in the throes of adolescent identity-seeking. In any case, the developmental period of adolescence brings a new level of parent/child interaction. Regina addresses these changes in "'You Aren't My Real Parent' . . . and Other Joys of Parenting Adopted Teenagers."

Many parents have explained adoption to their children in developmentally congruent ways when the children are young and find little conflict. Relieved that the task of "telling" went so well, the topic is sometimes put away. When parents originally adopted, their interest in adoption was very high. But as the years go by, the topic usually becomes less important to them as the child becomes "their child." Adoption is talked about less often. Conversely, the infant has little cognitive awareness of adoption, but as he grows older, he may have more questions and feel unable to bring them up.

Suddenly in the teen years, parents sometimes find their adopted child struggling with issues they felt were addressed and put to rest long ago. Oftentimes, they don't even realize that the child is struggling with adoption issues, because they believe those matters were already settled.

We must always remember that adoption has its roots in loss, and it is often in adolescence that adoptees begin to grieve the losses they now understand in a more adult way. How people grieve is very individual. Adoption losses can include national origin, identity, medical history, siblings (known and unknown), and language (for the internationally adopted child), to name a few. They *always* include the loss of the birth parents. Adoptees can often get trapped in the anger stage as they grieve, especially when their grief is unacknowledged.

An adopted child's adolescence is also a time for adoptive parents to face and reassess their own issues, such as infertility, loss of a birth child, feelings regarding entitlement, and their child's birth parents. A good essay to read is Erma Bombeck's "What Kind of a Mother Would Go in Search of Her Daughter's 'Real Mother'?"—which appears in her book, *Motherhood: The Second Oldest Profession*. Other appropriate adoption books that address your individual child's needs can be read by parents and shared with the child. After all, those preparation classes (if you had any) were many years ago, so it is time to brush up.

Television is another source that poses an opportunity to bring up issues. If a talk show is about reuniting birth parents and children, a comment from a parent could open up a child. Sometimes children do best with the indirect approach, such as, "I heard that some adoptees want to search for their birth parents. Do you ever think about that?"

Teenagers struggle with identity and often try on new and sometimes different hats while figuring out "Who am I?" Adoptees sometimes have a more difficult task forming their identity because of a lack of information about their roots. Some internationally adopted children do not even know their birth dates, much less any other information. Even adoptees who have information struggle with the ultimate question, "Why was I given up?"

It is difficult for adoptees with only a few pieces of the puzzle to get a clear picture of their identity. Parents can help this struggle by offering all the information available. Even though they feel they have shared it before, an adolescent may want it all again. There is no detail too small or insignificant to share. Writing down the information and telling the child where it is may be a good way to share, because this allows him to control when, if, and where he reads it. Do not assume that he is ready to search for his birth parents just because he is approaching the age of eighteen. That is a decision that is very individual. You should be supportive, but do not push your agenda.

If your child doesn't want the information, this should be acknowledged and respected. Not all teens are interested in adoption issues; some just want to be like everyone else. They may be experiencing feelings of loyalty conflict and fear that curiosity about their roots will hurt your feelings.

Now, too, is the time to ask if he wants you to reconnect with the adoption agency to be sure all available information is known. It is important to review agency policy and laws regarding confidentiality in your state, because they may have changed since the time of the adoption. This is a good time for you to reconnect with adoption support groups that may offer programs for teenagers or offer important support and training for parents. If there is a search group in your area, you should be in contact for current information. Many search groups offer group meetings that your family may want to attend. Adult adoptees can talk about their issues in ways that help the adopted child normalize his feelings about adoption.

Another important task of adolescence is separation and individuation. Some teens do this with grace, while others are quite bombastic. The refrain "You aren't my real parents anyway" is not too much different from a birth child's "I wish you weren't my mother." It is important for parents to allow some freedom while maintaining boundaries and expectations. This is not a time to abandon your child emotionally; he needs parents even as he pushes away.

Sexuality takes on new importance in teenage years. When your child was young, odds are she accepted the story that went something like, "Your birth parents couldn't take care of you, so we adopted you." This saga takes on new meaning when she's older and figures out that two people had sex, she grew inside her birth mother as a result, and then she was given away. At some point most adoptees feel "given away," and they struggle with questions such as, "What would I do if I had the same choice to make?"

If these adoption issues are impacting your child in a way that interferes with her life, development, or happiness, it may be necessary to find an adoption-sensitive counselor to help her. Do not assume every professional knows about adoption. Instead, check parent support groups and adoption agencies for referrals. Ask therapists what training and experience they have had with adoption. Your child may feel more comfortable talking to someone other than you.

If your child does not want to talk, maybe he doesn't need to do so right now. It may be best to open the door in a calm time with a comment like, "I was thinking of how proud your birth mother would be of you" or "I was so lucky to adopt you"—and let the child take the lead. Many teens like reviewing their baby books and hearing their adoption stories one more time.

Adolescents often have a favorite adult who is not their parent—an aunt, coach, neighbor, or family friend. They may feel more comfortable talking to that person, so it is important to share relevant information with that person without violating the child's privacy. If the child doesn't want people to know he is adopted, his wishes should be honored.

Adoption is a lifelong issue, and it is important for every individual to have the tools to deal with the issues in his own time. Forcing a child to talk about the adoption can be as destructive as ignoring the topic. Teenagers are mercurial, and Monday's "I never think about adoption" can become Tuesday's "I want to search for my birth parents." Adoptive parents need to respect their child's changing moods and be open, available, and knowledgable about adoption issues.

This article was first printed in the Fall 2000 issue of Adoption News, *the newsletter of Jewel Among Jewels Adoption Network, Inc.*

"AFFIRMING THE REALITY OF THE HURT ADOPTEE"

Recent trends in adoption lean toward openness, truth, and full disclosure. While most agencies share nearly all information with adoptive families, there is still not agreement on what constitutes the "total truth." This is particularly true in the case of adoptees who have experienced trauma prior to adoption. The concern is that they will be hurt when faced with the truth about physical or sexual abuse, neglect, parental drug addiction, or difficult circumstances surrounding their removal from the birth family. However, it isn't knowledge of a horrid past that causes their hurt—it's the hurtful experience itself. Most children who have been removed from a bad situation and finally adopted remember much of what occurred in their birth families. While their memories are not always well organized and intact, they are there in some form. Believing that complete disclosure will ultimately help the hurt child, Greg wrote "Affirming the Reality of the Hurt Adoptee."

The trauma of hurt children who are placed in adoptive homes is often so dramatic that the adults involved in the situation cannot deal with it. I believe that is why parents and social workers sometimes focus too much on what few "positives" there are about hurtful birth parents and inadvertently minimize the truth for the child.

Time after time, I see beautifully constructed life books with nice pictures of people from the child's early life. That is fine—especially if one is trying to create good feelings. However, the stark reality is that if everyone at home were always smiling around the birthday cake or playing happily in the park, the child would *not* have been removed from the family. In our attempt to be respectful to those who hurt their children, I believe we further confuse those children. We are not affirming their reality. We are, in essence, conspiring with those parents who plead, "I just lost control . . . I was drinking when I burned her with the cigarette!"

Children most often know the truth—they lived it! We need to validate their truth, document their truth, and where possible, show them the truth. Sometimes in therapy we have used police or hospital photos to show the child exactly what "bad touch" means. These photos do more to affirm the child's reality than the nice smiling photos taken at a supervised visit.

We have to remember that our perceptions often become our truths. Some things that happened to a child that we think are "bad" are viewed as "okay" or even "good" by the abusive parents.

Trauma is subjective. Therefore, we must present the facts as they *were,* and then allow it to become the child's "job" to reframe it, repackage it, and put it together in *his* understandable form. We can only affirm who he is when we give him the truths and allow him to integrate or discard them as he wishes.

In their efforts to protect the child emotionally, and perhaps to safeguard themselves as well, parents and professionals too often try to "make nice." But we cannot change reality. We shouldn't, nor should we try to make bad things good and good things bad. This attempt causes great cognitive dissonance, further perplexing the child and clouding his reality. It is neither the adoptive parent's job nor the professional's job to protect the child from his past. In fact, it is not possible to do this. It is, however, possible and necessary to protect the child from present and future dangers.

One such danger is the distortion of the reality. Full disclosure should apply to all aspects of the adoptive process. I don't feel that we should keep any information about a child from that child. And I don't think we have to wait until he is old enough to understand what happened to him. After all, most atrocities committed by parents are done before their children can truly understand them. We talk to babies. We explain to our children about being sorry long before they have a conscience or understand the concept. If parents waited for a child to "be ready" before they said or did something, no child would ever "get it."

The fact is—hurt children have been exposed to things we don't like. We need to help the child heal, and to do so we need to be honest—even when we don't like the truth. Affirmation requires the truth, and the truth is affirming. Like pieces of a puzzle, each piece of information begins to complete the very complicated picture. Even when the picture is ugly, one can see the *whole* when there are not too many *holes.*

This article was first printed in the Spring 1999 issue of Adoption News, *the newsletter of Jewel Among Jewels Adoption Network, Inc.*

"REACTIVE ATTACHMENT DISORDER
AND ITS TREATMENT"

*Many people ask, What exactly is Reactive Attachment
Disorder? How is it treated most effectively? They have
heard many things, read much, and done extensive
searches on the Internet. After finding it nearly impossible to answer these two questions in a brief phone call
between appointments, Greg decided to write the following description of Reactive Attachment Disorder
and its treatment.*

The types of problems that adoptive parents see in their children are most likely the result of breaks in attachment that occur
within the first three years. They are problems that impair, and
even cripple, a child's ability to trust and bond—or attach to
other human beings.

These issues with attachment are the ones that cause the
greatest problems in adopting a child with special needs. As adoptive parents attempt to attach to a child whose attachment ability
is impaired by developmental delays, the attachment will either be
nonexistent, distorted, or focused around negative behaviors.

Children who have suffered abuse or neglect severe enough
to bring them into the foster care/adoption system may meet the
diagnostic criteria for Reactive Attachment Disorder. This clinical
diagnosis identifies children who have not been able to attach
appropriately to a caregiver in a meaningful way.

Because many children who have experienced neglect,
abuse, and abandonment have not yet developed an internalized set of values by which they judge themselves and others,
they are not able to receive and experience empathy, nor can
they develop insight. They project blame onto others and onto
objects. They blame their adoptive parents for causing their
anger, and they blame toys for breaking. They blame things that
could not possibly be responsible for anything!

Most often, children or adolescents who engage in projecting blame are those who have not yet developed a conscience.
These same children are adept at engaging others in a superficial manner, thus therapists, teachers, and outsiders to the family feel that these children are easy to be around and that they

are truly misunderstood by those who should know them best—their parents.

"Unfreezing" Development

Developmental change occurs within the context of intense interpersonal relationships. The relationships forged in the birth family—although locked in faulty thinking and ultimately causing developmental arrest—were intense. As a result, a strong connection developed between the abused child and the abusing parent. It is important to remember this dynamic and to understand that our positive relationships must be equally intense if they are to counteract and compete with the abusive relationships that initiated and solidified the child's pathology.

Therapy with hurt children needs to include high energy and intense focus, close physical proximity, frequent touch, confrontation, movement, much nurturing and love, almost constant eye contact, and fast-moving verbal exchanges. One goal of therapy, then, is to approximate what occurs in the healthy attachment cycle, thus reworking the process that was so traumatically interrupted early in the child's life. Therapy that is detached, nondirective, and passive is seldom received by the child as it is intended by the therapist. It is most often viewed as cold, uncaring, uninvolved, boring, and useless.

Holding Therapy

Close physical proximity heightens the therapeutic process and the interpersonal contact. Holding the child or adolescent results in an intensity that cannot be duplicated in any other therapeutic format. We have found that therapeutic holdings—not restraint—mobilize development. Clearly, this is an intended outcome of therapy with those who have developmental delays.

Holding the child or adolescent is accomplished by having him lie across the laps of two therapists and/or his parents. His right arm is behind the back of the lead therapist, who is sitting closest to the head. His left arm is free, or may be restrained if he uses it to try to hit the therapist or to engage in self-stimulation such as scratching or fidgeting. Such self-stimulating activities may increase during holding as the child attempts to deflect contact with the therapist and to maintain awareness of self by avoiding others. This behavior is discouraged because the goal is to heighten the child's contact with others.

The lead therapist is responsible for guiding the session. Eye contact is critical and is enforced nearly all the time. The child is responsible for maintaining eye contact with the person with whom he is talking. When he doesn't, the therapist uses either verbal or physical cues—such as turning the child's head—to help him establish the connection he needs.

Most of the professionals who advocate holding therapy are in agreement about the following elements:

- Emotional contact between the child and the therapist/holder is heightened.
- Holding produces emotional responses that are unlikely to occur in any other kind of therapeutic intervention.
- Corrective emotional experiences may occur during, and as a result of, holding.
- Holding enhances the child's capacity to attach.
- Holding increases the child's attachment to the therapist/holder and facilitates the transfer of this connection to the parents.
- Holding provides physical containment, which is reassuring to the child whose feelings often frighten him.
- Therapists who do holding are more aware of this child's nonverbal experiences than they would be if they sat across from him with no physical contact.

Some people refer to holding therapy as rage reduction therapy. We think that the term "rage reduction" is a limited description of what holding encompasses. Of course, reducing the child's rage is a desirable and necessary outcome; however, most of the time spent in therapy is not focused on the provocative rage work that is often featured in television coverage of holding therapy. Rather, a variety of interventions and strategies are utilized.

Holding is a process that often reactivates delayed development. It is a vehicle that allows an intense interpersonal relationship to develop and consequently promotes, nurtures, and supports growth. Holding therapy does not result in a "quick fix," but rather in a "jump start." The child and therapist can access feelings that would not be available through talk therapy alone.

When treating rage-filled children and adolescents, holding promotes heightened emotional release. Not all children who have attachment issues operate out of a rage state; but for those who do, the releasing process helps to clear away the rubble so they can begin to experience other feelings. Emotions that they often attempt to ignore—sadness, hurt, and fear—can surface within a safe context, with safe people.

Most therapy attempts to correct past insults. While no therapy can change what has already happened, perceptions can be altered. Reframing one's circumstances and responses can help an individual gain mastery over his greatest fears and his most serious losses.

Therapy for a hurt child should provide corrective emotional experiences. Holding enhances the likelihood that this will happen, because it accesses the child's feelings and prior experiences almost immediately. A disturbed child's feelings related to early negative experiences are not usually managed well. He may have been avoiding them for years and/or projecting them onto his adoptive parents.

Reprinted from Adopting the Hurt Child by Gregory C. Keck, Ph.D., and Regina Kupecky, LSW. Used by permission of Piñon Press (Colorado Springs, CO). All rights reserved.

"GIRDLES, LAXATIVES, AND RESPITE"

Respite, respite, respite . . . familiar words of exhausted and frustrated parents with seriously disturbed children. While most everyone would agree that relief is sometimes needed, one needs to examine the many issues associated with it. In an attempt to help people look at respite from a variety of perspectives and think about the actual outcomes of respite, Greg wrote the following article. One thing that this brief article hopes to address is this fundamental question: Are you getting long-term benefit and developmental improvement and change from your use of respite?

You're probably wondering just what these three things have in common, and even more likely, you are questioning what they have to do with attachment! Excessive use of any of them may lead to further reliance upon them. In fact, ongoing use may increase the need for them.

Respite, the obvious focus of this article, has become sacred in some corners—hailed as the very thing, perhaps the only thing, that keeps some placements together. That may very well be true, but I think we should take another look at respite via these questions:

- Is respite supposed to improve the child's capacity to attach to the family?
- Is the ultimate goal of respite to no longer need/want respite?
- What is the message that respite sends to the child about the family's capacity to love, nurture, control, or manage him?
- Does respite mimic or parallel the child's own approach/avoidance attachment responses?
- How is respite different from the child's experiences in multiple placements?

I would hope that the goal of any respite plan is to do more than give people a "break." These breaks may actually be further damaging to the attachment breaks that the child has already experienced. They may concretize the child's thinking that he needs to be able to function only for short periods of time—then he can go elsewhere for another short period of time. I would also hope that one of the goals of respite should be related to enhancing the child's capacity for attachment, as well as helping family members address the difficulties they face.

I assume that people would like to be with their children. I assume that parents want to have fun with their kids. And I would hope that kids would like to be with their families. That is the purpose of adoption! Therefore, I think the ultimate goal of respite ought to be the elimination—or at least a reduction—in the frequency of it.

While it is difficult to estimate just what message any child gets about anything, particularly if he is disturbed, I think it is critical to attempt to evaluate this issue. If the child gets the idea that he has to go to respite because the parents *can't* handle him anymore, that may be giving him too much power. We need to remember that children and adolescents who have been hurt so much in their early lives fear vulnerability. If parents seem to be vulnerable, the child will have extreme difficulty ever attaching.

Children with attachment difficulties will identify with, and attach to, only powerful images. After all, if the parents are too weak (in the child's view) to handle the child, how could they ever be counted on to protect him? Who would want to attach to someone who might not be able to protect (read: control, manage, love, nurture) him?

I do think ongoing use of respite parallels the child's own fragmented attachment responses. It seems to me that regularly scheduled respite allows, and perhaps even promotes, ongoing dysfunction. If parents end up feeling and thinking, "Oh well, at least she'll be gone for the weekend," they may also be accepting behaviors that they would not tolerate if they knew "the break" wasn't coming. They may avoid yet another conflict, just to "hang in there" for another day. The child's already well-developed (although not healthy) temporal thinking patterns inevitably get reinforced.

Everyone working with individuals with attachment problems knows that yesterday was the distant past, and tomorrow doesn't exist. Fragmentation in the child's life has led to this development, and I think regular utilization of respite may perpetuate this kind of thinking pattern. Continuity of environment helps to bring about continuity of thought, which will lead to improved cause-and-effect thinking, which evolves into conscience.

Respite should be different from a child's pre-adoptive experience of moving around. Children and adolescents who have had child welfare experiences get accustomed to moving about. It, in a way, allows them to remain irresponsible and unaccountable in their current setting. After all, "If I'm making bad choices today (Friday), I won't have too much to worry about because I'll be going to respite tonight!" And we all know that by Monday, Friday will be ancient history.

In closing, I wanted to write this to help us reexamine an assumption that I see developing. Parents and professionals frequently talk about just how important respite is. I agree that some families feel they could not exist without it. However, just like the girdles and laxatives in the title of this article, too much use of respite, or unfocused use of it, may prove to be habituating. Excessive use may further complicate what I believe that parents and professionals truly desire—children who can attach to and live with them comfortably. Temporary relief may not be the solution to a permanent situation.

Before I hear myself misquoted—as I frequently do—let me say the following:

- I am not saying that a respite plan is *never* helpful.
- I am not in a position to judge what/who other people can live with nor for how long at a stretch. Only families can decide that.
- I do think respite is temporary relief that may become habit-forming.
- I do think the goals of any respite plan should include an attachment rationale.
- I do think the ultimate goal of respite should be its elimination.

I hope that people will start to more carefully evaluate the issues of respite and not simply accept what we keep hearing so much about. Remember, what is accepted practice now will probably be critically evaluated by others in the future. Once upon a time, not very long ago, foster parents were discouraged from allowing the infants in their care to attach to them; that was to be done later with an adoptive family. Now, how wrong was that?

This article originally appeared in the March 2000 issue of Connections, *a newsletter of ATTACh, the Association for Treatment and Training in the Attachment of Children, Columbia, SC.*

"OPEN LETTER DISPUTING THE RAD ACRONYM"

As people have become more familiar with the diagnosis of Reactive Attachment Disorder, they have been quick to abbreviate it as RAD and place it among the alphabet soup of diagnoses. In response to this, Greg wrote the following caution in Connections.

Several years ago, in the Message from the President's column, I warned of the potential damage that the use of the acronym RAD or "RAD Kid" might cause. I can think of no other disorder or condition referred to in the same way.

While many diagnoses have acronyms, only the one referring to attachment problems has developed its own singular word—as opposed to a series of letters that signifies something. In other words, people do talk about ODD (Oppositional Defiance Disorder), but they do not refer to those who experience the problem as "odd" kids. They simply mention all three letters.

I have yet to hear someone say, "I'm a cancer mom, and I have three cancer kids. These cancer kids sure can cause stress for the entire family. People even get divorced over these cancer kids!" Yet this is what I hear about every time I speak at a conference about children with attachment difficulties.

The use of the aforementioned acronym (I hate to give it any more print than it already gets!) does a number of things:

- It degrades the child.
- It discounts the disorder.
- It demeans the diagnosis.
- It refers to the child as if the child *is* the disorder as opposed to the child's *having* the disorder.
- It suggests that the disorder is a permanent or stagnant condition, like boy, girl, Asian, and so on.

We don't treat people for what or who they are, but rather for what they *have*. All three words in the diagnostic nomenclature are critical to the condition's understanding and treatment. Reactive—reminds us that the disorder was developed in *reaction* to trauma. Attachment—helps us focus on what the child was unable to do as a result of the trauma. Disorder—tells us that the result of the trauma is not part of normal development, and that is what we need to treat.

This article originally appeared in the May 2000 issue of Connections, *a newsletter of ATTACh.*

RESOURCES

Resources have changed so much since we wrote *Adopting The Hurt Child*. The amount of information that is now available on the Internet is staggering. There are chat rooms and information (some mentioned in this book in chapter 8, "Life Preservers") on every type and every aspect of adoption. If you do not have access to the Internet, your local library can help.

Listed here are support groups, organizations, and information available on adoption and attachment. The addresses, telephone numbers, and organizations change constantly, so if these are outdated, please try referrals from other resources.

Remember . . . although information is on the Web, in a book, or declared at a conference, each family is unique. There are no one-size-fits-all solutions or easy answers.

We have not investigated all of these organizations, so inclusion on this list does not reflect our recommendation. Lack of inclusion merely reflects our lack of awareness. We offer the information to you as you start your own exploration. Begin with the resources below, and it is likely you will discover many more.

ABC
Attachment and Bonding Center of Ohio
12608 State Road, Suite One
Cleveland, OH 44133
(440) 230-1960
www.abcofohio.net
Provides pre- and post-adoption counseling, as well as intensive attachment therapy; authors can be contacted at this location

ADOPTION/ATTACHMENT PARTNERS
4300 Evergreen Lane, Suite 300
Annandale, VA 22003
(703) 658-7103

ADOPTION EMAIL LISTS DIRECTORY
www.comeunity.com
Annotated directory of adoption e-mail lists for adoptive families; other parent support

ADOPTIVE FAMILIES MAGAZINE
2472 Broadway, Suite 377
New York, NY 10025
(800) 372-3300
www.adoptivefamiliesmagazine.com

ADOPTION NETWORK
291 East 222nd Street
Euclid, OH 44123
(216) 261-1511
www.adoptionnetwork.org
Triad member support group for help with search for biological families

ADOPTION NEWSFLASH
www.adopt.org/news.html
Keeps readers current on adoption news

ADOPTNET
Support for Adoptive Families
www.adoptnet.org

AMERICAN ACADEMY OF ADOPTION ATTORNEYS
P.O. Box 33053
Washington, DC 20033
(202) 832-2222
www.adoptionattorneys.org

AMERICAN ADOPTION CONGRESS
P.O. Box 42730
Washington, DC 20015
(202) 483-3399
www.americanadoptioncongress.org
Committed to truth in adoption and adoption reform

AMERICAN SPEECH-LANGUAGE-HEARING ASSOCIATION
10801 Rockville Pike
Rockville, MD 20852
(800) 638-TALK
www.asha.org

ANXIETY DISORDERS ASSOCIATION OF AMERICA
11900 Parklawn Drive, Suite 100
Rockville, MD 20852
(301) 231-9350

ARCH NATIONAL RESOURCE CENTER FOR RESPITE & CRISES CARE
(888) 671-2594
www.chtop.com/archbroc.htm
Training and technical assistance to respite providers

ASSOCIATION OF EDUCATIONAL THERAPISTS
14852 Ventura Boulevard, Suite 207
Sherman Oaks, CA 91403
(818) 788-3850

ASSOCIATION ON HIGHER EDUCATION AND DISABILITY
P.O. Box 21192
Columbus, OH 43221-0192
(614) 488-4972

ATTACH
Association for Treatment and Training in the Attachment of Children
P.O. Box 11347
Columbia, SC 29211
(866) 453-8224
www.attach.org

International coalition of professionals and parents who work together to promote identification, intervention, and treatment for those with attachment difficulties; informative yearly conference; audio tapes of past conferences; links to many parent resources (organizations and therapists) by state

ATTACH-CHINA
www.members.aol.com/RADchina
Web site devoted to educating parents about Reactive Attachment Disorder in children adopted from China

ATTACHMENT CENTER AT EVERGREEN
27618 Fireweed Drive
Evergreen, CO 80439
(303) 674-1910
Attachment therapy and adoption-related psychological services

ATTACHMENT CENTER NORTHWEST
8011 118th Avenue., N.E.
Kirkland, WA 98033
(425) 889-8524
e-mail: attachnw@earthlink.net

ATTACHMENT DISORDER NETWORK
contacts:
Gail Trenberth
Attachment Disorder Network
P.O. Box 18475
Boulder, CO 80308
(303) 443-1446
GailADPN@aol.com
–and–

Nancy Spoolstra
17572 Bridle Trail Rd.
Gurnee, IL 60031
(847) 855-8676
saanda@aol.com
www.radzebra.org
Non-profit parent support group providing information and resources for parents, professionals, and others who are dealing with children with attachment issues; quarterly newsletter; information packets on request

ATTACHMENT DISORDER SITE
www.attachmentdisorder.net
Information and support regarding Reactive Attachment Disorder

ATTACHMENT DISORDER SUPPORT
GROUP (ADSG)
www.syix.com/adsg

AUTISM NETWORK INTERNATIONAL
(ANI)
www.students.uiuc.edu/~bordner/
nai.html

CHILD WELFARE LEAGUE OF AMERICA
440 1st Street NW, Third Floor
Washington, DC 20001-2085
(202) 638-2952
www.cwla.org

CHILDREN'S DEFENSE FUND
25 E Street NW
Washington, DC 20001
(202) 628-8787
www.childrensdefense.org

CHILDREN WITH ATTENTION DEFICIT
DISORDERS (CHADD)
499 NW 70th Avenue, Suite 101
Plantation, FL 33317
(800) 233-4050
www.chadd.org

CHILDREN UNLIMITED
1825 Gadsden Street
P.O. Box 11463
Columbia, SC 29211
(803) 799-8311

COUNCIL FOR EXCEPTIONAL CHILDREN
1920 Association Drive
Reston, VA 22091
www.cec.sped.org

COUNCIL FOR LEARNING DISABILITIES
P.O. Box 40303
Overland Park, KS 66204
(913) 492 8755

DAVE THOMAS FOUNDATION FOR
ADOPTION
4288 West Dublin-Granville Road
Dublin, OH 43017
(614) 764-3100
nac.adopt.org/wendy.html

DISCOVERY SCHOOL.COM
http://school.discovery.com

DISTANCE LEARNING
www.educating.net

EASTERN EUROPEAN ADOPTION
COALITION, INC.
www.eeadopt.org
Adoptive family support organization

EDUWEB: ADVENTURES
www.eduweb.com/adventure.html

FAMILY ATTACHMENT & COUNSELING
CENTER OF MINNESOTA
18322 C Minnetonka Blvd.
Deephaven, MN 55391
(952) 475-2818

FEDERATION OF FAMILIES FOR
CHILDREN'S MENTAL HEALTH
1021 Prince Street
Alexandria, VA 22314-2971
(703) 684-7710
www.fcmh.org

FOREST HEIGHTS LODGE
P.O. Box 789
Evergreen, CO 80439
(303) 674-6681
Residential treatment

GLADE RUN LUTHERAN SERVICES
P.O. Box 70, Beaver Road
Zelienople, PA 16063
(724) 452-4453

HEAL THE HEART FOUNDATION
www.healtheheart.org
Promotes education, understanding, and support of families of children with Reactive Attachment Disorder

HOLT INTERNATIONAL CHILDREN'S
SERVICES
P.O. Box 2880
1195 City View
Eugene, OR 97402
(541) 687-2202
www.holtintl.org

HOMES FOR KIDS
www.homes4kids.org
*Information and links; essays,
advocacy, getting started, disruption, subsidy*

INTERMOUNTAIN HOME
500 Lamborn
Helena, MT 59601

INTERNATIONAL ADOPTION CLINIC
P.O. Box 211
UMHC
420 Delaware Street SE
Minneapolis, MN 55455
(612) 626-2928
Contact: Dana Johnson, M.D.

INTERNATIONAL DYSLEXIA ASSOCIATION
Chester Building, Suite 382
8600 La Salle Road
Baltimore, Maryland 21204
(410) 296-0232

INTERNET PUBLIC LIBRARY
www.ipl.org

JEWEL AMONG JEWELS ADOPTION
NETWORK
www.adoptionjewels.org
mail@adoptionjewels.org
*Bible-based organization that
advocates for adoptees by educating prospective adoptive parents,
adoptive parents, birth parents,
mental health professionals, and
others; newsletter and twelve-step
workbook for adult adoptees
adopted as children*

LEARNING DISABILITIES ASSOCIATION OF
AMERICA (LDAA)
4156 Library Road
Pittsburgh, PA 15234
(412) 341-1515
(888) 300-6710
www.ldanatl.org

NATIONAL ADOPTION CENTER
1500 Walnut St., Suite 701
Philadelphia, PA 19102
(800) 862-3678
www.adopt.org
*Referrals and information about
special-needs adoption; waiting
children listed on Web site*

NATIONAL ADOPTION INFORMATION
CLEARINGHOUSE
330 C Street, SW
Washington, DC 20447
(888) 251-0075 or (703) 352-3488
www.calib.com/naic
*Current information regarding
adoption*

NATIONAL CLEARINGHOUSE FOR
PROFESSIONALS IN SPECIAL EDUCATION
1800 Diagonal Road, Suite 320
Alexandria, VA 22314
(703) 519-3800

NATIONAL INFORMATION CENTER FOR
CHILDREN AND YOUTH WITH
DISABILITIES (NICHCY)
P.O. Box 1492
Washington, DC 20013
(800) 695-0285
www.nichy.org

NATIONAL RESOURCE CENTER ON
SPECIAL NEEDS ADOPTION
16250 Northland Drive #120
Southfield, MI 48075
(248) 443-7080
Videos, books, curriculum, statistics, newsletter, and current and past resources

NORTH AMERICAN COUNCIL ON
ADOPTABLE CHILDREN (NACAC)
970 Raymond Avenue, Suite 106
St. Paul, MN 55114-1149
(651)644-3036
www.nacac.org
Well-respected special-needs advocacy group whose annual conference is well attended by many parents and professionals; many audio tapes available; information on subsidy state by state; excellent resource room; yearly membership fee includes newsletter

ONLINE SUBSTANCE TREATMENT
PROGRAM
(866) HELP-999
www.eGetgoing.com

PARENTS' EDUCATIONAL RESOURCE
CENTER
1660 South Amphlett Boulevard,
Suite 200
San Mateo, CA 94402-2508
(415) 655-2410

RAINBOW CENTER FOR INTERNATIONAL
CHILD HEALTH
Adoption Health Service
11100 Euclid Avenue
Cleveland, OH 44106-6038
(216) 844-3224

RESOLVE
www.resolve.org
Infertility and adoption information and support

SPECIAL CHILDREN
www.specialchildren.about.com
A Web site offering over seven hundred sites with information for parents

STUDY SITE FOR LITERATURE, SAT
www.pinkmonkey.com

TAPESTRY PRESS CATALOG
(800) 765-2367
www.tapestrybooks.com
Complete catalog of adoption books and tapes for children, parents, and professionals

THE THERAPLAY INSTITUTE
3330 Old Glenview Rd., Suite 8
Wilmette, IL 60091
www.Theraplay.org

THREE RIVERS ADOPTION COUNCIL
307 Fourth Avenue, Suite 710
Pittsburgh, PA 15222
(412) 471-8722
Inexpensive guidebooks on a variety of special-needs adoption topics

TRESSLER ADOPTION SERVICES
The Lutheran Center
700 Light Street
Baltimore, MD 21230
(410) 230-2849

VILLA SANTA MARIA
P.O. Box 156
Cedar Crest, NM 87008
(800) 453-5037 or (505) 281-3609

VOICE FOR ADOPTION
P.O. Box 77496
Washington, DC 20013
(202) 543-7372
Organization that lobbies for
legislation and laws regarding
adoption

RELATED READINGS

Adler, Alfred. *The Problem Child.* Capricorn Books, New York, 1963.

Ainsworth, Mary D., et al. *Patterns of Attachment: A Psychological Study of the Strange Situation.* Erlbaum Association, Hillsdale, NJ, 1978.

Ainsworth, M. "Object Relations, Dependency and Attachment: A Theoretical Review of the Infant-Mother Relationship." *Child Development,* 1969, pp. 969-1025.

Askin, Jayne. *Search: A Handbook For Adoptees and Birth Parents.* Oryx, Phoenix, AZ, 1992.

Ayers, A. J. *Sensory Integration and The Child.* Western Psychological Services, Los Angeles, 1979.

Bailey, Julie Jarrell, and Lynn N. Giddens, MA. *The Adoption Reunion Survival Guide: Preparing Yourself for the Search, Reunion, and Beyond.* New Harbinger Publication Inc., Oakland, CA, 2001.

Barnard, K. E., and T. B. Brazelton. *Touch: The Foundation of Experience.* International University Press, Madison, CT, 1990.

Barth, Richard P., and Marianne Berry. *Adoption and Disruption: Rates, Risks, Responses.* Aldine de Gruyter, Hawthorne, NY, 1988.

Belesky, Jay, and Teresa Nezworski. *Clinical Implications of Attachment.* Lawrence Erlbaum Associates, Hillsdale, NJ, 1987.

Bettelheim, Bruno. *A Good Enough Parent.* Vintage Books, New York, 1988.

Boneh, Carol. *Disruptions in Adoptive Placements: A Research Study.* Massachusetts Department of Public Welfare, Boston, MA, 1979.

Bostrom, J. "Fostering Attachment in Post-Institutionalized Adopted Children Using Group Theraplay." *The Theraplay Institute Newsletter,* Fall 1995, pp. 7-8.

Bowlby, John. *Attachment and Loss, vol. I, vol. II, vol. III.* Basic Books, New York, 1969, 1973, 1980.

Bowlby, John. *The Making and Breaking of Affectional Bonds.* Tavistock Publications, London, UK, 1979.

Boyd, Brian (photographs by Stephen Wunrow). *When You Were Born in Korea: A Memory Book for Children Adopted from Korea.* Yeong & Yeong Book Co., St. Paul, MN, 1993.

Boyles, Nancy S., and Darlene Contadino, MSW. *Parenting a Child with Attention Deficit/Hyperactivity Disorder.* Lowell House, Los Angeles, 1999.

Brazelton, T. B., M.D. *Infants and Mothers: Individual Differences in Development.* Delacorte Press, New York, 1969.

Brazelton, T. B., M.D. *Touchpoints: Your Child's Emotional and Behavioral Development.* Addison-Wesley, Reading, MA, 1992.

Brazelton, T. B., M.D. *What Every Baby Knows.* Addison-Wesley, Reading, MA, 1987.

Brodzinsky, David M., and Marshall D. Schecter, ed. *The Psychology of Adoption.* Oxford University Press, New York, 1990.

Brooks, Barbara, Ph.D., and Paula M. Siegel. *The Scared Child.* John Wiley and Sons, New York, 1996.

Carter, Jean and Michael. *Sweet Grapes: How to Stop Being Infertile and Start Living Again.* Perspectives Press, Wayne, IN, 1989.

Clarke, Jean Illsely, and Connie Dawson. *Growing Up Again.* Harper & Row, San Francisco, 1989.

Cline, Foster W., M.D. *Hope For High Risk and Rage Filled Children.* Foster W. Cline, M.D., Evergreen, CO, 1992.

Cline, Foster W., M.D. *Learning Disorders and School Problems* (the "Red Book"). Evergreen Consultants in Human Behavior, Evergreen, CO, 1979.

Cline, Foster W., M.D. *Parent Education Text* (the "Yellow Book"). Evergreen Consultants in Human Behaviors, Evergreen, CO, 1982.

Cline, Foster W., M.D. *Understanding and Treating the Difficult Child* (the "Blue Book"). Evergreen Consultants in Human Behavior, Evergreen, CO, 1981.

Cline, Foster W., M.D. *Understanding and Treating the Severely Disturbed Child* (the "Green Book"). Evergreen Consultants in Human Behavior, Evergreen, CO, 1979.

Cline, Foster W., M.D., and Jim Fay. *Parenting with Love and Logic.* Piñon Press, Colorado Springs, CO, 1990.

Cline, Foster W., M.D., and Jim Fay. *Parenting Teens with Love and Logic.* Piñon Press, Colorado Springs, CO, 1992.

Cline, Foster W., M.D., and Cathy Helding. *Can This Child Be Saved? Solutions for Adoptive and Foster Families.* World Enterprises, Ashland, Wisconsin, 1999.

Confer, Charles. *Letters to Foster Parents: On Managing Angry Behavior.* American Foster Care Resources, Inc., P.O. Box 271, King George, VA 22485, 1989.

Confer, Charles. *Letters to Foster Parents: More On Discipline.* American Foster Care Resources, Inc., P.O. Box 271, King George, VA 22485, 1990.

Cooper, Scott. *Sticks and Stones.* Random House, New York, 2000.

Cox, Susan. "Search and Reunion in International Search," 1998. Available through Holt International Children's Services (see Resources).

Davis, Ronald D. *The Gift of Dyslexia.* The Berkeley Publishing Group, New York, 1997.

DeGangi, G. A. "Assessment of Sensory, Emotional, and Attentional Problems in Regulatory Disordered Infants: Part 1." *Infants and Young Children,* 1991.

Delaney, Richard, Ph.D. *Fostering Charges: Treating Attachment Disordered Foster Children.* Corbett, Fort Collins, CO, 1991.

Delaney, Richard, Ph.D., and Frank R. Kunstal. *Troubled Transplants.* University of Southern Maine, Portland, ME, 1993.

Dorow, Sara (photographs by Stephen Wunrow). *When You Were Born in China: A Memory Book for Children Adopted from China.* Yeong & Yeong Book Co., St. Paul, MN, 1997.

Eldridge, Sherrie. *20 Things Adopted Kids Wish Their Adoptive Parents Knew.* Dell Publishing, New York, 1999.

Ellison, Sheila, and Barbara Ann Barnett, Ph.D. *365 Ways to Help Your Children Grow.* Sourcebooks, Naperville, IL, 1996.

Elkind, David. *All Grown Up and No Place to Go: Teenagers In Crisis.* Addison-Wesley, Reading, MA, 1998.

Elkind, David. *The Hurried Child: Growing Up Too Fast Too Soon.* Addison-Wesley, Reading, MA, 1981.

Eyre, Linda and Richard. *Teaching Your Child Values.* Simon and Schuster, New York, 1993.

Fahlberg, Vera, M.D. *Attachment and Separation.* Spaulding for Children, P.O. Box 337, Chelsea, MI, 48118, 1979.

Fahlberg, Vera, M.D. *The Child in Placement.* Spaulding for Children, P.O. Box 337, Chelsea, MI, 48118, 1981.

Fahlberg, Vera, M.D. *A Child's Journey Through Placement.* Perspective Press, Indianapolis, IN, 1991.

Fahlberg, Vera, M.D. *Helping Children When They Must Move.* Spaulding for Children, P.O. Box 337, Chelsea, MI, 48118, 1979.

Fahlberg, Vera, M.D., ed. *Residential Treatment, a Tapestry of Many Therapies.* Perspective Press, Indianapolis, IN, 1990.

Fay, Jim. *Helicopters, Drill Sergeants and Consultants.* Cline/Fay Institute, 2207 Jackson St., Golden, CO, 80401, 1988.

Fay, Jim. *Tickets to Success.* Cline/Fay Institute, 2207 Jackson St., Golden, CO, 80401, 1988.

Fay, Jim, and Foster W. Cline, M.D. *Grandparenting with Love and Logic: Practical Solutions to Today's Grandparenting Challenges.* Love and Logic Press, Golden, CO, 1995.

Fisher, Antwone Quenton. *Finding Fish.* William Morrow, New York, 2001.

Geerars, Hetty, René Hoksbergen and Janneke Rooda. *Adoptees on Their Way to Adulthood.* University Utrecht, The Netherlands, 1996.

Geidman, J., and L. Brown. *Birthbond: Reunions Between Birth Parents and Adoptees, What Happens After.* New Horizons Press, New Jersey, 1995.

Gilman, Louis. *The Adoption Resource Book* (3rd ed.). HarperCollins, New York, 1992.

Glenn, Stephen H., and Jane Nelson, Ed.D. *Raising Self-Reliant Children in a Self-Indulgent World.* Prima Publishing and Communications, Rocklin, CA, 1989.

Gold, Michael. *And Hannah Wept: Infertility, Adoption and the Jewish Couple.* JPS, Philadelphia, PA, 1988.

Goldstein, Joseph, et al. *Beyond the Best Interests of the Child.* Free Press, New York, 1984.

Grandin, Temple. *Journal of Child and Adolescent Psychopharmocology,* vol. 2, November 1, 1992. Mary Ann Liebert, Inc., Publishers.

Grandin, Temple. *Thinking in Pictures and Other Reports from My Life with Autism.* Vintage Books, Larchmont, New York, 1995.

Grandin, Temple, and M. Scariano. *Emergence: Labelled Autistic.* Arena Press, Navato, CA, 1986.

Gravelle, Karen, and Susan Fischer. *Where Are My Birth Parents? A Guide for Teenage Adoptees.* Dalker and Co., New York, 1993.

Green, Gordon W. Jr., Ph.D. *Helping Your Child Learn.* Citadel Press, New York, 1994.

Greene, Ross W., Ph.D. *The Explosive Child.* HarperCollins, New York, 1998.

Grow, I., and D. Shapiro. *Black Children, White Parents: A Study of Transracial Adoption.* Child Welfare League of America, Washington, DC, 1974.

Grow, I., and D. Shapiro. *Transracial Adoption Today: Views of Adoptive Parents and Social Workers.* Child Welfare League of America, Washington, DC, 1975.

Hallowell, Edward M., M.D., and John J. Ratey. *Driven to Distraction.* Simon and Schuster, New York, 1994.

Healy, Jane M., Ph.D. *Endangered Minds: Why Children Don't Think—and What We Can Do about It.* Simon & Schuster, New York, 1990.

Hochman, Gloria, Ellen Feathers-Acuna, and Anna Huston. *The Sibling Bond: Its Importance in Foster Care and Adoptive Placement.* Adoption Information Clearinghouse, Rockville, MD, n.d.

Hoksbergen, R. A. C. *Adopting a Child: A Guidebook for Adoptive Parents and Their Advisors.* University Utrecht, The Netherlands, 1994.

Hopkins-Best, Mary. *Toddler Adoption: The Weaver's Craft.* Perspectives Press, Indianapolis, IN, 1997.

Hughes, Daniel A. *Building the Bonds of Attachment: Awakening Love in Deeply Troubled Children.* Jason Aronson, Inc., Northvale, NJ, 1998.

Hughes, Daniel A. *Facilitating Developmental Attachment.* Jason Aronson, Inc., Northvale, NJ, 1997.

Hurford, Daphne M. *To Read or Not to Read.* Simon and Schuster, New York, 1999.

Jernberg, Ann M., and Phyllis B. Booth. *Theraplay: Helping Parents and Children Build Better Relationships through Attachment-Based Play.* Jossey-Bass, San Francisco, 1999.

Jewett, Claudia L. *Adopting the Older Child.* The Harvard Common Press, Boston, 1978.

Jewett, Claudia L. *Helping Children Cope with Separation and Loss.* The Harvard Common Press, Harvard, MA, 1982.

Johnston, Patricia. *Adopting After Infertility.* Perspective Press, Wayne, IN, 1993.

Johnston, Patricia. *Perspectives on a Grafted Tree.* Perspective Press, Wayne, IN, 1983.

Jordan, Barbara. *Preparing Foster Parents' Own Children for the Fostering Experience.* American Foster Care Resources, Inc., King George, VA, 1989.

Kadushin, Alfred. *Adopting Older Children.* Columbia University Press, New York, 1970.

Kamin, Ben. *Raising a Thoughtful Teenager.* Penguin Books, New York, 1996.

Karen, Robert. *Becoming Attached: Unfolding the Mysteries of the Infant Mother Bond and Its Impact on Later Life.* Warner Books, New York, 1994.

Karen, Robert. "Become Attached." *Atlantic Monthly,* Feb. 1990. pp. 35-70.

Karr-Morse, Robin, and Meredith Wiley. *Ghosts from the Nursery.* Atlantic Monthly Press, New York, 1997.

Keck, Gregory C., Ph.D, and Regina M. Kupecky, LSW. *Adopting the Hurt Child: Hope for Families with Special Needs Kids.* Piñon Press, Colorado Springs, CO, 1995.

Keefer, Betsy, and Jayne E. Schooler. *Telling the Truth to Your Adopted or Foster Child: Making Sense of the Past.* Bergin & Garvey, Westport, Connecticut, 2000.

Klaus, Marshall H., M.D. *Amazing Talents of the Newborn.* Videotape. Johnson & Johnson, 1998.

Klaus, Marshall H., M.D., Phyllis H. Klaus, and John H. Kennell, M.D. *Bonding: Building the Foundations of Secure Attachment and Independence.* Addison-Wesley Publishing, Reading, MA, 1995.

Klaus, Marshall H., M.D., and John H. Kennell, M.D. *Maternal Infant Bonding.* C.V Mosby, Saint Louis, MO, 1976.

Kralovec, Etta, and Jon Buell. *The End of Homework.* Beacon Press, Boston, 2000.

Kranowitz, Carol Stock. *The Out-Of-Sync Child: Recognizing and Coping with Sensory Integration Dysfunction.* Perigee Books, New York, 1998.

Krementz, Jill. *How It Feels to Be Adopted.* Knopf, New York, 1982.

Kupecky, Regina M. "Siblings Are Family, Too." Three Rivers Adoption Council, Pittsburgh, PA, 1993.

Lifton, Betty Jean. *Lost and Found—the Adoption Experience.* Harper & Row, New York, 1979.

Lifton, Betty Jean. *Twice Born: Memoirs of an Adopted Daughter.* Penguin, New York, 1977.

Magid, Ken, Ph.D., and Carole A. McKelvey. *High Risk . . . Children without a Conscience.* Bantam Books, New York, 1988.

Mansfield, Lynda G., and Christopher H. Waldmann. *Don't Touch My Heart: Healing the Pain of an Unattached Child.* Piñon Press, Colorado Springs, CO, 1994.

Marindin, Hope, ed. *Handbook for Single Adoptive Parents.* Committee of Single Adoptive Parents, Chevy Chase, MD, 1992.

McKelvey, Carole A., ed. *Give Them Roots, Then Let Them Fly: Understanding Attachment Therapy.* Attachment Center Press, Evergreen, CO, 1995.

McNamara, Joan. *Adoption and the Sexually Abused Child.* Family Resources Adoption Program, 226 N. Highland Ave., Ossining, NY, 10562, 1990.

Melina, Louis Ruskai. *Making Sense of Adoption: A Parent's Guide.* Harper & Row, San Francisco, 1989.

Melina, Louis Ruskai. *Raising Adopted Children: A Manual for Adoptive Parents.* Harper & Row, San Francisco, 1986.

Meyer, Donald J., ed. *Uncommon Fathers.* Woodbine House, Bethesda, MD, 1995.

Miller, Alice. *For Your Own Good.* The Noonday Press, New York, 1990.

Miller, Margi, MA, and Nancy Ward, MA. *With Eyes Wide Open: A Workbook for Parents Adopting International Children Over Age One. Children's Home Society of Minnesota,* LN Press Incorporated, Minneapolis, MN, 1996.

O'Hanlon, Tim, Ph.D. *Accessing Federal Adoption Subsidies after Legalization.* Child Welfare League of America, Washington, DC, 1995.

Papolos, Demitri F., M.D., and Janice Papolos. *Bipolar Child.* Broadway Books, New York, 1999.

Peacock, Carol Antoinette. *Mommy Far, Mommy Near.* Albert Whitman & Co., Morton Grove, Illinois, 2000.

Pertman, Adam. *Adoption Nation: How the Adoption Revolution Is Transforming America.* Basic Books, New York, 2000.

Randolph, Elizabeth. *Children Who Shock and Surprise: A Guide to Attachment Disorders.* RFR Publications, 8655 Water Rd., Catati, CA, 94931, 1994.

Reitz, Miriam, and Ken Watson. *Adoption and the Family System: Strategies for Treatment.* Guilford Press, New York, 1991.

Roberts, Monty. *Horse Sense for People.* Penguin Press, New York, 2001.

Rosenberg, Elinor B. *Adoption Life Cycle: The Children and Their Families through the Years.* Free Press, New York, 1992.

Samenow, Stanton E., Ph.D. *Before It's Too Late.* Times Books, New York, 1991.

Sandmaier, Marian. *When Love Is Not Enough: How Mental Health Professionals Can Help Special Needs Adoptive Families.* Child Welfare League of America, Washington, DC, 1988.

Schafer, Carol. *Other Mother: A Woman's Love for the Child She Gave Up for Adoption.* Soho Press, New York, 1991.

Schooler, Jayne E. *The Whole Life Adoption Book: Realistic Advice for Building a Healthy Adoptive Family.* Piñon Press, Colorado Springs, CO, 1993.

Seligman, Martin E. P., Ph.D. *The Optimistic Child.* Houghton Mifflin, New York, 1995.

Shapiro, Francine. *Eye Movement Desensitization and Reprocessing—Basic Principles, Protocols, and Procedures.* The Guilford Press, New York, 1995.

Smith, Sally L. *No Easy Answers.* Bantam Books, New York, 1995.

Smith, Sally L. *Succeeding Against the Odds.* Penguin Putnam, New York, 1991.

Staub, Debbie, Ph.D. *Delicate Threads.* Woodbine House, Bethesda, MD, 1998.

Stevens, Suzanne H. *The LD Child and the ADHD Child.* John E. Blair, Publisher, Winston-Salem, NC, 1997.

Thomas, Nancy. *When Love Is Not Enough: A Guide to Parenting Children with Attachment Disorder.* Families by Design, Glenwood Springs, Colorado, 1997.
Thompson, Michael M., Ph.D. *Who's Raising Whom?* McClean Publishing Group, Dublin, OH, 1994.

Trott, Maryann C., Marci K. Laurel, and Susan L. Windeck. *SenseAbilities—Understanding Sensory Integration.* Therapy Skill Builders, San Antonio, TX, 1993.

Vail, Priscilla L. *Smart Kids with School Problems.* Penguin Books, New York, 1989.

Van der Kolk, Bessel A., Alexander C. McFarlane, and Lars Weisaeth, eds. *Traumatic Stress: The Effects of Overwhelming Experience on Mind, Body, and Society.* The Guilford Press, New York, 1996.

Van Gulden, Holly, and Lisa Bartels Rabb. *Real Parents, Real Children: Parenting the Adopted Child.* Crossroads Publishing Company, New York, 1993.

Verny, Thomas, M.D. *Nurturing Your Unborn Child.* Delecorte Press, New York, 1991.

Verny, Thomas, M.D. *Parenting Your Unborn Child.* Doubleday-Canada, Toronto, 1988.

Verny, Thomas, M.D. *The Secret Life of the Unborn Child.* Summit Books, New York, 1981.

Verrier, Nancy Newton. *The Primal Wound.* Gateway Press, Baltimore, MD, 1993.

Watkins, Mary, and Susan Fischer. *Talking with Young Children About Adoption.* Yale University Press, New Haven, CT, 1993.

Watson, Kenneth. *"Substitute Care Providers Helping Abused and Neglected Children."* U.S. Department of Health and Human Services, Washington, DC, 1994.

Welch, Martha G., M.D. *Holding Time.* Simon & Schuster, New York, 1988.

AUTHORS

GREGORY C. KECK, PH.D., founded the Attachment and Bonding Center of Ohio, which specializes in the treatment of children and adolescents who have experienced developmental interruptions. In addition, he and his staff treat individuals and families who are faced with a variety of problems in the areas of adoption, attachment, substance abuse, sexual abuse, and adolescent difficulties.

Dr. Keck is certified as a Diplomate and Fellow by the American Board of Medical Psychotherapy and is a Diplomate in Professional Psychotherapy. He has taught at Case Western Reserve University's Mandel School of Applied Social Sciences and the University of Akron, and is involved in training for a diversity of agencies, hospitals, and organizations, both nationally and internationally.

His memberships include the Cleveland Psychological Association, the Ohio Psychological Association, the American Psychological Association, and the National Association of Social Workers. He was president of the board of directors of the Association for Treatment and Training in the Attachment of Children (ATTACh) from 1991 to 1998.

In 1993, Dr. Keck was given the adoption Triad Advocate Award by the Adoption Network of Cleveland, Ohio.

He is a parent and has appeared on numerous television and radio talk shows to discuss a broad spectrum of adoption issues.

REGINA M. KUPECKY, LSW, has worked in the adoption arena for over twenty-five years as an adoption placement worker. She is currently a co-therapist with Dr. Gregory C. Keck, Ph.D., at the Attachment and Bonding Center of Ohio, where she works with children who have attachment disorders.

Mrs. Kupecky authored a resource guide, *Siblings Are Family, Too,* which is available through the Three Rivers Adoption Council in Pittsburgh, Pennsylvania. She has presented at local, national, and international conferences on a variety of adoption topics and holds a Master of Arts degree from John Carroll University.

INDEX